Windows Networking Tools

The Complete Guide to Management,
Troubleshooting, and Security

IT MANAGEMENT TITLES
FROM AUERBACH PUBLICATIONS AND CRC PRESS

Windows
Networking Tools

The Complete Guide to Management, Troubleshooting, and Security

Gilbert Held

CRC Press
Taylor & Francis Group
Boca Raton   London   New York

CRC Press is an imprint of the
Taylor & Francis Group, an **Informa** business
AN AUERBACH BOOK

CRC Press
Taylor & Francis Group
6000 Broken Sound Parkway NW, Suite 300
Boca Raton, FL 33487-2742

© 2013 by Taylor & Francis Group, LLC
CRC Press is an imprint of Taylor & Francis Group, an Informa business

No claim to original U.S. Government works

Printed in the United States of America on acid-free paper
Version Date: 2012920

International Standard Book Number: 978-1-4665-1106-4 (Paperback)

Library of Congress Cataloging-in-Publication Data

Held, Gilbert, 1943-
  Windows networking tools : the complete guide to management, troubleshooting, and security / Gilbert Held.
      p. cm.
  Includes bibliographical references and index.
  ISBN 978-1-4665-1106-4 (pbk.)
  1. Computer network protocols. 2. Microsoft Windows server. 3. TCP/IP (Computer network protocol) 4. Operating systems (Computers) I. Title.

TK5105.55.H456 2012
004.6--dc23   2012030989

Visit the Taylor & Francis Web site at
http://www.taylorandfrancis.com

and the CRC Press Web site at
http://www.crcpress.com

Contents

1

INTRODUCTION

This chapter is a guide to the contents of this book, allowing readers to preview what is to come. Because this book is focused upon Windows networking tools and the use of the Internet is the primary method associated with networking, we first turn our attention to obtaining an appreciation for the TCP/IP protocol suite, which can be considered the glue that binds the Internet together. In briefly examining the composition of this protocol suite, we primarily focus our attention upon gaining an appreciation for existing and emerging applications as well as discuss some of the problems associated with some applications. In later chapters we significantly enmesh ourselves in the details of the protocol suite; however, as an introduction, we focus our attention upon applications. This provides material to discuss in later chapters, for example, how the protocol suite has the ability to distinguish between applications flowing over a common communications path. In the second portion of this introduction we briefly preview succeeding chapters, providing readers with a road map to information contained in this book.

1.1 The TCP/IP Protocol Suite

The TCP/IP protocol suite evolved from a primarily academic and research communications protocol sponsored by the U.S. Department of Defense's Advanced Projects Agency (APA) into a protocol that affects the lives of most individuals around the globe. Although most, if not all, readers are familiar with the Internet, that network of interconnected networks represents only one use of the TCP/IP protocol suite. Today there are many organizations either creating or operating private networks based upon the use of the TCP/IP protocol suite that collectively are referred to as intranets. In addition, the Internet is used to interconnect geographically separated networks through a technology referred to as virtual private networking (VPN), where security is of paramount importance since two or more private networks are connected over the public Internet. Recognizing the versatility of the TCP/IP protocol suite, the Internet Protocol (IP) is now being used to transport voice, video, and data. That transmission can occur over both wired and wireless communications, and as such provides mobile users with the ability to access email and surf the web from their mobile phones. Thus the TCP/IP protocol suite represents the key protocol for both existing and potential communications users.

In this chapter, we first turn our attention to the role of the TCP/IP protocol suite. We begin by focusing our attention upon common and emerging applications supported by this technology. Next, we preview succeeding chapters. This information, either by itself or in conjunction with the index, can be used to rapidly locate particular information of interest.

1.1.1 Applications

When the TCP/IP protocol suite was initially developed, it was used to support a relatively small number of applications. Those applications included electronic mail, file transfer, and remote terminal operations. Since the initial development of the TCP/IP protocol suite, its modular architecture has enabled literally hundreds of applications to be developed that use the protocol suite as a transport for communications. In this section we briefly review a core set of current and emerging applications to obtain an appreciation for the role of the TCP/IP protocol suite.

We can subdivide TCP/IP applications into three general categories: obsolete or rarely used, current, and emerging. Although obsolete or rarely used applications are interesting from a historical basis, their value for the networking professional is minimal, and for the most part we focus our attention upon current and evolving applications.

1.1.1.1 Current Applications   There is a core set of TCP/IP applications that are used by most persons. Those applications include electronic mail, file transfer, remote terminal operations, and web surfing. Although not directly used by most persons, the domain name service (DNS) is crucial for the operation of TCP/IP-based networks because it provides the translation process between host names and

IP addresses. For example, what would you prefer to enter into your web browser—www.yahoo.com as the domain name or the IP address 209.191.122.70? If you are like the vast majority of rational web surfers, you can easily remember domain names, whereas remembering IP addresses might be a completely different story. To illustrate this, do you know the IP addresses of google.com or bing.com? Since the vast majority of persons that use TCP/IP-based networks enter host addresses, while routing is based upon the use of IP addresses, DNS provides the crucial link between the two. In the remainder of this section, we briefly review the operation and utilization of the core set of current applications commonly used by persons on TCP/IP-based networks. This information is presented to ensure readers with different networking backgrounds obtain a common level of appreciation for the majority of current applications used on TCP/IP-based networks.

1.1.1.1.1 Electronic Mail The TCP/IP protocol suite dates to the 1960s, when government laboratories (Advanced Research Projects Agency [ARPA]) and research universities required a method to share ideas in an expedient manner. Among the first applications developed for the protocol suite was a text-based electronic mail system. Over the past thirty plus years the use of electronic mail has evolved from a text-based messaging system into the development of sophisticated, integrated calendar, messaging, and documenting systems that work with electronic mail. One example of a popular integrated email system is Microsoft's Outlook. Figure 1.1 shows a screenshot of the inbox of the author's version of Outlook running on one of his computers. Note that the left portion of the screen shows a listing of emails with one highlighted. The right portion of the screen illustrates the contents of the highlighted email. In the lower left corner of Figure 1.1 you will notice a series of six icons stacked vertically, one above the other. As you move your cursor over each icon, your display will note Mail, Calendar, Contacts, Tasks, Notes, and Folder List, indicating the major options available for selection. Through the use of Outlook, you can send and receive conventional text-based messages, embed graphic images and word processing documents within your message, develop the equivalent of an electronic rolodex via the use of a contact folder, and use its calendar facility as a reminder to perform different tasks.

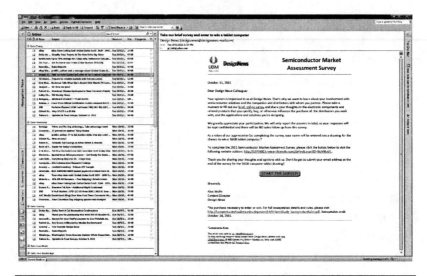

Figure 1.1   Viewing the electronic mail display of Microsoft's Outlook program.

Figure 1.2 illustrates a portion of the additional capability obtained through the use of Outlook. In this example we use the program's calendar feature that enables us to schedule events as well as define tasks and indicate the status of different tasks. To arrive at Figure 1.2 we initially clicked on the Calendar icon, which is below the highlighted envelope icon in the lower left portion of Figure 1.1. This action brings up the Calendar display for the current day. We can then select

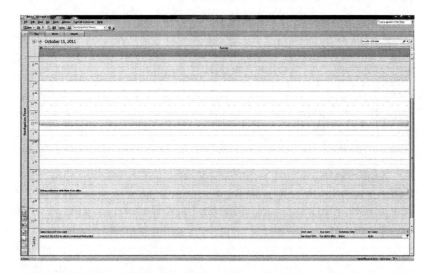

Figure 1.2   Using Microsoft's Outlook calendar and task pad.

Week or Month from the resulting display to view scheduled meetings as well as enter or adjust the time of a meeting. For example, in Figure 1.2 we established the time for a videoconference with the New York office at 7 p.m., as well as indicated a task for completion on the indicated day, which is to obtain the telephone number to establish the conference.

Unlike the early versions of electronic mail that depended on the TCP/IP protocol suite for communications, Microsoft's Outlook, as well as competitive products such as Lotus Notes and Novell's GroupWise, initially supported many communications protocols. In fact, just a decade ago IBM's System Network Architecture (SNA) and Novell's NetWare IPX and SPX protocols accounted for approximately 70% of the communications market. The growth in the use of the Internet and the development of corporate intranets have more than reversed protocol utilization, with the TCP/IP protocol stack now accounting for approximately 70 to 90% of the communication's market. Although you can still find SNA and even IPX and SPX networks, the majority of non-TCP/IP networking is attributed to banking and other financial systems. As time progresses, even those systems are expected to migrate to a TCP/IP environment.

1.1.1.1.2 File Transfers A second application that traces its roots to the initial development of the TCP/IP protocol suite is file transfer. During the 1960s many research laboratories and universities required a mechanism to share what was then considered to be large quantities of data, resulting in the development of the File Transfer Protocol (FTP), which more accurately represents an application that facilitates file transfers.

Early versions of FTP applications were text based. Although several software developers introduced graphic user interface versions of FTP during the mid-1990s, the popular Windows operating system added a text-based FTP that represents one of the more popular methods for transferring files.

Let's examine an example of the use of a Windows FTP application, and in doing so we learn why we should become acquainted with the use of the Command Prompt, which allows us to use Disk Operating System (DOS) commands. Note that, with the exception of Windows version 3.1, all later versions of the ubiquitous Microsoft operating

Figure 1.3   An example of the use of a Windows FTP application.

system include FTP as an MS-DOS application. Although better known to modern Windows users as a Command Prompt application, in reality we are using software developed initially for the DOS. Thus in Figure 1.3 we observe the use of FTP built into Windows and accessed through the Command Prompt. In this example we simply entered FTP into the Command Prompt to invoke the application and then typed "help" to obtain a list of FTP commands. Later in this book we discuss how you can operate the Command Prompt.

Because it is free, the addition of a TCP/IP protocol stack with the introduction of Windows 95, to include several basic applications, caused many third-party software developers that concentrated on TCP/IP applications to undergo a severe contraction in sales. In fact, although there are several graphic user interface versions of FTP available, most such products are now shareware instead of commercial products. Thus the inclusion of the TCP/IP protocol suite in different versions of Windows had a significant impact upon the market for stand-alone applications.

The use of FTP has considerably diminished in tandem with the growing popularity of web browsing. Just about every web browser now has the ability to transfer files, as well as the capability to incorporate numerous add-ons and plug-in programs that enable special types of files to be both downloaded and opened within a browser. Figure 1.4 illustrates some of the plug-ins operating on this author's Firefox web browser. In this example the window illustrates the results obtained from checking the plug-ins to ascertain if they were up to date.

Figure 1.4 Checking the status of third-party plug-ins on the Firefox browser.

Scrolling down Figure 1.4 you observe that Microsoft has a variety of plug-ins that this author enabled on Firefox. In addition to Firefox, Microsoft's Internet Explorer (IE), as well as other browsers, includes the ability to add numerous types of plug-ins that can be used to customize a browser to the operating environment you select, such as adding plug-ins to enable different types of documents to be viewed within a browser, enhance printing, and perform a variety of other tasks, such as verifying a site's security certificate and automatically employing encryption to enable a secure communications link to certain websites. Figure 1.5 illustrates the display of some of the plug-ins used by this author within Microsoft's Internet Explorer. Note that Microsoft refers to plug-ins as add-ons, a semantic that provides gainful employment for some persons charged with explaining technological terms. By selecting Tools from the menu bar and then selecting the Manage add-ons entry, you can view and manage the add-ons in an Internet Explorer environment.

1.1.1.1.3 Web Browsing While most people correctly associate the use of the Internet with a web browser, this is only one portion of a rather complex story. The first commercial browser introduced to the marketplace had a limited capability and was primarily used for navigation to different websites and the display of web pages. As websites proliferated, they began to add new applications that required

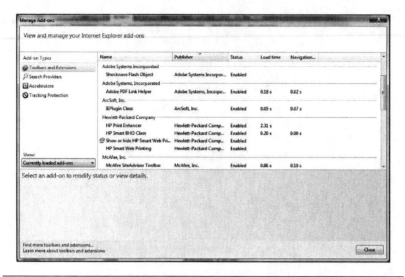

Figure 1.5   Managing add-ons in an Internet Explorer environment.

browser developers and third-party software developers to add plug-ins to extend the capabilities of browser software. Examples of some common plug-ins include video and audio conferencing, music playing, and authentication and encryption.

Figure 1.6 displays version 9 of Microsoft's Internet Explorer running on one of this author's many computers. In this example the author right-clicked on the shaded bar under the address bar and

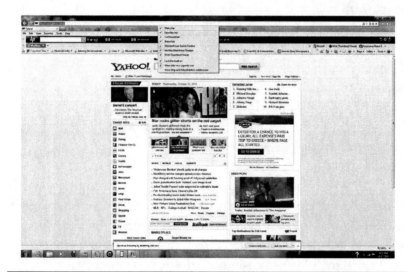

Figure 1.6   Every menu bar enabled in Internet Explorer version 9.

selected each option so that every menu bar supported by IE9 would be displayed. Note that at the bottom of the screen IE9 provides the user with the ability to speed up browsing by temporarily removing add-ons, a feature that can be extremely valuable for some readers. Concerning the address bar, yahoo.com was entered in Figure 1.6, which explains why the page shown was displayed. Through the use of 128-bit Secure Sockets Layer (SSL) connections Internet Explorer creates an automatically encrypted connection with websites run by banks, online stores, and other organizations that handle security-related data, allowing users of the browser to log in to each site and not worry about performing the required encryption or checking the certificate of the site. Note that once you are operating the browser in a secure mode a lock appears on the right side of the address bar, which when clicked upon displays a security report that identifies the website being accessed as well as providing data about its certificate and your connection to the website.

Internet Explorer is similar to most modern browsers in that it represents an integrated program that can be tailored through the use of different add-ons to the specific requirements of users. In fact, this browser software can be considered to represent an integrated program that includes the built-in ability to interconnect to such popular programs as the Microsoft Excel spreadsheet by exporting data into that program, translate a web page via Microsoft's Bing search engine, manage add-in programs, and even transmit a web page to a Bluetooth device, assuming the computer operating Windows has a Bluetooth capability. In fact, by simply right-clicking on a web page you can view the list of a few of the options available under Internet Explorer. While this program, as well as its various competitors, represents sophisticated programs that have considerably evolved over the years, we leave a comparison of programs to other books and conclude our overview of browsing by simply stating the obvious: Browsing, whether by computer or cell phone, tablet, or notebook, has profoundly altered our lives. Over the past decade electronic commerce on the web grew from under 10 million to over a billion transactions, with the TCP/IP protocol suite facilitating the growth in online sales due to the flexibility of the protocol suite to accommodate new protocols and applications necessary to support electronic commerce. This is why the well-publicized Black Friday is now followed by a Cyber Monday where billions of dollars in sales occur online in one 24-hour period.

Now that we have an appreciation for the role of a core set of TCP/IP applications, let us turn our attention to several emerging applications.

1.1.1.2 Emerging Applications There are several emerging applications that have the potential to alter the manner by which persons perform daily activities. While such applications are interesting from the perspective of a book on the evolution of the TCP/IP protocol suite, we also need to be aware of emerging applications because they create new demands upon network resources. Two emerging TCP/IP applications that deserve mention are audio-video communications and cloud computing.

1.1.1.2.1 Audio and Video Communications One of the major benefits of the Internet is its ability to function as a vast distribution center for information. While web surfing has been very popular for many years, within the past decade the distribution of music has literally skyrocketed with the introduction of MP3 players and various "stores" that enable customers to download individual songs for a dollar or less. Perhaps the defining moment in the annals of technology was October 23, 2001, when the original Apple iPod was introduced to the world. Since that time digitization has considerably evolved, to the point where the use of audio and video software-based players provide end users with the ability to enable their PCs to function like miniature televisions. Through the ability to digitize voice and video several calling or communications services have been developed. Such services enable low-cost to no-cost communications, with the latter popularized by Skype Communications, when a connection occurs between computers.

Figure 1.7 illustrates this author's Skype account as of October 2011, showing a balance of $7.30. Because most of this author's communications were computer to computer, the cost of audio and video calls was zero, explaining why an initial deposit of $10.00 into the account a few years earlier had hardly diminished.

One of the problems with Skype is similar to the problems users encounter when viewing cnn.com, yahoo.com, or another website

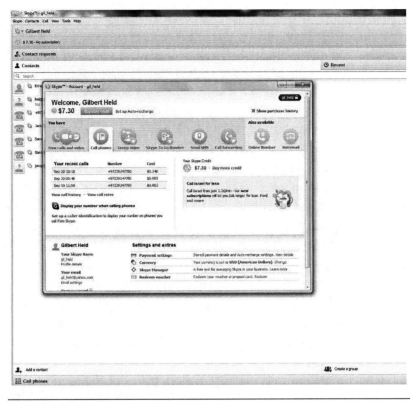

Figure 1.7 The author's Skype account, which enables no-cost computer-to-computer audio and video communications.

that incorporates audio and video that can be viewed by the click of a mouse. Because the video player buffers data to obtain the ability to eliminate random delays associated with the arrival of packets as they flow over the Internet and encounter different degrees of delay, any dropping of packets can adversely affect how the audio or video is reconstructed. This in turn may explain why a conversation will suddenly have an unnatural pause, or suddenly your view of your children on the other coast may become blocky and then revert to a good visual. For both situations lost packets probably caused the problem. Because routers, which can be considered the glue that holds the Internet together, are programmed to drop packets when high activity occurs that they cannot handle, only faster routers and additional bandwidth can alleviate this situation. However, due to the tremendous growth in Internet usage, we will probably have to live with this periodic problem for the foreseeable future.

While audio and video players can enable desktops to function like miniature televisions, they can also saturate the use of bandwidth on a network. When network congestion occurs this situation will result in some video players freezing their audio and video presentation and buffering data at a lower rate until a sufficient amount of data is buffered to allow playback. Because it is very easy for 50 to 100 employees to click on different music and news items, the cumulative effects of such actions can result in the necessity to either upgrade a network or restrict the use of audio and video players. To illustrate the importance of bandwidth, it is worth mentioning a video call this author made to his son located in a suburb of Seattle. While the video call was progressing smoothly and this author was able to both talk and see his grandson, all of a sudden video began to freeze and audio faded in and out. It turned out that the culprit was the other grandson, who had just begun an Xbox 360 communications session with a friend. While the author's local cable company and the Internet routing provided sufficient bandwidth, it was literally the last mile of cable connection in the Seattle suburb that could not handle both a video call and an Xbox 360 connection.

1.1.1.2.1.1 Problems with Technology   Both Voice over IP (VoIP) and Video over IP technology are extremely delay sensitive and do not tolerate lengthy packets transporting data interspersed between packets transporting digitized voice. Thus the ability to transmit Voice over IP and Video over IP can require equipment or software that prioritizes packets transporting voice or video over those transporting data, as well as fragmenting lengthy packets transporting data, so their transmission between voice and video carrying packets has a minimal effect upon the reconstruction of voice and video at the receiver.

1.1.1.2.2 *Cloud Computing*   Another emerging TCP/IP application is the use of the Internet as a VPN that enables access to computing facilities where such functions as the use of spreadsheets, word processing programs, and even the ability to synchronize data, including photographs and music, may be available. The latter, when offered by some cloud services, may allow users to synchronize data among computers, tablets, and even smart cell phones. The rationale for the use of the Internet in a cloud environment is economics. Leased lines are billed monthly based upon distance between interconnected locations and operation rate. In comparison, the use of the Internet is distance insensitive, with corporations primarily billed on a monthly basis based upon the operation rate of the access line that connects each corporate location to the Internet.

In addition to reducing the cost of communications, the use of cloud computing can save on equipment costs as well as the use of energy, resulting in cloud computing actually being a shade of green. This is because one connection to the Internet can support an almost unlimited number of virtual paths to different geographically separated corporate locations. In comparison, a private network requires routers at each location to have multiple ports to obtain the ability to interconnect one location with many other locations. Because router ports are relatively expensive, typically costing $1000 or more each, the ability to access cloud services via the use of the Internet can reduce the need for routers as well as computational facilities that are now shared among many organizations. Thus cloud computing can reduce the cost of both communications hardware and transmission facilities.

While cloud computing provides a mechanism to reduce both computer and networking costs, it opens up networks connected to the Internet to potential attack from a virtually unlimited population of hackers. Thus the use of cloud computing introduces the need to consider various security measures, to include firewalls, router access lists, and servers that perform authentication and encryption. Now that we have an appreciation for some of the emerging applications being developed for use under the TCP/IP protocol suite, we conclude this chapter by briefly previewing the focus of the succeeding chapters.

1.2 Book Preview

This book is divided into nine chapters. Here we review the focus of each chapter.

1.2.1 Examining the TCP/IP Protocol Suite

In Chapter 2 we present a detailed introduction to the major components of the TCP/IP protocol suite. Information presented shows the relationships of the various components of the protocol suite and their operations and functionality. By understanding the structure of the protocol suite, we can see its flexibility for adding new applications and protocols, as well as how its use has evolved over the past four decades.

1.2.2 IP and MAC Addressing

In Chapter 3 we commence our examination of protocol specifics by addressing the data link layer and the network layer. Referred to as layers 2 and 3 of the International Organization for Standardization (ISO) Open Systems Interconnection (OSI) Model, we can see how layer 2 addresses are resolved into layer 3 addresses for routing over the Internet or a company's intranet. We examine how the IP operates, its addressing method, to include IPv4 and IPv6, and several related protocols that are transported by either IP or at the data link layer. The two additional protocols we cover in Chapter 3 are the Internet Control Message Protocol (ICMP) and the Address Resolution Protocol (ARP).

1.2.3 Transport Layer Protocols

Chapter 4 focuses upon the transport layer, which represents the fourth layer of the ISO OSI Reference Model. We examine the operation of the two transport layer protocols included in the TCP/IP protocol suite, the Transmission Control Protocol (TCP) and the User Datagram Protocol (UDP). We note how each operates, the similarities and differences associated between the protocols, and how they are used by different applications. The reader will obtain an appreciation for how voice and video, as well as other types of digitized data, can be transported. In addition, we discuss how the network access rate and the use of local area networks (LANs) can affect the quality of transmission. This information is used in later chapters to describe the results of different network troubleshooting techniques that can be used to ascertain whether a voice or video application has sufficient bandwidth to operate, or if it would be appropriate to increase one's Internet connection prior to installing an application. Similarly, information from network troubleshooting can be used to ascertain why current applications have problems, as well as how to resolve such problems.

1.2.4 Working with the Command Prompt

Chapter 5 provides readers with information to assist in their use of Windows networking tools. Such tools primarily operate under the Command Prompt, and many were developed during the glory days of DOS. In this chapter we review the use of directories, how to control the Command Prompt display, as well as how to generate files of data or send such data to the printer to obtain a hard copy. In addition, some keyboard shortcuts that can be used to save time when performing different tasks are given.

1.2.5 Windows Built-In Networking Tools

Although many readers have either heard of or used ping and tracert, they represent only a small fraction of network troubleshooting tools built in to Windows. In Chapter 6 we turn our focus upon the operation and utilization of Windows built-in networking tools. We examine how certain tools can be used not only to gain insight into existing problems, but also as a mechanism to determine if a future bandwidth bottleneck or another problem can be expected to occur under different growth scenarios. Think about how you can possibly solve a problem before it actually becomes a problem, and you will realize how helpful the insight provided in various Windows networking tools in this chapter can be.

1.2.6 Network Monitoring

The ability to monitor the flow of data is a key element in a network technician's bag of tricks. In Chapter 7 we turn our attention to network monitoring and how a third-party tool can be used to understand traffic flow and the operational status of a network. We examine the Wireshark program, to include how we can capture and analyze traffic.

1.2.7 Network Security

Unfortunately, the growth in the use of networks resulted in the development of malicious software, ranging from keystroke loggers to viruses and other malware that make computers and even smart cell phones vulnerable. Because most TCP/IP networks include a connection to Internet security, it is an important topic. In Chapter 8 we examine the use of a number of software programs that can be used to enhance the security of a network.

1.2.8 Efficiency Methods

No book with the goal of providing readers with knowledge to diagnose networking problems would be complete without discussing the operation and utilization of a number of third-party and Windows-based tools that can enhance the performance of our computer. In Chapter 9 we turn our attention to the operation and utilization of several software products, some of which are included in Windows, which enable you to enhance the operational capability of your computer. For example, periodically running a built-in disk defragmentation program not only defragments your disks, but after use also speeds up disk reading and writing, which will enhance file uploads and downloads, as well as other disk operations. Thus while not directly related to networking operations, the tools covered in this chapter enhance many network operations.

Now that we have an appreciation for the orientation of this book, relax, grab your favorite beverage, and follow this author on a tour into the world of Windows networking tools.

2

Examining the TCP/ IP Protocol Suite

The primary objective of this chapter is to obtain an appreciation for the composition of the TCP/IP protocol suite. We first examine the International Organization for Standardization (ISO) Open Systems Interconnection (OSI) Reference Model, which was briefly mentioned in Chapter 1. Although the TCP/IP protocol suite predates the ISO's Reference Model, by examining the layering concept associated with communications defined by that model we can obtain a better appreciation for the functioning of the TCP/IP protocol suite. Let's examine the ISO Reference Model.

2.1 ISO Reference Model

During the 1970s, which was approximately a dozen years after the development of several popular communications protocols, to include TCP/IP, the ISO established a framework for standardizing communications systems. This framework was called the OSI Reference Model. One of the key goals behind the development of the OSI Reference Model was to define an architecture in which communications functions could be divided into seven distinct layers, with specific functions becoming the responsibility of a particular layer. By breaking communications into layers, it became easier for software and hardware developers to work on communications projects, as teams could be assigned to work on different layers of a protocol, which could then be linked together in a standardized manner.

Figure 2.1 illustrates the seven layers of the ISO Reference Model. Note that each layer, with the exception of the lowest, covers a lower layer, effectively isolating each layer from higher-layer functions. Similarly, with the exception of the topmost layer, which is the seventh in the model, each layer interconnects with a higher layer,

Layer 7	Application
Layer 6	Presentation
Layer 5	Session
Layer 4	Transport
Layer 3	Network
Layer 2	Data Link
Layer 1	Physical

Figure 2.1   The ISO's Open Systems Interconnection Reference Model.

facilitating interoperability. Layer isolation is an important aspect of the ISO Reference Model, as it allows the given characteristics of one layer to change without affecting the remaining layers of the model, provided that support services remain the same. This becomes possible since well-known interface points in a layered model enable one layer to communicate with another even though one or both layers may change. In addition, the layering process permits end users to mix and match OSI or other layered protocol-conforming communications products to tailor their communications system to satisfy a particular networking requirement. Thus the OSI Reference Model, as well as protocol suites that employ a layered architecture, provides the potential to directly interconnect networks based upon the use of different vendor products. This architecture, which is referred to as an open architecture when its specifications are licensed or placed in the public domain, can be of substantial benefit to both users and vendors.

An open architecture removes users from dependence upon a particular vendor, and may also be considered to be economically advantageous, as it fosters competition among vendors. For vendors, this open architecture enables products to reach the market and possibly gain widespread acceptance in comparison to proprietary systems. Thus the ability for vendors to easily interconnect their products with the products produced by other vendors opens up a wider market. This in turn fosters competition, which as many students of economics understand should result in a lowering of costs in a competitive environment, unless a nefarious activity such as price fixing occurs. Hopefully this is why governments exist and we can ignore such activities from consideration.

Now that we have an appreciation for the value of a layered architecture, let us turn our attention to the functions of the seven layers of the OSI Reference Model.

2.1.1 OSI Reference Model Layers

As noted, the OSI Reference Model consists of seven layers, with specific functions occurring at each layer. Here we turn our attention to obtaining an understanding of the functions performed at each layer in the OSI Reference Model. Once this is accomplished, we use the information gained in the next section to better understand the components of the TCP/IP protocol suite.

2.1.1.1 Layer 1: The Physical Layer   The physical layer, as shown in Figure 2.1, represents the lowest layer in the ISO Reference Model. Because the physical layer involves the connection of a communications system to a communications medium, the physical layer is responsible for specifying the electrical and physical connection between communications devices that connect to different types of media. At this layer such information as cable connectors and the electrical rules necessary to transfer data between devices is specified. A few examples of physical layer standards include the well-known RS-232, V.24, and V.35 interfaces.

2.1.1.2 Layer 2: The Data Link Layer   Moving up the ISO's OSI model we come to the data link layer, which is layer 2 in the model. The data link layer is responsible for defining the manner by which a device gains access to the medium specified in the physical layer. In addition, the data link layer is also responsible for defining data formats, to include the entity by which information is transported, error control procedures, and other link control procedures.

Most trade literature and other technically oriented publications reference the entity by which information is transported at the data link layer as a frame. Depending upon the protocol used, the frame will have a certain header composition with fields that normally indicate the destination address and the originator or source address of the frame. In addition, frames will have a trailer with a cyclic redundancy check (CRC) field that indicates the value of an error-checking mechanism algorithm performed by the originator on the contents of the frame. The receiver will apply the same algorithm to an inbound received frame and compare the locally generated CRC to the CRC in the trailer. If the two match, the frame is considered to be received without error, while a mismatch indicates a transmission error occurred, and the receiver will then normally request the originator to retransmit the frame. A key exception to the retransmission of error frames occurs when voice is digitized and transferred as 20 ms of digitized data. Here the retransmission of a frame containing an error would introduce a variable delay that would inhibit the reconstruction of the original conversation. Thus the receiver's software would either drop the frame or carefully examine the preceding and succeeding frames in an attempt to smooth out the conversation, with the procedure for handling errors usually differentiating one product from another. Examples of common layer 2 protocols include such local area network (LAN) protocols as Ethernet and Token-Ring, as well as such wide area network (WAN) like High-Level Data Link Control (HDLC).

2.1.1.3 Layer 2 Subdivision   The original development of the OSI Reference Model was targeted toward wide area networking. This resulted in its applicability to LANs requiring a degree of modification. The Institute of Electrical and Electronic Engineers (IEEE), which was delegated the responsibility for developing LAN standards by the American National Standards Institute (ANSI), subdivided the data link layer into two sublayers: Logical Link Control (LLC) and Media Access Control (MAC). The LLC layer is responsible for generating and interpreting commands that control the flow of data and performing recovery operations in the event errors are detected. In comparison, the MAC layer is responsible for providing access to the local area network, which enables a station on the network to transmit information. The subdivision of the data link layer allows a common LLC layer to be used regardless of differences in the method of network access. Thus a common LLC is used for both Ethernet and Token-Ring, although their access methods are dissimilar.

2.1.1.4 Layer 3: The Network Layer   Once again let's move up the ISO Reference Model, this time to the third layer, the network layer.

This layer is responsible for arranging a logical connection between a source and destination on the network. This action includes the selection and management of a route for the flow of information between the source and destination based upon the available paths within a network. Note that the source and destination can be any type of computational device, ranging from a conventional desktop computer to a router, tablet, or even smart phone.

Services or functions provided at the network layer are associated with the movement of data through a network. Thus this can include addressing, routing, switching, sequencing, as well as flow control procedures to enable the orderly flow of data. At the network layer units of information are placed into packets that have a header and trailer similar to frames at the data link layer. Thus the network layer packet will contain addressing information as well as a field that facilitates error detection and correction. Between the data link layer and network layer we have frames and packets, each with unique addresses. Thus we need a mechanism to resolve one address to another address at a different layer. In a TCP/IP environment this technique is referred to as address resolution and occurs using the Address Resolution Protocol (ARP), which we discuss later in this chapter and the next.

Returning to our discussion of the network layer, it's important to note that in a complex network, the source and destination may not be directly connected by a single path. Instead a path may be required to be established through the network that consists of several sub-paths. Thus the routing of packets through the network, as well as the mechanism in the form of routing protocols that provide information about available paths, is an important feature of this layer.

Currently there are over 20 protocols that are standardized for layer 3, which can be subdivided into operating protocols and management protocols. Examples of the former include the International Telecommunications Union Telecommunications (ITU-T) body X.25 packet switching protocol, the ITU-T X.75 gateway protocol, Internet Protocol versions 4 and 6, IPSec or IP Security, and the Internet Control Message Protocol (ICMP). It should be noted that X.25 governs the flow of information through the packet network, whereas X.75 governs the flow of information between packet networks. Examples of the latter include Open Shortest Path First

(OSPF), Routing Information Protocol (RIP), and Border Gateway Protocol (BGP), all of which are routing protocols.

When we examine the TCP/IP protocol suite later in this chapter, as well as in succeeding chapters, we note that there are two operating versions of the Internet Protocol (IP), IPv4 and IPv6, both of which represent the network layer protocol used in the TCP/IP protocol suite. IPv4 is the primary mechanism used on the Internet; however, the last IPv4 address was used and there are no longer any IPv4 addresses available. Thus the Internet is gravitating to the use of IPv6.

2.1.1.5 Layer 4: The Transport Layer   Continuing our tour of the ISO Reference Model, the transport layer is responsible for governing the transfer of information after a route has been established through the network by the network layer protocol. There are two general types of transport layer protocols: connection oriented and connectionless. A connection-oriented protocol first requires the establishment of a connection prior to the actual data transfer occurring. This type of transport layer protocol performs error control, sequence checking, and other end-to-end data reliability functions. A second type or category of transport layer protocol operates as a connectionless, best-effort protocol. This type depends upon higher layers in the protocol suite for error detection and correction. When we examine the TCP/IP protocol suite we note that TCP represents a layer 4 connection-oriented protocol, while the User Datagram Protocol (UDP) represents a connectionless layer 4 protocol. Other examples of transport layer protocols include Authentication Header (AH) over IP or IPSec, Encapsulating Security Payload (ESP) over IP or IPSec, and Generic Routing Encapsulation (GRE) for tunneling.

2.1.1.6 Layer 5: The Session Layer   Continuing our tour of the OSI Reference Model, the fifth layer is the session layer. This layer is responsible for providing a set of rules that govern the establishment and termination of data streams flowing between nodes in a network. The services that the session layer can provide include establishing and terminating node connections, message flow control, dialog control, and end-to-end data control. In the TCP/IP protocol suite layers 5 through 7 are grouped together as an application layer. Examples of session layer protocols include the Netware Core Protocol (NCP) and the Network File System (NFS).

2.1.1.7 Layer 6: The Presentation Layer The sixth layer of the OSI Reference Model is the presentation layer. This layer is concerned with the conversion of transmitted data into a display format appropriate for a receiving device. This conversion can include data codes as well as display placement. Other functions performed at the presentation layer can include data compression and decompression and data encryption and decryption.

2.1.1.8 Layer 7: The Application Layer The top layer of the OSI Reference Model is the application layer. This layer functions as a window through which the application gains access to all of the services provided by the model. Examples of functions performed at the application layer include electronic mail, file transfers, resource sharing, and database access. Although the first four layers of the OSI Reference Model are fairly well defined, the top three layers can vary considerably between networks. As previously mentioned, the TCP/IP protocol suite, which is a layered protocol that predates the ISO Reference Model, combines layers 5 through 7 into one application layer. Thus while the File Transfer Protocol (FTP), Telnet, the remote access protocol, and the web browsing protocols Hypertext Transfer Protocol (HTTP) and its security version Hypertext Transfer Protocol Secure (HTTPS) are many times listed as layer 7 protocols, in reality they cover the upper three layers of the ISO Reference Model.

2.1.2 Data Flow

The design of an ISO Reference Model-compatible network is such that a series of headers are appended to each data unit as packets are transmitted and delivered at layer 2 by frames. At the receiver, the headers are removed as a data unit flows up the protocol suite, until the headerless data unit is identical to the transmitted data unit. In the next section, we will examine the flow of data in a TCP/IP network that follows the previously described ISO Reference Model data flow.

The ISO Reference Model never lived up to its intended goal, with ISO protocols achieving a less than anticipated level of utilization.

The concept of the model made persons aware of the benefits that could be obtained by a layered open architecture as well as the functions that would be performed by different layers of the model. Thus the ISO can be considered as succeeding in making networking personnel aware of the benefits that could be derived from a layered open architecture and more than likely contributed to the success of the acceptance of the TCP/IP protocol suite. We now turn our attention to the TCP/IP protocol suite.

2.2 The TCP/IP Protocol Suite

The Transmission Control Protocol/Internet Protocol (TCP/IP) can be considered to represent two distinct protocols within the TCP/IP protocol suite, although in actuality there are numerous protocols, most of which are seldom used. Due to the popularity of those two protocols, and the fact that a majority of traffic is transferred using them, the members of the protocol suite include TCP and IP and are collectively referred to as TCP/IP.

In Figure 2.2 a general comparison of the structure of the TCP/IP protocol suite to the OSI Reference Model is provided. "General comparison" is used because the protocol suite consists of hundreds of applications, of which only a handful are shown. A second reason that Figure 2.2 represents a general comparison is because the TCP/IP protocol suite actually begins above the data link layer. Although the physical and data link layers are not part of the TCP/IP protocol suite, they are shown in Figure 2.2

ISO Reference Model Layer	TCP/IP Protocol Suite						
Application / Presentation / Session	FTP	HTTP	Telnet	SMTP	DNS	SNMP	Other Applications
Transport	TCP				UDP		
Network	ICMP / IP / ARP						
Data Link	Ethernet	Token Ring		X.25	Frame Relay		Other
Physical	Physical Layer						

Figure 2.2   Comparing the TCP/IP protocol suite to the ISO Reference Model.

to provide a frame of reference to the ISO Reference Model as well as to facilitate an explanation of the role of two special protocols within the TCP/IP protocol suite. For example, Ethernet local area networks, which are defined at the first two layers of the ISO OSI Reference Model, are IEEE standards that, although they interact with TCP/IP, are not defined as TCP/IP standards. As a matter of digression but of interest, ANSI, which was tasked with developing communications standards, literally passed the buck and tasked the IEEE with developing LAN standards. This is how the IEEE's efforts in the area of 802.x standards became recognized around the world.

2.2.1 The TCP/IP Network Layer

The TCP/IP protocol suite actually begins at the third layer of the ISO OSI Reference Model, which is the network. The network layer of the TCP/IP protocol stack primarily consists of the IP, a messaging protocol referred to as the ICMP and an ARP, which resolves layer 2 and layer 3 addresses, as we shortly note.

The IP protocol includes an addressing scheme that identifies the source and destination address of the packet being transported. In TCP/IP terminology the unit of data being transmitted at the network layer is referred to as a datagram, although it is also commonly referred to as a packet.

2.2.2 IP

The IP provides the addressing capability that allows datagrams to be routed between networks. The current version of IP is IPv4, under which IP addresses consist of 32 bits. As this book goes to press the last IPv4 addresses were assigned, which has resulted in a growing emphasis for Internet service providers (ISPs) as well as major websites to migrate to IPv6, which has a 128-bit addressing capability. This expanded addressing capability ensures that every person on the globe can be assigned a unique address for multiple devices with extra capacity to spare. Thus the primary goal for expanding IP addressing was accomplished through the development and deployment of IPv6. As an additional rationale, IPv6 enables security and other functions to occur more naturally and will be described later in this book. For now we simply become familiar with IP addressing.

2.2.2.1 IPv4 Addressing   There are five classes of IPv4 addresses, referred to as Class A through Class E, with Classes A, B, and C having their 32 bits subdivided into a network portion and a host portion. The network portion of the address defines the network where a particular host resides, while the host portion of the address identifies a unique host on the network. In Chapter 4 we examine the Internet Protocol in detail, to include its current method of 32-bit addressing as well as the 128-bit addressing of IPv6.

2.2.2.2 IPv6 Addressing   The primary motivation for creating IPv6 was to rectify the addressing limitations associated with the use of IPv4. In addition to expanding the number of available addresses, backward compatibility was required, as well as developing a mechanism to incorporate design evolutions through the use of a header that enables additional subheaders to be incorporated into data flow.

2.2.2.2.1 IPv6 Address Size   In IPv4, IP addresses are 32 bits long; these are usually grouped into four octets of 8 bits each. Thus the theoretical IPv4 address space is 2^{32}, or 4,294,967,296 addresses. Since each extra bit assigned to the address size doubles the address space, expanding IP addresses to 128 bits results in a significant increase in possible addresses to 2^{128}, or 340,282,366,920,938,463,463,374,607,431,768,211,456 addresses for those of us mathematically inclined to work with powers of two. Because this number by far exceeds the number of grains of sand on the earth, IPv6 addresses provide multiple levels of hierarchy that are lacking in IPv4. For example, a unicast address where communications occur directly from an originator to a receiver is indicated by the prefix 001 in the first three bits of the address. The remaining 125 bits can be used as a global routing prefix (64 bits, to include the first three bits set to 001 for a unicast address), which indicates a network ID or prefix of the address used for routing, 16 bits for a subnet identifier, and the remaining 64 bits functioning as an interface identifier. In Chapter 4 we examine the wonderful world of IP addressing, to include the types of IP addresses supported under IPv4 and IPv6.

2.2.2.3 ARP One of the more significant differences between the data link layer and the network layer is the method of addressing used at each. At the data link layer, LANs such as Ethernet and Token-Ring networks use 48-bit MAC addresses. In addition, most tablet computers have a built-in Ethernet port that is commonly used for connecting to a cable or DSL modem in the home. In comparison, TCP/IP currently uses either 32-bit or 128-bit addresses depending upon the version of IP in use. Thus the delivery of a packet or datagram flowing at the network layer to a station on a LAN, even when the computer is directly connected to a network via a cable or DSL modem, requires an address conversion. That address conversion is performed by the ARP, whose operation is covered in detail in Chapter 4.

2.2.2.4 ICMP The ICMP, as its name implies, represents a protocol used to convey control messages. Such messages range in scope from routers responding to a request that cannot be honored, with a "destination unreachable" message flowing back to the requestor, to messages that convey diagnostic tests and responses. An example of the latter is the echo request/echo response pair of ICMP datagrams that is more popularly referred to collectively as ping.

ICMP messages are conveyed with the prefix of an IP header to the message. Thus we can consider ICMP to represent a layer 3 protocol in the TCP/IP protocol suite. We will examine the structure of ICMP messages as well as the use of certain messages in Chapter 4 when we look at the network layer of the TCP/IP protocol suite in detail. As you might surmise, there are two versions of ICMP, ICMPv4 and ICMPv6, with the one in use dependent upon which version of TCP/IP is in use. In Chapter 4 we will cover both ICMPv4 and ICMPv6.

2.2.3 The Transport Layer

As indicated in Figure 2.2, there are two transport layer protocols supported by the TCP/IP protocol suite: TCP and UDP.

2.2.3.1 TCP TCP is an error-free, connection-oriented protocol. This means that prior to data being transmitted by TCP the protocol requires the establishment of a path between source and destination as well as an acknowledgment that the receiver is ready to receive information. After the flow of data commences, each unit, which is referred to as a TCP segment, is checked for errors at the receiver. If an error is detected through a checksum process, the receiver will request the originator to retransmit the segment. Thus TCP represents an error-free, connection-oriented protocol where error correction is performed by retransmission.

The advantages associated with the use of TCP as a transport protocol relate to its error-free, connection-oriented functionality. For the transmission of relatively large quantities of data or important information, it makes sense to use this transport layer protocol. The connection-oriented feature of the protocol means that it will require a period of time for the source and destination to exchange handshake information. In addition, the error-free capability of the protocol may be redundant if the higher layer in the protocol suite also performs error checking. Recognizing the previously mentioned problems, the developers of the TCP/IP protocol suite added a second transport layer protocol referred to as UDP.

2.2.3.2 UDP   The UDP is a connectionless, best-effort, non-error-checking transport protocol. UDP was developed in recognition of the fact that some applications, such as the transport of real-time digitized voice, may require small pieces of information to be transferred, and the use of a connection-oriented protocol would result in a significant overhead to the transfer of data. Because a higher layer in the protocol suite could perform error checking, error detection and correction could also be eliminated from UDP. Because UDP transmits a piece of information referred to as a UDP datagram without first establishing a connection to the receiver, it is also called a best-effort protocol. To ensure that a series of UDP datagrams are not transmitted into a black hole if a receiver is not available, the higher layer in the protocol suite using UDP as a transport protocol will wait for an acknowledgment. If one is not received within a predefined period of time, the application can decide whether to retransmit or cancel the session. For example, in a Voice over IP environment the retransmission of a datagram transporting voice would result in a delay distortion that would make the reconstructed voice sound awkward, which explains why real-time Voice over IP implementations do not retransmit datagrams.

In examining Figure 2.2 you will note that certain applications use TCP as their transport protocol, while other applications use UDP. In general, applications that require data integrity, such as remote terminal transmission (Telnet), file transfer (FTP), secure web browsing (HTTPS), and electronic mail, use TCP as their transport protocol. In comparison, applications that transmit relatively short packets, such as the Domain Name Service (DNS) and the Simple Network Management Protocol (SNMP) that is used to perform network management operations, use UDP.

Two relatively new TCP/IP applications take advantage of both the TCP and UDP transport protocols. Those applications are Voice over IP (VoIP) and Video over IP. VoIP commonly uses TCP to set up a call and convey signaling information to the distant party. After all, it's extremely important to be able to access the correct distant party. Because real-time voice cannot be delayed by retransmission if an error is detected, there is no need to perform error detection. Thus digitized voice samples are commonly transmitted using UDP once a session is established using TCP. Similarly, video applications, which include digitization of output from web cams and other types of cameras and digitized voice from microphones, initiate a call using TCP and then transmit digitized video and voice via UDP.

2.2.4 *The Application Layer*

The development of the TCP/IP protocol suite predated the development of ISO's OSI Reference Model. At the time the TCP/IP protocol suite was initially developed functions above the transport layer were combined into one entity that represented an application. Thus the TCP/IP protocol suite does not include separate session and presentation layers. Now that we have an appreciation for the manner by which the TCP/IP protocol stack can be compared and contrasted to the OSI Reference Model, we conclude this chapter by examining the flow of data within a TCP/IP network.

2.3 Data Flow within a TCP/IP Network

Data flow within a TCP/IP network commences at the application layer, where data are provided to an applicable transport layer protocol, such as TCP or UDP. At layer 4, the transport layer opens either a TCP or a UDP header to the application data depending upon the transport protocol used by the application layer.

The transport layer protocol uses a port number to distinguish the type of application data being transported. Through the use of port numbers, it becomes possible to distinguish one application from another that flows between a common source and destination. For lay personnel not familiar with TCP or IP, this explains how a common hardware platform, such as a Windows-based server, can support both web and FTP services. That is, although the server's interface has a common IP address contained in an IP header, the port number in the TCP or UDP header indicates the application.

Application data flowing onto a network is first formed into a TCP segment or UDP datagram. The resulting UDP datagram or TCP segment is then passed to the network layer where an IP header is opened. The IP header contains network addressing information that is used by routers to route datagrams through a network.

When an IP datagram reaches a LAN, the difference between the network layer and LAN address is first resolved through ARP. Once this is accomplished, the IP datagram is placed into a LAN frame using an appropriate MAC address in the LAN header. Figure 2.3 illustrates the data flow within a TCP/IP network for delivery to a

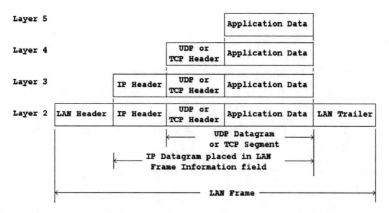

Figure 2.3   Data flow on a TCP/IP network to a station on a local area network.

station on a LAN. Here the term *station* is used to denote any type of computational device, to include an adapter card connected to a LAN-based printer.

2.4 Summary

The TCP/IP protocol suite represents a methodically considered and developed collection of protocols and applications. It includes a very flexible open architecture that allows new applications and protocols to be developed. In fact, although we are just beginning our examination of TCP/IP, we have already noted how Voice over IP and Video over IP can be considered additions to the flexibility of TCP/IP.

3

ADDRESSING AT LAYERS 2 AND 3 AND THE INTERNET PROTOCOL

In this chapter we continue to acquire a foundation of knowledge concerning both Ethernet LANs and the TCP/IP protocol suite by focusing attention upon the data link and network layer addressing as well as the Internet Protocol (IP), to include the Address Resolution Protocol (ARP) and both versions of Internet Control Message Protocol (ICMP). IP represents both the network layer protocol in the TCP/IP protocol suite and the data delivery mechanism, which enables packets to be routed from source to destination. However, when data are delivered to a device, such as a workstation on a LAN or even a computer accessing the Internet via a cable modem, the physical interface at the data link layer represents a 48-bit Media Access Control (MAC) address, while the IP address at the network layer is either a 48-bit IPv4 address or a 128-bit IPv6 address. Thus a mechanism is required to deliver the IP addressed data to the physical 48-bit hardware address. That mechanism is ARP.

In this chapter we first examine addressing at the second layer in the ISO Open Systems Interconnection (OSI) Reference Model, which is the data link layer. Next we gain familiarity with the various versions of gigabit and 10 Gigabit Ethernet transmission techniques, to include transmission over fiber and metallic conductors. While covering this topic may initially appear questionable, when you need to analyze a particular type of Ethernet transmission this information will be of considerable value. Once this is accomplished we move up one layer in the protocol stack and examine IP addressing. This includes a detailed examination of IP addressing since many network-related problems can be traced to this area. Then we examine the composition of the fields within the IPv4 and IPv6 headers. Because ICMP messages are transported via IP we also examine the ICMP.

3.1 Data Link Addressing

In this section we focus on the 48-bit addressing specified for LANs by the IEEE. Since there are several types of data link addressing, we narrow our focus to what is referred to as MAC addressing. As Ethernet is by far the dominant local area network in use, and both DSL and cable modems typically connect to a computer's built-in Ethernet port, the first portion of this chapter provides an examination of Ethernet frame operations.

3.1.1 Ethernet Frame Operations

We will turn our attention to the composition of different types of Ethernet frames. In actuality, there is only one Ethernet frame; the Carrier Sense Multiple Access with Collision Detection (CSMA/CD) frame format was standardized by the IEEE and is technically referred to as an 802.3 frame. Here the term *802.3* is used to indicate the IEEE standard for Ethernet. However, in this book we collectively reference CSMA/CD operations as Ethernet and, when appropriate, indicate differences between Ethernet and the IEEE 802.3 Ethernet-based CSMA/CD standard. One such area worthy of a comparison is the frame format, which differs between Ethernet and the IEEE 802.3 Ethernet-based CSMA/CD standard. Upon obtaining an understanding of the composition of Ethernet and IEEE 802.3 frames, we examine the function of fields within each frame, and then discuss the overhead of the frame with respect to its information transfer capability.

Ethernet has used a 1500-byte Data field and 26 bytes of Header and Trailer fields from its original development at 10 Mbps through Fast Ethernet operating at 100 Mbps and Gigabit Ethernet operating at 1 Gbit/s, as well as 10 Gigabit Ethernet (10GbE). If we first focus on Ethernet operating at 10 Mbps we note that while the field lengths remain uniform, their use varies with the result that we can consider those variations to represent changes in Ethernet's frame format. Similarly, Fast Ethernet retained the frame structure of its older Ethernet cousin but used a few tricks to maintain compatibility. When discussing GigaEthernet or Gbit/s Ethernet, although it dates to 1999 with the development of three IEEE standards, two additional standards for transport of data were introduced in 2004. By the time this book was written in 2012 there were nine varieties of Gigabit Ethernet, ranging from a twin-axial version for transmission up to 25 m to the use of a single-mode fiber that enables a transmission distance up to approximately 70 km. A higher-bandwidth version of Ethernet, referred to as 10 Gigabit Ethernet, was standardized in 2002 for fiber, while a twisted pair standard was developed in 2006. As of 2012 10 Gigabit Ethernet was replacing 1 Gigabit Ethernet as a backbone for corporate networks and the Internet and had migrated down to high-end server systems. With a need for speed due to hundreds of millions of tablets, smart phones, and other devices requiring Internet access 40 Gigabit Ethernet (40GbE) and 100 Gigabit Ethernet (100GbE) were developed. These standards support transmitting Ethernet at 40 and 100 Gbit/s over multiple 10 or 25 Gbit/s lanes. They were first examined in November 2007, proposed as the IEEE 802.3ba standard in 2008, and ratified in June 2010, while another variant was added in March 2011.

When the speed of Ethernet increased to 1 Gbit/s several vendors created support for what are now referred to as jumbo frames as a mechanism to enhance LAN and WAN performance. Although jumbo frames have not been officially recognized as a standard by the IEEE, they deserve mention and are discussed in this section. In addition, when operating in a half-duplex mode Gigabit Ethernet uses a carrier extension as a mechanism to increase the range of transmission.

Another area that modified the Ethernet frame was the standardization of virtual LANs by the IEEE. Because the standard requires a 4-byte virtual local area network (vLAN) tag, the use of Ethernet in a vLAN environment means that the Ethernet frame will be modified.

In this and succeeding chapters we use the terms *bytes* and *octets* to reference the width of different Header fields. The term *octet* was employed by standards organizations to explicitly reference 8 bits operated upon as an entity at a time when computers were manufactured with different numbers of bits per byte. To alleviate potential confusion when referencing a group of eight bits, standards organizations

Preamble	Destination Address	Source Address	Type	Data	Frame Check Sequence
Bytes: 8	6	6	2	46–1500	4

Figure 3.1   The Ethernet DIX frame.

turned to the term *octet*. Today essentially all computers use 8-bit bytes, and the terms *byte* and *octet* are commonly used synonymously.

3.1.1.1 Basic Ethernet   Prior to the IEEE 802.3 committee taking responsibility for the development of Ethernet this LAN was administered by the so-called DIX consortium, consisting of Digital Equipment Corporation, Intel, and Xerox Corporation. At that time the format of an Ethernet frame followed the DIX standard, and in some literature you might note that it is referred to as the Ethernet version II or DIX frame, which is illustrated in Figure 3.1.

3.1.1.1.1 The Ethernet II/DIX Frame   Because the Ethernet DIX frame provides a base for further modifications that occurred, we examine each field in the frame in detail.

3.1.1.1.1.1 Preamble Field   The Preamble field consists of 8 bytes of alternating binary 1s and 0s. The purpose of this field is to announce the frame as well as to enable receivers on the network to synchronize themselves to the incoming frame. In addition, the 8 bytes or 64 bits in this frame ensures that there is a minimum spacing of 9.6 μs at 10 Mbps between frames for error detection and recovery operations.

3.1.1.1.1.2 Destination Address Field   The Destination Address field identifies the recipient of the frame. Although this field appears to be simple, the first two bits are used to define how the following 46 bits are interpreted.

Figure 3.2 illustrates the subdivision of the Destination Address field into three subfields. As indicated, the setting of the I/G bit subfield to a binary 0 indicates that the 46-bit address is an individual or

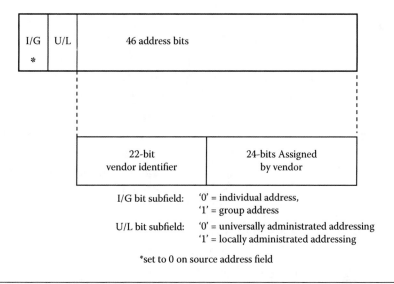

I/G *	U/L	46 address bits

22-bit vendor identifier	24-bits Assigned by vendor

I/G bit subfield: '0' = individual address,
                     '1' = group address

U/L bit subfield: '0' = universally administrated addressing
                     '1' = locally administrated addressing

*set to 0 on source address field

Figure 3.2   The Ethernet Destination Address field.

unicast address. When the value of the subfield is set to a binary 1, the address field represents a group address. One specific example of a group address is the assignment of all 1s to the address field. Here the address hex FFFFFFFFFFFF, where each F represents four set bits, is recognized as a broadcast address, and each station on a network receives and accepts frames with that address.

The second subfield, which is labeled U/L, is set to a binary 0 to represent the fact that the address is a universally administered address, while a setting of binary 1 indicates that the address is locally administered. As a refresher, a universally administrated address indicates that the address is unique and reflects a burnt-in read-only memory (ROM) address on a network interface card (NIC) or Ethernet chip set. Initially Xerox was responsible for administrating universal addresses by assigning one or more blocks representing the first 24 bits (3 bytes) to vendors. Later the IEEE became responsible for administrative functions, to include assigning blocks of 24-bit addresses to vendors. Vendors would then use the remaining 24 bits to assign unique addresses to one or more blocks of addresses based upon the popularity of their products. That is, once they used all $24^2 - 1$ addresses they would begin anew with a new vendor code.

3.1.1.1.1.3 Source Address Field   The Source Address field identifies the station that transmitted the frame. Similar to the destination address, the Source Address field is 6 bytes in length, with the first 3 bytes (actually the last 24 bits in the first three bytes) assigned initially by Xerox and later by the IEEE to the manufacturer for incorporation into each NIC's ROM. The vendor then normally assigns the last three bytes to each of its NICs or chip sets so that each 46-bit address is unique. Because the first three bytes are assigned to manufacturers, another term used to reference this subfield is the Manufacturer subfield.

3.1.1.1.1.4 Type Field   The 2-byte Type field was used by Xerox and later the DIX consortium to identify the protocol transported with an Ethernet frame. Since the minimum length of an Ethernet frame is 64 bytes, each of the higher-level protocols defined by a Type field value required either a larger minimum message length or an internal field that could be used to distinguish data from padding.

3.1.1.1.1.5 Data Field   The Data field must be a minimum of 46 bytes in length to ensure that an Ethernet frame, without considering the 8-byte preamble, is 64 bytes in length. This means that the transmission of 1 byte of information must be carried within a 46-byte Data field and results in the padding of the remainder of the field if the information to be placed in the field is less than 46 bytes. Although some publications subdivide the Data field to show a PAD subfield, the latter actually represents optional fill characters that are added to the information in the Data field to ensure a length of at least 46 bytes. The maximum length of the Data field is 1500 bytes, which results in the use of multiple frames to transport full-screen images, photographs, and almost all file transfers.

3.1.1.1.1.6 Frame Check Sequence Field   The Frame Check Sequence (FCS) is applied by the transmitter computing a cyclic redundancy check (CRC), which covers the two address fields, the Type field and the Data field. The transmitter then places the CRC in the 4-byte FCS field.

The CRC is developed by treating the composition of the previously named fields as one long binary number. The n bits to be covered by the

CRC are considered to represent the coefficients of a polynomial $M(x)$ of degree $n - 1$. Here, the first bit in the Destination Address field corresponds to the X^{n-1} term, whereas the last bit in the Data field corresponds to the x^0 term. Next, $M(x)$ is multiplied by X^{32} and the results of that multiplication process are divided by the following polynomial:

$G(X) = X^{32} + X^{26} + X^{23} + X^{22} + X^{16} + X^{12} + X^{11} + X^{10} + X^8 + X^7 + X^5 + X^4 + X^3 + X + 1$

Readers should note that the term X^n represents the setting of a bit to a 1 in position n. Thus part of the generating polynomial $X^5 + X^4 + X^3 + X$ represents the binary value 111011.

The result of the division produces a quotient and a remainder. The quotient is discarded and the remainder becomes the CRC value, which is placed in the 4-byte FCS field. The 32-bit CRC reduces the probability of an undetected error to 1 bit in every 4.3 billion, or approximately 1 bit in $2^{32} - 1$ bits.

Once a frame reaches its destination the receiver uses the same polynomial to perform the same operation upon the received data, resulting in the computation of a local CRC. If the locally generated CRC matches the one in the FCS field, the frame is accepted. Otherwise, the receiver discards the frame, as it is considered to have one or more bits in error. The receiver also considers a received frame to be invalid and discards it under two additional conditions. Those conditions occur when the frame does not contain an integral number of bytes or when the length of the Data field does not match the value contained in the Length field. The latter condition is only applicable to the IEEE 802.3 frame, which we examine next.

3.1.1.1.2 The 802.3 Frame The key differences between the Ethernet Type II/DIX frame and the IEEE 802.3 Ethernet frame are in the Preamble field, and the change from a 2-byte Type field to a 2-byte Length field.

3.1.1.1.2.1 Length Field   When the IEEE took over the standardization of Ethernet it needed to ensure a minimum frame length of 64 bytes to enable collision detection to work properly. While the Ethernet II/DIX frame solved the minimum frame length through the selection of higher-level protocols that resulted in a minimum frame length of 64 bytes, for Ethernet to be interchangeable with other types of LANs the IEEE needed to replace the Type field with a Length field to distinguish data from padding.

3.1.1.1.2.2 Preamble Field Modification   The second change to the Ethernet II/DIX frame occurred by splitting the 8-byte Preamble field into a 7-byte Preamble field and a 1-byte Start of Frame Delimiter (SFD) field. The 8-byte Preamble field consisted of a repeating sequence of binary 0s and 1s. When the field was split the new 7-byte Preamble field retained this sequence, which was then carried over into the Start of Frame Delimiter field with the exception of the last two bits, which were now both set to binary 1s. Thus the only difference between the old Preamble field and the new Preamble and Start of Delimiter fields is one set bit, which assists the synchronization effort.

3.1.1.1.2.3 Type/Length Field Values   When Xerox was the custodian of Ethernet it had not assigned any important protocols to have a value below 1500. Since the maximum length of an Ethernet Data field is 1500 bytes and the change in the Preamble field only enhances synchronization, in essence DIX and 802.3 frames are compatible. That is, any Ethernet frame with a Type/Length field value less than 1500 is an 802.3 frame, while any frame with a field value greater than 1500 must be in DIX format and the field represents a Type field. Thus many times this field is referred to as a Type/Length field.

3.1.1.1.3 The 802.2 Header   When the IEEE created the 802.3 Ethernet frame its desire for compatibility with fields in other types of LANs resulted in the 802.2 Logical Link Control (LLC) header following the 802.3 header. The 802.2 header is 3 bytes in length and is situated within the 1500-byte Data field, reducing the amount of information that can be transported in that field.

Figure 3.3 illustrates the 802.2 LLC header within an 802.3 frame. The first two bytes of the 3-byte 802.2 header identify the Destination Service Access Point (DSAP) and Source Service Access Point (SSAP). Later in this section we discuss the role of each field.

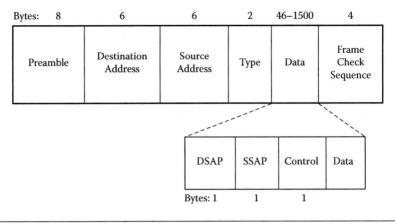

Figure 3.3   The 802.2 header.

The following Control field is 1 byte, resulting in the 802.2 header being 3 bytes in length. This LLC header is used for connectionless data transmitted by the older Ethernet II/DIX protocols. For connection-oriented data a 4-byte LLC header is used, with the two SAP fields set to hex 0404 for SNA and hex FOFO for NETBEUI.

3.1.1.1.3.1 Subnetwork Access Protocol   One of the problems associated with the IEEE 802.3 frame is that its use of a Length field precludes it from providing support for transporting multiple higher-layer protocols. Recognizing this limitation, the IEEE developed the Subnetwork Access Protocol (SNAP) as a mechanism for transporting multiple protocols over networks. SNAP can be considered a mechanism for multiplexing data on networks using the IEEE 802.2 LLC.

3.1.1.1.3.2 LLC Header Operation   The 802.2 LLC header follows the Data Link header. The purpose of the LLC header is to provide a position in buffer memory where an adapter can place the data frame. Thus the LLC header informs the upper layers where data can be stored and retrieved. Due to the placement and retrieval of data resembling the manner by which post office employees sort mail into post office boxes, the operation of the first two fields is often referenced with wording that resembles post office operations.

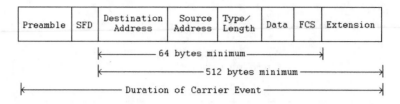

Figure 3.4   The Ethernet SNAP frame.

3.1.1.1.3.3 The SNAP Frame   SNAP can be considered an extension of the 802.2 LLC header that is inserted into the Data field of an 802.3 frame, as illustrated in Figure 3.4. The SNAP header consists of two fields that follow the LLC header, an Organization Code and an Ether Type field. Note from Figure 3.4 that the 8 bytes of additional LLC and SNAP subfields reduces the Data field to a value between a minimum of 38 bytes and a maximum of 1492 bytes.

In examining Figure 3.4 you might be a bit puzzled as to the rationale for having a separate subnetwork header. The reason for SNAP results from the fact that at the time the LLC was designed, most pundits thought that the use of a single byte to specify up to 256 values would be sufficient to register all protocol values. Unfortunately, as values began to be registered, the IEEE realized that the LLC header would soon run out of available values. Thus the hex values AA and AB were reserved and the SNAP subheader was developed.

To obtain an appreciation of the LLC header and SNAP let's turn our attention to each of the subfields that are placed into the beginning of the old 1500-byte Data field.

DSAP Subfield: The DSAP is a 1-byte field that acts as a pointer to a memory buffer in the receiving workstation. The DSAP value in effect tells the receiving NIC where data should be placed. A DSAP value of hex AA or BB indicates that the frame is a SNAP frame.

SSAP Subfield: The SSAP is similar to the DSAP, specifying the Service Access Point (SAP) of the sending process. To specify that this is a SNAP frame, the SSAP is set to a value of hex AA or BB.

Control Subfield: The control subfield is 1 byte in length. The purpose of this field is to specify the type of LLC frame.

When SNAP is present the value of the Control field is set to hex 03.

Organization Code Subfield: The Organization Code (OC) field is 3 bytes in length. Usually this field has the same value as the first three bytes in the Source Address field, although upon occasion it is set to zero.

Ether Type Subfield: The 2-byte Ether Type subfield specifies which protocol is encapsulated within the IEEE 802 network. This field provides backward compatibility with the Ethernet version II/DIX frame.

Data Field: Because the LLC and SNAP fields use 8 bytes within the Data field its information carrying capacity is reduced. That reduction results in a Data field with a minimum of 38 bytes and a maximum of 1492 bytes. That Data field typically consists of upper-layer headers, such as TCP/IP or IPX, followed by user data. For example, an Ether Type value of 2048 decimal (hex 0800) denotes IP, while a value of 2054 decimal (hex 0806) indicates ARP is being transported.

3.1.1.1.4 IPX over Ethernet   In concluding our examination of the initial series of Ethernet frames designed for legacy 10 Mbps LANs, this author would be remiss if he did not mention the transmission of IPX over Ethernet.

3.1.1.1.5 The 802.3 Raw Frame   The transmission of IPX over Ethernet is commonly referred to as an 802.3 raw frame. Here IPX data immediately commence after the 802.3 header. Because the first two bytes in IPX are set to hex FF, it's a relatively simple matter to examine the composition of the bytes following the Length field to determine that it is an 802.3 frame.

3.1.1.1.6 Other Encapsulations   In addition to being transmitted within an 802.3 frame, IPX can be encapsulated within an Ethernet II frame, an 802.2 frame, and an 802.3 SNAP frame. In the first situation (Ethernet II/DIX frame) the Ether Type value of hex 8137 will denote IPX is being transported. In an 802.2 frame the 802.3 frame header (Destination Address, Source Address, Length) is followed by

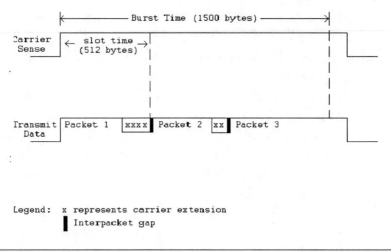

Figure 3.5   Ethernet 802.3 SNAP transporting IPX.

the 3-byte LLC header. When the 3-byte LLC header is set to hex E0, E0, 03 IPX data will be in the Data field as the hex E0 values in DSAP and SSAP indicate the Novell protocol is being transported.

The third additional method used to transport IPX is via an Ethernet SNAP frame. In this situation DSAP and SSAP subfield values are each hex AA and the Control field value is hex 03 to denote a SNAP frame. Then the Ether Type value of hex 8137 is used to denote IPX encapsulation, as shown in Figure 3.5.

3.1.1.2 Full Duplex and the PAUSE Frame   Originally Ethernet used the CSMA/CD protocol that resulted in transmission occurring in a half-duplex mode of operation. This resulted from the fact that when a station needed to transmit information it first had to listen to the media and wait for an idle period to occur due to the shared media design of the protocol.

With the introduction of 10BASE-T it became possible for the physical media to support the simultaneous transmission and reception of data. In fact, in 1997 the IEEE released the 802.3x standard, which defined full-duplex transmission on point-to-point links that connect exactly two stations. In addition, the standard also incorporated DIX framing, which eliminated the 802.3/DIX frame split.

Under the IEEE 802.3 standard both stations on the link must be both capable of and configured to support full-duplex operations.

3.1.1.2.1 Advantages   The ability of two stations to simultaneously transmit and receive data in effect doubles the potential data transfer capability. For example, assume a 10BASE-T station is connected to a 10BASE-T switch port and both support and are configured to operate in a full-duplex mode. Then the maximum bandwidth of the link is 20 Mbps even though the station can only transmit at 10 Mbps due to the ability to simultaneously transmit and receive data.

Because full-duplex operations enable a device to transmit without first listening to the media, the efficiency of the link is improved. In addition, because no collisions can occur on a full-duplex link the delays due to initiating a back-off algorithm are eliminated, further enhancing the efficiency of the point-to-point link.

Perhaps the key advantage associated with full-duplex operations is that segment lengths are not limited. Under half-duplex Ethernet the segment length was fixed to ensure collisions propagated to all stations within 512 bit times. Because no collisions are possible under full duplex, that constraint is eliminated.

3.1.1.2.2 Flow Control   With the addition of a full-duplex mode of operation the IEEE recognized that the continuous transmission from one device to another could result in the inability of some devices to keep up with received data. In this event the receiving device's buffers could fill, resulting in a loss of data. The solution to this problem was obtained through an optional flow control mechanism that could be used to regulate the flow of data. To implement flow control the IEEE developed the PAUSE frame.

3.1.1.2.2.1 PAUSE Frame   The function of the PAUSE frame is to enable one station to temporarily stop all traffic other than MAC control frames originating from the other station on a point-to-point link. To do so the PAUSE frame contains a field whose value specifies the duration of the PAUSE event in units of 512 bit times.

> **Overview:** PAUSE frame support is an option limited to full-duplex operations. Once a PAUSE frame is transmitted by a station to another station the receiving station can only issue a PAUSE frame if it is in a paused state. To further complicate

Bytes

7	1	6	6	2	2	2	42	4
Preamble	SFD	Destination Address (01-80-C2-00-00-01) or unique DA	Source Address	Type/Length 802.3 MAC Control (88-08)	MAC Control OP Code (00-01)	MAC Control Parameters (00-00 to FF-FF)	Reserved Set to zeros)	FCS

Figure 3.6   The PAUSE frame.

operations, a station may be able to issue PAUSE frames without having the ability to decode such frames, in other words, limited to supporting half of the protocol.

Frame Fields: Figure 3.6 illustrates the format of the PAUSE frame. The Preamble and Start of Frame Delimiter fields are the same as their IEEE 802.3 frame fields. The Destination Address field can be assigned to either the address of the station to be paused or the globally assigned multicast address of hex 01-80-C2-00-00-01. The Length/Type field value is set to hex 88-08 to indicate that the frame is a MAC control frame. Next, the following two bytes in a MAC control Opcode (Operational Code) field are set to hex 00-01 to indicate that the type of MAC control frame is a PAUSE frame. The following field (MAC Control Parameters) uses 16 bits to define the duration of the PAUSE event in units of 512-bit times. Valid values are hex 00-00 to hex FF-FF. A PAUSE with a value of zero in this field informs the station at the other end of the link to resume transmission. The next-to-last field of 42 bytes is reserved, while the last field is the FCS field.

3.1.1.3 vLAN Tagging   A year after the development of the 802.3z standard the IEEE in 1998 approved its 802.3ac standard. This standard defines the frame format for the extension of an Ethernet frame to support virtual local area network (vLAN) tagging. In actuality, there are two IEEE standards associated with vLANs. The IEEE 802.1Q standard defines how vLANS operate, while the 802.3ac standard defines how the vLAN protocol elements that are specific to Ethernet are implemented.

3.1.1.3.1 The 802.1Q Standard   The IEEE 802.1Q standard was developed to enable multiple bridged networks to share the same physical network link without the occurrence of leakage of data between networks. To accomplish this task the 802.1Q standard defined how a virtual LAN would operate with respect to bridging at the MAC layer and with respect to the 802.1D spanning tree protocol.

The result of the 802.1Q effort was a tagging mechanism that allows switches to differentiate frames based upon the value of the tag. As a result of the 802.1Q effort a vLAN can be considered to represent a single logical broadcast domain consisting of interfaces on one or more switches.

3.1.1.3.2 Advantages   A major benefit of vLANs is the ability to subdivide one physical switch into multiple logical networks. Because broadcasts are restricted to the interfaces associated with the vLAN this action can reduce broadcasts as well as enhance efficiency. The v in vLAN results from the fact that multiple virtual networks can be formed from one physical switch, such as assigning accountants to one vLAN while engineers are assigned to another.

3.1.1.3.3 Frame Format   The vLAN tag, when present, is inserted into an Ethernet frame between the Source Address field and Length/Type field. The first two bytes of the vLAN tag are its tag protocol ID (TPID), which is always set to a value of hex 8100. This is actually a reserved Length/Type field value that indicates the presence of the vLAN tag and indicates to software processing the frame that the normal Length/Tag field value can be found 4 bytes further into the frame.

The last two bytes of the vLAN tag consist of three fields: User-Priority, Canonical Format Indicator (CFI), and vLAN Identifier (VID). The User-Priority field is 3 bits in length and is used to assign a priority level to the Ethernet frame. The CFI is a 1-bit field that is always set to zero for Ethernet switches. CFI is used to provide compatibility between Ethernet and Token-Ring networks, resulting in a frame with a CFI set to 1 being received at an Ethernet port not being forwarded, as it is being sent to an untagged port.

The third field is the VID. This 12-bit field specifies the vLAN that the frame belongs to. If the value is 0, then the frame does not belong

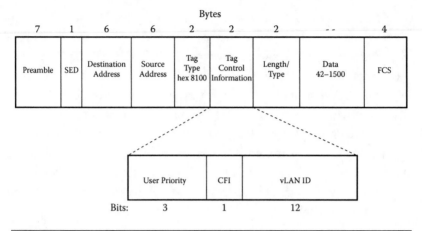

Figure 3.7 vLAN-tagged Ethernet frame format.

to any vLAN. Instead, the tag only specifies a priority and is then referred to as a priority tag.

Figure 3.7 illustrates the Ethernet frame extended to support vLAN tagging. Note that the 802.3ac standard resulted in the maximum Ethernet frame being extended from 1518 bytes to 1522 bytes. Because some software and ROM chips consider a frame length beyond 1518 bytes to be in error, older adapter cards need to be carefully checked to determine if they can work in a modern vLAN environment.

Currently a hex value of FF in the vLAN ID is reserved. All other values can be used as vLAN identifiers, enabling up to 4094 vLANs. Because 4 bytes is now added to a tagged frame the original FCS field must be recalculated.

3.1.1.4 SNAP Frames For IEEE 802.2 SNAP frames the use of tagging is similar to the previously described method. That is, the Ether Type value in the SNAP header is set to hex 8100 and the 4-byte tag is then inserted after the SNAP header.

3.1.1.5 Frame Determination A simple examination of the value in the Length/Type field followed by the value of the following two bytes can be used to determine the type of frame flowing on the LAN. Figure 3.8 illustrates the tests performed by software to determine the type of Ethernet frame.

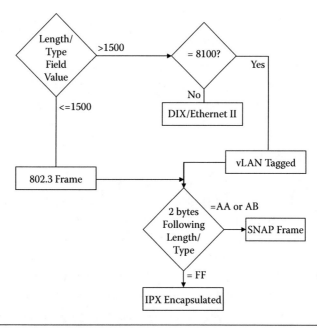

Figure 3.8   Determining the frame type.

The differences between Ethernet and IEEE 802.3 frames, although minor, make the two technically incompatible with one another. Originally, this meant that a network must contain either all Ethernet-compatible NICs or all IEEE 802.3-compatible NICs. During the late 1980s and early 1990s software was developed that enabled multiple protocols to be simultaneously transmitted on a LAN, to include different versions of Ethernet. Such software represents multiprotocol drivers, which enables different types of frames to be supported by a common network adapter. Examples of multiprotocol drivers include the Open Data Interface (ODI) and the Network Data Interface Specification (NDIS). Today, the fact that the IEEE 802.3 frame format represents a standard resulted in just about every communications vendor now marketing 802.3-compliant hardware and software. Although a few vendors continue to manufacture Ethernet or dual functioning Ethernet/IEEE 802.3 hardware, such products are primarily used to provide organizations with the ability to expand previously developed networks without requiring the wholesale replacement of NICs. Although the IEEE 802.3 standard has essentially replaced Ethernet due to their similarities and the fact that 802.3 was based upon Ethernet, we can consider both to be Ethernet.

3.2 Fast Ethernet

When Fast Ethernet (100BASE-TX) was developed for transmission at 100 Mbps the 802.3 frame was left intact; however, prefix and suffix bytes referred to as Start of Stream Delimiter (SSD) and End of Stream Delimiter (ESD) were used to surround the frame.

3.2.1 4B5B Coding

The SSD results from the use of 4B5B encoding, under which groups of 4 bits are mapped into groups of 5 bits. Because there are 32 possible combinations of 5 bits and 16 combinations of 4 bits, the 16 groups of 5 bits with the most transitions are used to provide clocking information for the signal.

Table 3.1 illustrates the manner by which groups of 4 bits can be mapped into groups of 5 bits, enabling enough transitions so that the clock signal can be recovered at a receiver. Because there are 16 unused characters, they can be used to detect errors for a special purpose, such as the SSD and ESD.

Table 3.1   Mapping 4B5B

4B BINARY		5B BINARY
0000	0	11110
0001	1	01001
0010	2	10100
0011	3	10101
0111	4	01010
1001	5	01011
1010	6	0110
1011	7	01111
1000	8	10010
1001	9	10011
1010	A	10110
1011	B	10111
1100	C	11010
1101	D	11011
1110	E	11100
1111	F	11101
N/A	Idle	11111

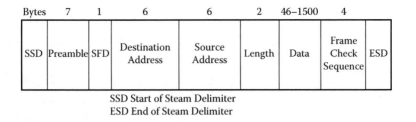

Bytes	7	1	6	6	2	46–1500	4	
SSD	Preamble	SFD	Destination Address	Source Address	Length	Data	Frame Check Sequence	ESD

SSD Start of Steam Delimiter
ESD End of Steam Delimiter

Figure 3.9   The 100BASE-TX frame format.

3.2.2 Delimiters

Figure 3.9 illustrates the 100BASE-TX frame. Note that this frame differs from the 802.3 frame through the addition of a byte to mark the beginning and end of the frame. Because at 100 Mbps the frames are known as streams, this resulted in the names assigned to the two delimiters.

3.2.3 Interframe Gap

Another difference between the 802.3 frame and the 100BASE-TX frame concerns the interframe gap. At 10 Mbps the interframe gap is 9.6 μs between frames, while at 100 Mbps idle codes are used to mark a 0.96 μs interframe gap. Although there are minor differences, note that the addressing fields remain the same.

The SSD 5B symbols are 11000 10001, while the ESD has the 5B symbols 01101 00111. Both SSD and ESD fields can be considered to fall within the interframe gap of Fast Ethernet frames. Thus computation between Ethernet/IEEE 802.3 and Fast Ethernet becomes simplified, as the latter has an operating rate 10 times the former and an interframe gap 1/10 the former.

3.3 Gigabit Ethernet

In this section we first focus on the various types of Gigabit Ethernet technologies, ranging from transmission over fiber to the transmission of data over copper. Once this is complete, we turn our attention to the modification of the Ethernet frame to enable a data rate 10 times faster than that of Fast Ethernet.

3.3.1 Standards Evolution

Gigabit Ethernet was standardized by the IEEE in June 1998 as IEEE 802.3z, and required the use of optical fiber as a transport mechanism. The 802.3z standard is commonly referred to as 1000BASE-X, where X refers to either -CX, -SX, -LX, or -ZX, all varieties of the standard we will examine. In 1900 the IEEE 802.3ab standard was promulgated. This standard defines Gigabit Ethernet transmission over unshielded twisted pair (UTP) category 5, 5e, or 6 cabling and became known as 1000BASE-T. With the ratification of 802.3ab, Gigabit Ethernet became a desktop technology as organizations found that they could use their existing copper cabling infrastructure at a factor of 10 over Fast Ethernet.

In 2004 the IEEE 802.3ah standard was ratified. This standard added two more gigabit fiber standards, 1000BASE-LX10 and 1000BASE-BX10. Although Gigabit Ethernet was initially deployed in high-capacity backbone network connections, such as peering points, in 2000, Apple added 1000BASE-T to its PowerMacG4 and PowerBookG4 personal computers. Within a short period 1000BASE-T was added to most new servers and personal computers. Gigabit NICs (1000BASE-T) are now included in most desktop, laptop, and server computer systems. With the promulgation of 10 Gigabit Ethernet as a fiber-based standard in 2002 and a twisted pair standard in 2006 the faster Ethernet was rapidly replacing 1 Gbit in backbone networks as well as becoming available for use in servers.

3.3.1.1 Varieties There are five physical layer standards for Gigabit Ethernet using optical fiber (1000BASE-X), a twisted pair cable standard (1000BASE-T), and a balanced copper cable standard (1000BASE-CX). Below we briefly discuss each standard. However, prior to doing so a few words about the two primary types of fiber used in the Gigabit Ethernet standards are warranted. Those types of fiber are single-mode fiber (SMF) and multimode fiber (MMF). In SMF light follows a single path through the fiber, while in MMF, as its name implies, light takes multiple paths, resulting in differential mode delay. SMF is used for long-distance communication, while MMF is used for shorter distances. SMF has a narrower core, which requires a more precise termination and connection method, while MMF has a wider core.

3.3.1.1.1 1000BASE-X   1000BASE-X refers to Gigabit Ethernet transmission over fiber, where options include 1000BASE-CX, 1000BASE-LX, 1000BASE-SX, 1000BASE-LX10, 1000BASE-BX10, and the non-standard -ZX implementations.

3.3.1.1.2 1000BASE-CX   1000BASE-CX represents the initial standard for Gigabit Ethernet connections over twin-axial cabling. This standard has a maximum transmission distance of 25 m using balanced shielded twisted pair. This relatively short segment length is due to the very high signal transmission rate. Although it is still used for some specific applications, the use of 1000BASE-T has succeeded it for general copper wiring use.

3.3.1.1.3 1000BASE-SX   1000BASE-SX represents a fiber optic Gigabit Ethernet standard for operation over multimode fiber using a 770 to 860 nm, near-infrared (NIR) light wavelength. This standard specifies a distance capability between 220 m (62.5/125 μm fiber with low modal bandwidth) and 550 m (50/125 μm fiber with high modal bandwidth). This standard is typically employed as an intrabuilding link in large office buildings, co-location facilities, and Internet point of presence (POP) Internet exchanges. The optical power specifications of SX interface include a minimum output power of –9.5 dBm and a minimum receive sensitivity of –17 dBm.

3.3.1.1.4 1000BASE-LX   1000BASE-LX represents a fiber optic Gigabit Ethernet standard that uses a long-wavelength laser (1270–1355 nm), and a maximum root mean square (RMS) spectral width of 4 nm.

1000BASE-LX is specified to work over a distance of up to 5 km over a 10 μm single-mode fiber and can also run over common types of multimode fiber with a maximum segment length of 550 m. For link distances greater than 300 m, the use of a special launch conditioning patch cord may be required to spread the transmission across the diameter of the fiber core.

1000BASE-CX, 1000BASE-SX, and 1000BASE-LX standards use 8B/10B encoding, which inflates the line rate by 25%, from 1000 Mbit/s to 1250 Mbit/s, to ensure a DC balanced signal. The symbols are then sent using non-return to zero (NRZ) signaling.

3.3.1.1.5 1000BASE-LX10   1000BASE-LX10 was standardized in 2004, 6 years after the initial gigabit fiber versions, as part of the Ethernet in the First Mile task group. While very similar to 1000BASE-LX, it achieves longer transmission distances of up to 10 km over a pair of single-mode fiber due to higher-quality optics. Prior to being standardized, 1000BASE-LX10 was in use by many vendors as a proprietary extension called either 1000BASE-LX/LH or 1000BASE-LH.

3.3.1.1.6 1000BASE-BX10   1000BASE-BX10 represents a standard capable of transmission at a distance up to 10 km over a single strand of single-mode fiber, with a different wavelength going in each direction. The terminals on each side of the single-mode fiber are not equal, as the one transmitting downstream uses a 1490 nm wavelength, while the one transmitting upstream uses a 1310 nm wavelength.

3.3.1.1.7 1000BASE-ZX   1000BASE-ZX represents a non-standard but industry-accepted term used to refer to Gigabit Ethernet transmission employing a 1550 nm wavelength to achieve a transmission distance of at least 70 km over single-mode fiber.

3.3.1.1.8 1000BASE-T   1000BASE-T was developed by the IEEE as the 802.3ab standard for Gigabit Ethernet over copper wiring. This standard uses a different encoding scheme in order to keep the symbol rate as low as possible, allowing transmission over twisted pair. Each 1000BASE-T network segment can be a maximum length of 100 m (328 ft), and must use category 5 or better cable. 1000BASE-T uses all four cable pairs for simultaneous transmission in both directions with data transmitted over four copper pairs 8 bits at a time. First, 8 bits of data is expanded into four 3-bit symbols, with the resulting symbols then mapped to voltage levels that vary continuously during transmission.

3.3.1.1.8.1 Autonegotiation   When using 1000BASE-T autonegotiation is a required feature. Because negotiation occurs using only two pairs of wires, if two gigabit devices are connected through a cable with only two pairs this will result in the devices selecting gigabit as the highest common denominator (HCD); however, the link will never become active. Fortunately, most gigabit physical devices have a specific register to diagnose this behavior.

3.3.1.1.8.2 Automatic MDI/MDI-X Configuration   Automatic MDI/MDI-X represents an optional feature in the 1000BASE-T standard. When specified this enables the use of straight-through cables between gigabit-capable interfaces, eliminating the need for crossover cables. In addition, it results in the ability to avoid the use of legacy uplink ports and manual selector switches found on many older hubs and switches, as well as reduces installation errors.

3.3.1.1.9 1000BASE-TX   The 1000BASE-TX standard represents the effort of the Telecommunications Industry Association (TIA), which created and promoted a standard similar to 1000BASE-T but was simpler to implement. While the resulting simplified design could, in theory, reduce the cost of electronics by only using one pair of wires in each direction, its implementation required category 6 cable. Due to the stringer cabling requirement as well as the rapidly falling cost of 1000BASE-T products 1000BASE-TX has never reached a commercial level of adaption.

3.3.2 Frame Format Modifications

The introduction of the IEEE 802.3z standard for Gigabit Ethernet was accompanied by several changes to the Ethernet frame format. At a data rate of 1 Gbit/s maintaining a minimum frame length of 64 bytes (72 when the Preamble and Start of Frame Delimiter fields are considered) would reduce the network diameter to approximately 20 m. While this distance might be suitable for connecting a switch to a group of stations within close proximity of one another, it is not suitable for supporting horizontal wiring within a building where a 10 m distance is allowed from a wall faceplate to the desktop. To enable Gigabit Ethernet to support a network diameter of up to 200 m, a technique referred to as carrier extension was added to the technology.

3.3.2.1 Carrier Extension   Carrier extension results in an extension of the Ethernet slot time from 64 bytes (512 bits) to a new value of 512 bytes (4096 bits). To accomplish this extension, frames less than 512

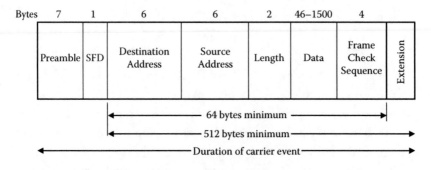

Figure 3.10   Carrier extension on a Gigabit Ethernet frame.

bytes in length are padded with special carrier extension symbols. Note that under Gigabit Ethernet the minimum frame length of 64 bytes is not changed. All frames less than 64 bytes in length are first padded out to a minimum of 64 bytes. The carrier signal placed on the network is then extended to provide a minimum carrier length of 512 bytes.

The preceding discussion of frame length is based upon the IEEE use of technology and does not consider the 8 bytes associated with the Preamble and Start of Frame Delimiter fields. Figure 3.10 illustrates the Gigabit Ethernet frame to include the location where non-data symbols are added. Note that the FCS is calculated only on the original, non-extended frame. At the receiver the extension symbols are removed before the FCS value is checked.

3.3.2.2 Half-Duplex Use   Carrier extension is only applicable to half-duplex transmission. This is because full-duplex transmission eliminates the possibility of collisions. Because carrier extension can significantly degrade the performance associated with short-packet transmission, a second modification to the Gigabit Ethernet frame, referred to as frame bursting, was developed.

3.3.2.3 Frame Bursting   Frame bursting represents a Gigabit Ethernet technique developed as a mechanism to compensate for performance degradation associated with carrier extension. Under frame bursting a station with more than one frame to send can transmit multiple frames if the first is successfully transmitted. If the first frame is less than 512 bytes in length carrier extension

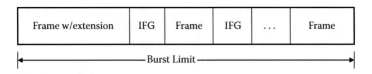

Figure 3.11 Frame bursting.

is applied to that frame. Succeeding frames in the burst are limited until a burst limit of 65,536 bit times (8192 bytes) is reached. An interframe gap period is inserted between each frame in the burst. However, instead of allowing the medium to be idle between frames, the transmitting station fills the interframe gaps with non-data symbols that maintain an active carrier and which are then discarded by receiving stations.

Bursting is only applicable to gigabit and higher Ethernet speeds when transmission is half duplex. Figure 3.11 illustrates an example of Gigabit Ethernet frame bursting. In this example the first frame in the burst is transmitted successfully with an extension and is assumed to have additional frames that need to be transmitted. Thus transmission continues until either all frames are transmitted or 8192 byte times are reached, whichever comes first.

3.3.2.4 Jumbo Frames Without considering the use of a vLAN tag or an Ethernet SNAP frame the maximum Data field in a frame is 1500 bytes. While this amount of data was sufficient during the 1970s, when text-based email prevailed, let's fast-forward to today. The inclusion of signature blocks in email, the attachment of photographs and motion picture files, and a general increase in organizational data storage resulted in the common occurrence of large emails and lengthy file transfers. Moving such data in 1500-byte fields can also result in a processing load on computers that hinders other multitasking operations. For example, consider moving a 1 Gbyte file from a server to a workstation via a Gigabit Ethernet connection. This action would require the processing of approximately 666,667 frames that could consume 20 to 40% of the processing power of a computer just to handle associated network interrupts.

Based upon the preceding, in 1998 Alteon Networks proposed an initiative to increase the maximum length of the Ethernet Data field from 1500 bytes to 9000 bytes. Although this initiative was not adopted by the IEEE it was implemented by a large number of hardware vendors as a jumbo frame option.

3.3.2.4.1 Operation   In the Alteon Networks proposal, which as adopted as an option by several hardware vendors, the Ethernet Data field is extended by a factor of 6, from a maximum of 1500 bytes to 9000 bytes. This extension can reduce the number of frames required to move a file by a factor of 6, increasing application throughput while decreasing host CPU utilization. Because the resources used by a server to handle network traffic are proportional to the number of frames transmitted and received, using larger frames improves performance when compared to the use of smaller frames.

3.3.2.4.2 Length Rationale   One of the key considerations in sizing a jumbo frame was the CRC-32 algorithm. To maintain a level of compatibility with Ethernet, jumbo frames only changed the size of the Data field. Due to the manner by which the CRC-32 algorithm operates, the probability of an undetected error is relatively unchanged until frames exceed 12,000 bytes. Thus to maintain the same undetected bit error rate jumbo frames should not exceed 12,000 bytes. In the opposite direction, certain applications have a low maximum size for a network file. For example, the maximum size for a Network File System (NFS) datagram is approximately 8000 bytes. Thus a jumbo data frame of 9000 bytes appears to be a good compromise.

3.3.2.4.3 Advantages   In addition to reducing the number of frames required to transport files and network overhead, the use of jumbo frames can result in other benefits. Those additional benefits can include a reduction in fragmentation, enhancing TCP throughput as well as the efficiency of switches and routers.

Reducing fragmentation reduces fragmentation overhead. This will result in a lower overhead associated with CPU processing. In a TCP environment, throughput has been shown to be directly proportional to the maximum segment size (MSS). Since the MSS is equal to the maximum transmission unit (MTU) less the TCP/IP headers, you can enhance throughput by increasing the Ethernet Data field, which enables larger packets to be transported. Concerning switches and routers, since their efficiency is primarily a function of how much time they spend examining headers, a reduction in frames needing processing will make these hardware devices more efficient.

3.3.2.4.4 Problems and Solutions One of the problems associated with the use of jumbo frames is intermediate hardware that uses a 1500 byte MTU. Because the smallest MTU used by any device in a given network path determines the maximum MTU for all traffic traveling along that path, frames traversing such hardware cannot be expanded. Thus an organization with connections to other offices and the Internet may only be able to use a small portion of a local switch for jumbo frames. Although replacement routers and switches could be purchased, they are not inexpensive, and in certain situations economics might prevent more than a token replacement of hardware each year.

One method that can be used to implement jumbo frames is to isolate the use of such frames to a portion of one's network that has compatibility with such frames. To accomplish this the IEEE 802.1Q vLAN tagging specification could be used to enable jumbo frames and standard Ethernet frames to be separate from each other, even when traversing the same physical link if the endpoints support jumbo frames. Thus through the use of vLAN tagging jumbo-compatible hardware could communicate with each other using jumbo frames, while communicating with other network devices using standard Ethernet frames. Then as funds become available to upgrade additional equipment the vLAN can be modified.

3.4.10 Gigabit Ethernet

The 10 Gigabit Ethernet computer networking standard, referred to as 10GigE or 10GbE, was first published in 2002. This standard defines a version of Ethernet with a data rate of 10 Gbit/s that is 10 times faster than Gigabit Ethernet. 10GbE defines only full-duplex point-to-point links that are typically connected by network switches and routers. Half-duplex operation, hubs, and CSMA/CD are not defined for use in 10GbE. Similar to Gigabit Ethernet, the 10 Gigabit Ethernet standard defines a number of different physical layer (PHY) standards. Let's examine 10GbE standards, first turning our attention to fiber standards and then copper standards.

3.4.1 Fiber Standards

There are five IEEE 10GbE standards as well as a pseudo industry-developed standard. In the following sections we will briefly examine each.

3.4.1.1 10GBASE-SR 10GBASE-SR, where SR stands for short range, represents a port type for multimode fiber and uses 850 nm lasers over obsolete FDDI-grade 62.5-micron multimode fiber (MMF) cabling; it has a maximum transmission range of 26 m. When transmission occurs over 62.5-micron OM1 it has a range of 33 m, while over 50-micron OM2 a range of 82 m is obtainable. When transmission occurs over OM3 a range of 300 m is obtainable, while over OM4 400 m can be obtained. Note that OM3 and OM4 are preferred for structured optical cabling within buildings. MMF has the advantage over SMF of having lower-cost connectors because of its wider core. A non-standard lower-cost, lower-power variant, sometimes referred to as 10GBASE-SR, is interoperable with 10GBASE-SR but is restricted to a range of 100 m.

3.4.1.2 10GBASE-LR 10GBASE-LR, where LR stands for long reach, represents a port type for single-mode fiber and uses 1310 nm lasers. It delivers serialized data at a line rate of 10.3125 Gbit/s. 10GBASE-LR has a specified reach of 10 km or 6.2 miles.

3.4.1.3 10GBASE-LRM 10GBASE-LRM, where LRM represents long-reach multimode, was originally specified in the IEEE 802.3aq standard as a port type for multimode fiber and uses 1310 nm lasers. It delivers serialized data at a line rate of 10.3125 Gbit/s. 10GBASE-LRM supports transmission distances up to 220 m on FDDI-grade multimode fiber and the same 220 m maximum reach on OM1, OM2, and OM3 fiber types. Although some 10GBASE-LRM transceivers support transmission distances up to 300 m on standard single-mode fiber, this is not part of the IEEE specification.

3.4.1.4 10GBASE-ER 10GBASE-ER, where ER refers to extended reach, represents a port type for single-mode fiber and uses 1550 nm lasers. It results in serialized data at a line rate of 10.3125 Gbit/s and has a transmission distance of 40 km over engineered links and 30 km over standard SMF links.

3.4.1.5 10GBASE-ZR   10GBASE-ZR represents a non-standard 10 Gpbs Ethernet that has a transmission rage of 80 km. Note that the physical layer is not specified within the IEEE 802.3ae standard, and manufacturers created their own specifications based upon the 80 km PHY described in the OC-192/STM-64 SDH/SONET specifications.

3.4.1.6 10GBASE-LX4   10GBASE-LX4 represents a port type for both multimode fiber and single-mode fiber. It uses four separate laser sources operating at 3.125 Gbit/s and employs wavelength division multiplexing (WDM) with four unique wavelengths around 1310 nm. This technology supports a range of 300 m over FDDI-grade, OM1, OM2, and OM3 multimode cabling that has a minimum modal bandwidth of 500 MHz*km at 1300 nm. 10GBASE-LX4 can support a transmission range of 10 km over SMF. Until approximately 5 years ago 10GBASE-LX4 optical modules were less expensive than 10GBASE-LR optical modules and were used by persons who wanted to support both MMF and SMF with a single optical module. Today 10GBASE-LX4 is considered to represent an expensive and near-obsolete technology.

3.4.2 Copper

10 Gigabit Ethernet can operate over three types of copper cabling, twin-ax cabling, twisted pair cabling, and backplanes. Below we will briefly discuss each standard.

3.4.2.1 10GBASE-CX4   10GBASE-CX4 represents the first 10 Gbit copper standard published by the IEEE as the 802.3ak standard, which was promulgated in 2004. Under this standard transmission is specified to work at a distance of up to 15 m, which limits its usefulness. However, 10GBASE-CX4 provides the advantages of low power, low cost, and low latency. A considerable disadvantage is its form factor, which results from the use of bulkier cables than the newer SFP+ standard has, as well as a much shorter transmission distance than that of various fiber optic standards or 10GBASE-T.

3.4.2.2 10GSFP+Cu 10GSFP+Cu, which is also known as 10GBase-CR and 10GBase-CX1, uses a passive twin-ax cable assembly and connects directly into an SFP+ housing. This standard has a transmission range of 7 m and, similar to 10GBASE-CX4, has the advantage of low power, low cost, and low latency. In addition, unlike 10GBASE-CX4, this standard has the added advantages of using less bulky cables and having the small form factor.

3.4.2.3 Backplane 10 GBps Ethernet Backplane 10 GBps Ethernet, which is known by its IEEE task force name of 802.3ap, is designed for use in backplane applications such as blade servers, routers, and switches. 802.3ap implementations must operate in an environment consisting of up to 1 m of copper-printed circuit board with two connectors. The 802.3ap standard defines two port types for 10 Gbit/s operations, 10GBASE-KX4 and 10GBASE-KR, as well as a 1 Gbit/s port type referred to as 1000BASE-KX. The 802.3ap standard also defines an optional layer for forward error correction (FEC), a backplane autonegotiation protocol, and link training for 10GBASE-KR, where the receiver can set a three-tap transmit equalizer. The autonegotiation protocol selects between 1000BASE-KX, 10GBASE-KX4, 10GBASE-KR, or 40GBASE-KR4 operations. 40GBASE-KR4 is defined in the IEEE 802.3ba standard, which provides a data rate of 40 Gbit/s.

3.4.2.3.1 10GBASE-KX4 The 10GBASE-KX4 standard operates over four backplane lanes and uses the same physical layer coding as 10GBASE-CX4.

3.4.2.3.2 10GBASE-KR Equipment compliant with this standard operates over a single backplane lane and uses the same physical layer coding as 10GBASE-LR, GBASE-ER, and 10GBASE-SR. Today a majority of backplane designs use 10GBASE-KR.

3.4.2.4 10GBASE-T 10GBASE-T represents the IEEE 802.3an-2006 standard released in 2006 to provide 10 Gbit/s connections over unshielded or shielded twisted pair cables at distances up to 100 m. One of the key advantages associated with 10GBASE-T is that cable infrastructure can also be used for 1000BASE-T, enabling a gradual upgrade from 1000BASE-T using autonegotiation to select which speed to use.

```
0     4      8              16                         31
 Vers   Hlen    Service Type |       Total Length
        Identification        | Flags | Fragment Offset
   Time to Live Protocol      | Header  |   Checksum
              Source IP Address
            Destination IP Address
              Options + Padding
```

Figure 3.12   The IPv4 header.

Another advantage is that 10GBASE-T uses the RJ45 connector, which is in wide use with other types of copper-based Ethernet.

Now that we have an overview of the structure of Ethernet, let's probe deeper and examine the composition of the two IP headers and IP addressing.

3.5 The IPv4 Header

As noted at the beginning of this chapter, the current version of the Internet Protocol is version 4. Thus we will commence our examination of the network layer of the TCP/IP protocol suite by turning our attention to the IPv4 header, to include becoming familiar with IPv4 addressing. The fields in the IPv4 header are illustrated in Figure 3.12. Note that the header contains a minimum of 20 octets of data. Also note that the width of each field is shown in Figure 3.12 with respect to a 32-bit word.

3.5.1 Vers Field

The Vers field consists of 4 bits that identify the version of the IP protocol used to create the datagram. The current version of the IP protocol is 4, and the next generation of the IP protocol is assigned version number 6. As we will note later the Vers field retains its meaning in both the IPv4 and IPv6 headers. Table 3.2 lists the assignment of numbers to the Version field.

3.5.2 Hlen and Total Length Fields

The second and fourth fields in the IPv4 header indicate the length of the header and the total length of the datagram, respectively. The Hlen field indicates the length of the IPv4 header in 32-bit words. In

Table 3.2   Assigned Internet Version Numbers

NUMBERS	ASSIGNMENT
0	Reserved
1–3	Unassigned
4	IP
5	Streams
6	IPv6
7	TP/IX
8	P Internet Protocol (PIP)
9	TUBA
10–14	Unassigned
15	Reserved

comparison, the Total Length field indicates the total length of the datagram, to include its header and higher-layer information, such as a following TCP or UDP header and application data following either of those headers. Because the total Length field consists of 16 bits, an IP datagram can be up to 2^{16}, or 65,535 octets in length.

3.5.3 Type of Service Field   The Type of Service (TOS) field is one octet or 8 bits in length. The purpose of this field is to denote the importance of the datagram (precedence), delay, throughput, and reliability requested by the originator.

Figure 3.13 illustrates the assignment of bit positions within the TOS field. Because the TOS field provides a mechanism to define priorities for the routing of IP datagrams, the TOS field could be used to provide a quality of service (QoS) for IP. Applications can set the appropriate values in the TOS field to indicate the type of

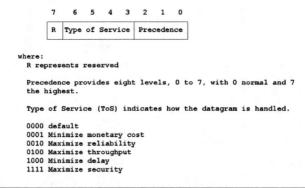

Figure 3.13   The Type of Service field.

routing path they would like. For example, a file transfer would probably request normal delay, high throughput, and normal reliability. In comparison, a real-time video application would probably select low delay, high throughput, and high reliability. While this concept appears to provide a QoS, this is not the case, as it does not provide a mechanism to reserve bandwidth. For example, 10 stations, each requiring 512 Kbps, could all define an immediate priority for flowing through a router connected on a T1 circuit operating at 1.544 Mbps. Another problem associated with the TOS field is that many routers ignore its settings. This is due to the fact that to support the TOS field a router would have to construct and maintain multiple routing tables, which in the era of relatively slow processors when the Internet evolved was not an attractive option with router manufacturers. Thus, although this field provides precedence definition capability, its use on a public network can be limited. Recognizing this limitation, plans were developed to reuse the TOS field as a mechanism to differentiate services requested when a data stream enters a network. This action resulted in a proposal to rename the TOS byte as a Diff Service field, and an RFC was developed to define its use.

3.5.4 Identification Field

The Identification field is two octets or 16 bits in length. This field is used to identify each fragmented datagram and is one of three fields that govern fragmentation. The other two fields that govern fragmentation are the Flags field and the Fragmentation Offset field.

IP fragmentation results when data flow between networks encounters different size MTUs. The MTU is commonly set when a device driver initializes an interface and represents the payload portion of a frame, i.e., the frame length less frame overhead. Most protocol stacks support MTUs up to 64,000 − 1 octets (65,535). Another MTU is a per route MTU, which represents the MTU that can be used without causing fragmentation from source to destination. Per route MTUs are usually maintained as a value in a host's routing table and set either by manual configuration or via a discovery process. When a route has interfaces with different MTUs and a large datagram must be transferred via an interface with a smaller MTU, the routing entity will either fragment the packet or drop it. As we note in the next

Table 3.3   Flag Field Values

Bit 0	Reserved (set to 0)
Bit 1	0 = may fragment, 1 = don't fragment
Bit 2	0 = last fragment, 1 = more fragments follow

section, if the DON'T_FRAGMENT bit is set in the Flags field, the router will drop the datagram. This will result in the router generating an ICMP "Destination Unreachable—Fragmentation Needed" message to the originator, which will cause the MTU discovery algorithm to select a smaller MTU for the path and subsequent transmissions.

3.5.5 Flags Field

This 3-bit field indicates how fragmentation will occur. Bit 0 is reserved and set to zero, while the values of bits 1 and 2 define whether or not fragmentation can occur and if the present fragment is the last fragment or one or more fragments follow. Table 3.3 lists the values associated with the 3 bits in the Flags field.

3.5.6 Fragment Offset Field

The third field in the IPv4 header that is involved with fragmentation is the Fragment Offset field. It is 13 bits in length and indicates where the fragment belongs in the complete message. The actual value placed in this field is an integer that corresponds to a unit of eight octets and provides an offset in 64-bit units.

IP fragmentation places the burden of effort upon the receiving station and the routing entity. When a station receives an IP fragment it must fully reassemble the complete IP datagram prior to being able to extract the TCP segment, resulting in a requirement for additional buffer memory and CPU processing power at the receiver. In doing so it uses the values in the Fragment Offset field in each datagram fragment to correctly reassemble the complete datagram. Because the dropping of any fragment in the original datagram requires the original datagram to be re-sent, most vendor TCP/IP protocol stacks set the DON'T_FRAGMENT bit in the Flags field. Setting that bit causes oversized IP datagrams to be dropped and results in an ICMP "Destination Unreachable—Fragmentation Needed" message transmitted to the originator. This action results in the MTU discovery algorithm selecting a smaller MTU for the path and using that MTU for subsequent transmissions.

3.5.7 Time to Live Field

The Time to Live (TTL) field is one 8-bit byte or octet in length. This field contains a value that represents the maximum amount of time a datagram can live. The use of this field prevents a misaddressed or misrouted datagram from endlessly wandering the Internet or a private IP network.

The value placed in the Time to Live field can represent router hops or seconds, with a maximum value for either being 255. Because an exact time is difficult to measure and requires synchronized clocks, this field is primarily used as a hop count field. That is, routers decrement the value in the field each time a datagram flows between networks. When the value of this field reaches zero the datagram is sent to the great bit bucket in the sky. The current recommended default time-to-live value for IP is 64.

3.5.8 Protocol Field

The purpose of the Protocol field is to identify the higher-layer protocol being transported within an IP datagram. By examining the value of this field, networking devices can determine if they have to look further into the datagram or should simply forward the datagram toward its destination. For example, a router that receives an IP datagram whose Protocol field value is 6 and which indicates the higher-layer protocol is TCP would simply forward the datagram toward its destination.

The 8-bit positions in the Protocol field enable up to 256 protocols to be uniquely defined. Table 3.4 lists the assignment of IP Protocol field values. Although TCP and UDP by far represent the vast majority of upper-layer protocol transmission, other protocols can also be transported that govern the operation of networks, such as the Exterior Gateway Protocol (EGP) and Interior Gateway Protocol (IGP) that govern the interconnection of autonomous networks. In addition, a large block of numbers is currently unassigned. In comparison, IPv6

Table 3.4 Assigned Internet Protocol Numbers

DECIMAL	KEYWORD	PROTOCOL
0	HOPOPT	IPv6 Hop-by-Hop Option
1	ICMP	Internet Control Message
2	IGMP	Internet Group Management
3	GGP	Gateway-to-Gateway
4	IP	IP in IP (encapsulation)
5	ST	Stream
6	TCP	Transmission Control Protocol
7	CBT	CBT
8	EGP	Exterior Gateway Protocol
9	IGP	Any private interior gateway (used by Cisco for its IGRP)
10	BBN-RCC-MON	BBN RCC Monitoring
11	NVP-II	Network Voice Protocol version 2
12	PUP	PUP
13	ARGUS	ARGUS
14	EMCON	EMCON
15	XNET	Cross Net Debugger
16	CHAOS	Chaos
17	UDP	User Datagram
18	MUX	Multiplexing
19	DCN-MEAS	DCN Measurement Subsystems
20	HMP	Host Monitoring
21	PRM	Packet Radio Measurement
22	XNS-IDP	XEROX NS IDP
23	TRUNK-1	Trunk-1
24	TRUNK-2	Trunk-2
25	LEAF-1	Leaf-1
26	LEAF-2	Leaf-2
27	RDP	Reliable Data Protocol
28	IRTP	Internet Reliable Transaction
29	ISO-TP4	ISO Transport Protocol Class 4
30	NETBLT	Bulk Data Transfer Protocol
31	MFE-NSP	MFE Network Services Protocol
32	MERIT-INP	MERIT Internodal Protocol
33	SEP	Sequential Exchange Protocol
34	3PC	Third-Party Connect Protocol
35	IDPR	Interdomain Policy Routing Protocol
36	XTP	XTP
37	DDP	Datagram Delivery Protocol
38	IDPR-CMTP	IDPR Control Message Transport Protocol
39	TP++	TP++ Transport Protocol

(continued)

Table 3.4   Assigned Internet Protocol Numbers (continued)

DECIMAL	KEYWORD	PROTOCOL
40	IL	IL Transport Protocol
41	IPv6	Ipv6
42	SDRP	Source Demand Routing Protocol
43	IPv6-Route	Routing Header for IPv6
44	IPv6-Frag	Fragment Header for IPv6
45	IDRP	Interdomain Routing Protocol
46	RSVP	Reservation Protocol
47	GRE	General Routing Encapsulation
48	MHRP	Mobile Host Routing Protocol
49	BNA	BNA
50	ESP	Encapsulating Security Payload for IPv6
51	AH	Authentication Header for IPv6
52	I-NLSP	Integrated Net Layer Security
53	SWIPE	IP with Encryption
54	NARP	NBMA Address Resolution Protocol
55	MOBILE	IP Mobility
56	TLSP	Transport Layer Security Protocol (using Kryptonet key management)
57	SKIP	SKIP
58	IPv6-ICMP	ICMP for IPv6
59	IPv6-NoNxt	No Next Header for IPv6
60	IPv6-Opts	Destination Options for IPv6
61		Any host internal protocol
62	CFTP	CFTP
63		Any local network
64	SAT-EXPAK	SATNET and Backroom EXPAK
65	KRYPTOLAN	Kryptolan
66	RVD	MIT Remote Virtual Disk Protocol
67	IPPC	Internet Pluribus Packet Core
68		Any distributed file system
69	SAT-MON	SATNET Monitoring
70	VISA	VISA Protocol
71	IPCV	Internet Packet Core Utility
72	CPNX	Computer Protocol Network Executive
73	CPHB	Computer Protocol Heart Beat
74	WSN	Wang Span Network
75	PVP	Packet Video Protocol
76	BR-SAT-MON	Backroom SATNET Monitoring
77	SUN-ND	SUN ND PROTOCOL-Temporary
78	WB-MON	WIDEBAND Monitoring

(continued)

Table 3.4 Assigned Internet Protocol Numbers (continued)

DECIMAL	KEYWORD	PROTOCOL
79	WB-EXPAK	WIDEBAND EXPAK
80	ISO-IP	ISO Internet Protocol
81	VMTP	VMTP
82	SECURE-VMTP	SECURE-VMPT
83	VINES	VINES
84	TTP	TTP
85	NSFNET-IGP	NSFNET-IGP
86	DGP	Dissimilar Gateway Protocol
87	TCF	TCF
88	EIGRP	EIGRP
89	OSPFIGP	OSPFIGP
90	Sprite-RPC	Sprite RPC Protocol
91	LARP	Locus Address Resolution Protocol
92	MTP	Multicast Transport Protocol
93	AX.25	AX.25 Frames
94	IPIP	IP-within-IP Encapsulation Protocol
95	MICP	Mobile Internetworking Control Protocol
96	SCC-SP	Semaphore Communications Security Protocol
97	ETHERIP	Ethernet-within-IP Encapsulation
98	ENCAP	Encapsulation Header
99		Any private encryption scheme
100	GMTP	GMTP
101	IFMP	Ipsilon Flow Management Protocol
102	PNNI	PNNI over IP
103	PIM	Protocol-Independent Multicast
104	ARIS	ARIS
105	SCPS	SCPS
106	QNX	QNX
107	A/N	Active Networks
108	IPPCP	IP Payload Compression Protocol
109	SNP	Sitara Networks Protocol
110	Compaq-Peer	Compaq Peer Protocol
111	IPX-in-IP	IPX in IP
112	VRRP	Virtual Router Redundancy Protocol
113	PGM	PGM Reliable Transport protocol
114		Any 0-hop protocol
115	L2TP	Layer 2 Tunneling Protocol
116	DDX	D-II Data Exchange (DDX)
117–254		Unassigned
255	Reserved	

uses a Next Header field in place of the Protocol field, but uses the values contained in Table 3.4.

3.5.9 Checksum Field

The tenth field in the IPv4 header is the Checksum field. This 16-bit or two-octet field protects the header and is also referred to as the Header Checksum field.

3.5.10 Source and Destination Address Fields

Both the Source and Destination Address fields are 32 bits in length. Each field contains an address that normally represents both a network address and a host address on the network. Because it is extremely important to understand IP addressing we focus on this topic below.

3.5.11 Options and Padding Fields

Included in IPv4 is a provision for adding optional Header fields. Such fields are identified by a value greater than zero in the field. IPv4 Option field values are based upon the manner by which the Option field is subdivided. That subdivision includes a 1-bit copy flag, a 2-bit Class field, and a 5-bit option number.

Options whose values are 0 and 1 are exactly one octet long, which is their Type field. All other options have their one-octet Type field followed by a one-octet Length field followed by one or more octets of option data. The optional padding occurs when it becomes necessary to expand the header to fall on a 32-bit word boundary.

3.6 IPv4 Addressing

IP addressing provides the mechanism that enables packets to be routed between networks as well as to be delivered to an appropriate host on a destination network. As noted above, there are two versions of the Internet Protocol. The current version that has a majority of use is IPv4, while the so-called next-generation Internet Protocol, which is currently being migrated to many networks, is

IPv6. Because there are significant differences in the method of addressing used by each version of IP, we cover both versions in this section. First, we focus upon the 32-bit addressing scheme employed under IPv4. Once we obtain an appreciation for the manner by which IPv4 addresses are formed and used, we then turn our attention to IPv6.

3.6.1 Overview

IPv4 uses 32-bit IP addresses to identify distinct device interfaces, such as interfaces that connect computers, tablets, routers, workstations, and gateways to networks, as well as to route data to those devices. Each device interface in an IP network must be assigned a unique IP address to enable it to receive communications addressed to the interface. Normally workstations have a single interface in the form of a LAN connection, which would be assigned an IP address. However, routers typically have more than one interface, and some high-performance servers may have two or more network connections. In such instances each device interface would have a separate IP address.

Each IPv4 header contains a 32-bit source and 32-bit destination address. The use of a 32-bit binary number provides an address pace that is capable of supporting 2,294,967,296 distinct addressable devices. When the TCP/IP protocol suite was developed the address space exceeded the world's population. However, the proliferation of workstations connected to LANs, the growth in the use of cable modems that require individual IP addresses, and the fact that every interface on an IP network must have a distinct IP address contributed to a rapid depletion of available IP addresses. In fact, during 2011 all available IPv4 addresses had been assigned.

Recognizing the possibility that hundreds of millions to billions of to-be-developed communications appliances may need access to the Internet, the Internet Activities Board (IAB) commenced work on a replacement for IPv4 during 1992. While the addressing limitations of IPv4 were of primary concern, the efforts of the IAB resulted in a complete revamp of the next-generation version of IP known as IPv6. Improvements in IPv6 include the use of 128-bit addresses for source and destination devices as well as a next header indicator that facilitates the daisy-chaining of headers to perform different functions. The latter enables intermediary devices along a path to note whether or not they have to look further into the contents of a datagram or simply relay the datagram toward its destination. The ability to avoid looking further into a datagram considerably enhances the packet processing capability of routers and can be expected to enhance the flow of data through the Internet. Because this section is focused upon IP addressing, we examine the addressing schemes, address notation, host address restrictions, and special addresses associated with both IPv4 and IPv6.

3.6.2 Addressing

The Internet Protocol was standardized in September 1981. At that time the standard included a requirement for each host connected to an IP-based network to be assigned a unique, 32-bit address value for each network connection. This resulted in some networking devices that have multiple interfaces, such as routers, gateways, and servers, being assigned a unique IP address for each network interface.

To illustrate the assignment of IP addresses to interfaces, consider Figure 3.14, which shows for simplicity a bus-based Ethernet LAN

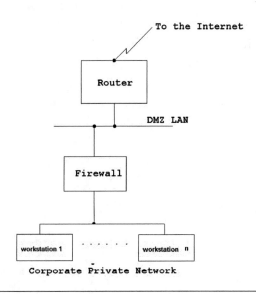

Figure 3.14   A common corporate LAN connection to the Internet where a router and firewall have multiple interfaces, each with a distinct IP address.

with attached workstations that are connected to the Internet via a corporate firewall and a router. Note that each workstation has a single interface in this example. Thus each of those devices would be associated with a single IP address by the assignment of one IP address to each device interface. Each router and firewall has two interfaces. For the router one interface is connected to a non-populated special type of LAN, called a demilitarized LAN or DMZ, while a second interface represents a serial port used to interconnect routers via a WAN. Thus each router would be assigned two IP addresses, one assigned to its LAN interface and the other assigned to its serial interface. Similarly, the firewall has two LAN connections and would be assigned two IP addresses, one for each interface. Through the assignment of addresses to each device interface, this method of addressing enables datagrams to be correctly routed when a device has two or more network connections.

3.6.3 Basic Addressing Scheme

During the development of the TCP/IP protocol suite it was recognized that internetworking two or more networks required distinct network addresses to differentiate one network from another. Because each host on a network also required a distinct address, a mechanism was required to identify a network as well as a host connected to a network. Although some protocols, such as NetWare's IPX, use separate network and host addresses, the designers of the TCP/IP protocol suite looked for a method to subdivide the IP address space so that one address field in the IP header could identify the network and the host on the network, with the latter actually the interface since IP addresses are assigned to interfaces. The result was the development of a two-level addressing hierarchy, which is illustrated in Figure 3.15.

Under the two level IPv4 addressing hierarchy the 32-bit IPv4 address is subdivided into network and host portions. The composition of the first 4 bits of each 32-bit word specifies whether the network portion i: 1, 2 or 3 bytes in length, resulting in the host portion being either 3, 2 or 1 bytes in length.

Figure 3.15   The two-level IPv4 addressing hierarchy.

Under the two-level IPv4 addressing scheme all hosts on the same network must be assigned the same network prefix; however, each host must have a unique address to differentiate it from another host on the same network. Similarly, two hosts on different networks must be assigned different network prefixes; however, the hosts can have the same host address.

3.6.3.1 Address Classes The two-level IPv4 addressing scheme shown in Figure 3.15 represents the most common method of routing data from source to destination over an IP network. However, as we will soon note, IPv4 supports other addressing schemes. Those schemes, as well as the two-level IP addressing scheme, were developed in recognition of the fact that the use of a single method of subdivision of the IPv4 32-bit address space would be wasteful with respect to the assignment of addresses. For example, if the address space was split evenly into a 16-bit network and a 16-bit host number, the result would be a maximum of 65,535 (2^{16}) networks, with up to 65,535 hosts per network. In actuality there are certain host addresses that cannot be used, which slightly reduces the number of hosts that can reside on an IP network. Later in this section we turn our attention to those addresses. However, returning to our address splitting example, the assignment of a network number to an organization that only has 200 computers would result in a waste of 65,334 host addresses that could not be assigned to another organization. Recognizing this problem, as well as recognizing the need to obtain flexibility in assigning address space to different organizations, resulted in the subdivision of the 32-bit address space into different address classes. Today, IPv4 address space consists of five address classes, referred to as Class A through Class E. Of these, Classes A through C are subdivided into a network identifier and host identifier. Classes D and E do not incorporate two-level addressing, as they represent special IP addressing. Class D addresses are used for IP multicasting, where a single message is distributed to a group of hosts dispersed across one or more networks that join a multicast group to receive the message. Through IP multicasting a single voice or video data stream can be transmitted to multiple recipients on the same or different networks, significantly reducing the use of precious bandwidth. For example, the well-known annual Victoria's Secret video represents a common

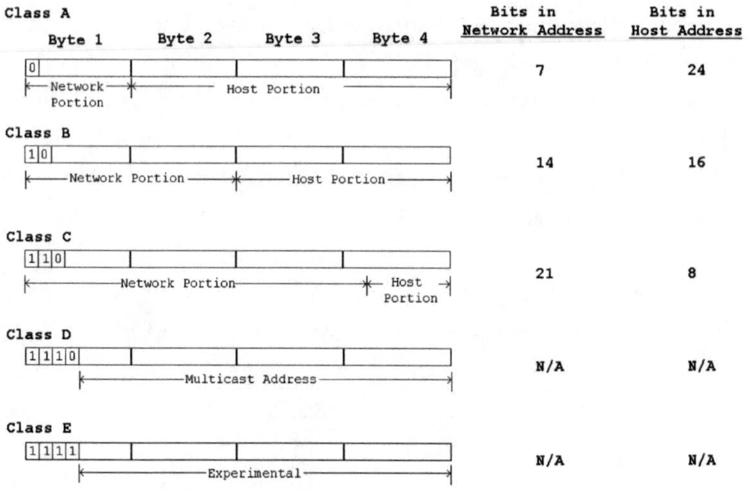

	Bits in Network Address	Bits in Host Address
Class A	7	24
Class B	14	16
Class C	21	8
Class D	N/A	N/A
Class E	N/A	N/A

Figure 3.16 IPv4 addresses.

multicast transmission method. Class E addresses are reserved for experimental use. Although Class D and Class E addresses are single-level addresses, they are similar to Class A through C addresses in that they are 32 bits in length and are identified in the same manner.

3.6.3.2 Address Formats   Figure 3.16 illustrates the five IPv4 address formats, to include the bit allocation in the first byte of each format, which identifies the address class. Once an address class is identified the subdivision of the remainder of the address into network and host address portions can be automatically noted.

To obtain an appreciation for the use of each address class let's first turn our attention to the composition and notation of IPv4 addresses. Once this is accomplished, we then examine special IPv4 addresses and each address class.

3.6.3.3 Address Composition and Notation   IPv4 addresses are specified in terms of 32 bits for source and destination. Because we would prefer not to work with 32-bit strings, dotted decimal notation was developed as a method to facilitate specifying IP address.

Under dotted decimal notation the binary value of an 8-bit byte is expressed as a decimal number between 0 and 255. Because a 32-bit IPv4 address is equivalent to 4 bytes, the use of dotted decimal notation permits four decimal numbers to be used in place of a 32-bit binary string. Since periods are used to separate each decimal number the term *dotted decimal notation* is used to reference the use of a string of four decimal numbers separated from one another by periods to represent a 32-bit binary IP address.

To illustrate the use of dotted decimal notation, consider the following IP address expressed as a 32-bit binary number:

11001111 00000010 10000000 10101010

If you remember, the bit values of a byte are as follows:

128 64 32 16 8 4 2 1

Then the dotted decimal address for the above 32-bit binary IP address becomes:

207.2.128.170

3.6.3.4 Special IPv4 Addresses   There are several special IP addresses that have predefined functions. Those addresses and their meanings are listed in Table 3.5. In examining the entries in Table 3.5 note that a subnet represents a subdivision of a network obtained by the expansion of the network portion of the address to the detriment of the host portion of the address. The expanded portion of the network address is used to denote a subnet that is only applicable internally within an organization's network structure. Later in this chapter we examine subnets in detail.

Note in Table 3.5 that an IP address of either all 0s or all 1s has a special meaning. Because a host value of all 0s and all 1s is part of the first two special addresses in Table 3.5, they cannot be used for a host address. This means that when we compute the number of possible hosts on a Class A, B, or C network we must reduce the total by two. Similarly, we must reduce the number of hosts on a subnet by two to

Table 3.5   Special IPv4 Addresses

ADDRESS	DESCRIPTION
Network = 0, host = 0	This host on this network
Network = all 1s, host = all 1s	Direct broadcast to network
Subnet = all 1s, host = all 1s	Direct broadcast to all subnets on the network
Host = all 1s on any subnet	Direct broadcast to all hosts on the specified subnet
Network = 127, host = any	Internal host loopback address

take into account a host value of zero and a host value of all 1s that has special subnet meanings.

Note also in Table 3.5 that any address with all 0s in the network portion is used to represent "this" network. Also note that an old form of broadcasting known as the all 0s takes the form of 0.0.0.0. You should not use this old broadcasting address because it is now used in a routing table to indicate a default route.

Finally, note that an address prefix of 127 represents an internal host loopback address and cannot be assigned to any host as a unique address. This address can be used to determine if a host's TCP/IP protocol stack is operational. For example, in a Windows 7, Windows NT, or/Windows 2000 environment you can ping yourself by using 127.0.0.1. In fact, because 127.*anything* represents a loopback, you could also use 127.0.0.2 or even 127.255.255.255. In the event you're not familiar with the Windows built-in ping networking tool, it is covered in depth in Chapter 6. Now that we have an appreciation for special IP addresses, let's turn our attention to the five IPv4 classes.

3.6.3.4.1 Class A Addresses   A Class A IPv4 address is defined by a 0-bit value in the high-order bit position of the 32-bit address. This setting indicates that the address has the following 4-byte format:

<network number.host.host.host>

Because the network portion of the Class A address uses one bit for identification, only 7 bits in the first byte are available for network addressing. Out of the 128 combinations all 0s and all 1s cannot be used. This is because all 0s represent "this host on this network" and all 1s provide an internal loopback address. Thus a maximum of 126 network addresses is permitted. Those addresses range from 1 to 126.

The 3-byte host field of a Class A address cannot have all 0s or all 1s. Thus it supports $2^{24} - 2$, or 16,277,214 hosts per network. Due to the relatively small number of Class A networks that can be defined and the large number of hosts that can be supported per network, Class A addresses were primarily assigned to large organizations and countries that have national IP-based networks. Another use of Class A addresses is by Internet service providers as a mechanism to issue

Classless Interdomain Routing (CIDR) protocol addresses. CIDR addressing is covered later in this section.

3.6.3.4.2 Class B Addresses   The setting of the two high-order bits in an IPv4 address to a value of 10 indicates a Class B address. This address takes the following form:

<network number.network number.host.host>

The network portion of a Class B address cannot use the first two bit positions, as they identify the network class. Thus the number of distinct networks becomes 2^{14} or 16,384 network numbers. Each network number is capable of supporting $2^{16} - 2$, or 65,354 hosts.

Because the first two bits in the Class B address are set to a value of 10, network numbers are restricted to the decimal range of 128 to 191 in the first portion of the dotted decimal notation for Class B addresses. Since a Class B address supports a large but not extravagant population of hosts, such addresses were normally assigned to relatively large organizations with tens of thousands of employees. Today all Class B addresses are allocated and only when a previously allocated Class B address is returned is it possible to obtain the use of this type of IPv4 address.

3.6.3.4.3 Class C Addresses   A Class C address is identified by the setting of the three high-order bits in a 32-bit IPv4 address to a value of 110. Thus the form of the Class C address being noted follows:

<network number.network number.network number.host>

The use of 3 bits to identify the network address as a Class C address reduces the number of bits that can be used to identify a particular network address from 24 to 21. This enables 2^{21} or 2,097,152 possible network addresses to be supported. Because a Class C address uses 8 bits for the portion of the host address, this means that each Class C address can support up to $2^8 - 2$, or 254 hosts.

The first byte of a Class C address will always have the composition 110xxxxx, where x represents any binary value. Thus the allowable network range is decimal 192 – 233 in the first field, used for dotted decimal representation of a Class C address. Class C addresses were primarily assigned for use by relatively small networks, such as an organizational LAN requiring a connection to the Internet. Because it is common for many organizations to have multiple LANs, it is also common for multiple Class C addresses to be assigned to organizations that require more than 254 host addresses.

3.6.3.4.4 Class D Addresses The assignment of a value of 1110 to the first four bit positions in a 32-bit IPv4 address defines a Class D address. The remaining 28 bits in the address are used to define 2^{28} or approximately 268 million possible multicast addresses.

Multicasting is an addressing technique that allows a source to send a single copy of a datagram to a specific group of recipients through the use of a multicast address. Each recipient dynamically registers to join the multicast group. As multicast traffic flows through a network, only a recipient registered to receive an appropriate multicast session will read the traffic denoted by the lower-order 28 bits within a 32-bit Class D address. Other stations that are not members of a multicast group only have to read the first four bits of the address to note it is a Class D address and can then ignore the remainder of the address.

To obtain an appreciation for the manner by which a Class D address conserves bandwidth, consider a digitized audio or video presentation routed from the Internet onto a private network for which a dozen employees on the network wish to receive the presentation. Without a multicast transmission capability a dozen separate audio or video data streams would be transmitted onto the private network, with each stream containing packets with a dozen distinct host addresses. In comparison, the use of a multicast address allows one data steam to be routed to the private network on which each registered station reads appropriate traffic. Because audio or video data streams can require a relatively large amount of bandwidth, the ability to eliminate multiple data streams via multicast transmission can prevent networks from becoming saturated, as well as considerably reduce traffic on the Internet. Since the first four bits in a Class D address are set to a value of 1110, the range of Class D addresses lies between 224 and 239 for the first decimal position when the address is expressed as a dotted decimal number.

Table 3.6   IPv4 Address Class First Byte Values

ADDRESS CLASS	FIRST BYTE ADDRESS RANGE
Class A	1–126
Class B	128–191
Class C	192–223
Class D	224–239
Class E	240–255

3.6.3.4.5 Class E Addresses   The assignment of the binary value 1111 to the first four bits in a 32-bit IPv4 address denotes a Class E address. This address is reserved for experimentation.

Class E addresses range between 240 and 254 in their first decimal position when the IPv4 address is expressed as a dotted decimal number. Table 3.6 summarizes IPv4 address classes based upon values permissible in the network or first byte portion of the address when expressed in dotted decimal notation.

3.6.3.4.6 Reserved Addresses   No discussion of IPv4 address classes would be complete without focusing attention upon three blocks of reserved addresses. Such addresses were originally reserved for networks that would not be connected to the Internet and are defined in RFC 1918, "Address Allocation for Private Internets."

Table 3.7 lists the three address blocks defined in RFC 1918. The use of addresses in one or more address blocks defined by RFC 1918 is primarily based upon security considerations as well as the difficulty organizations can face in attempting to obtain relatively scarce Class B or Class A IPv4 addresses.

Because the use of any private RFC 1918 Internet address by two or more organizations connected to the Internet would result in addressing conflicts and the unreliable delivery of information, those addresses are not directly used. Instead, organizations either use a router with a network address translation (NAT) capability or a proxy

Table 3.7   Reserved IPv4 Addresses for Private Internet Use from RFC 1918

ADDRESS BLOCKS
10.0.0.0–10.255.255.255
172.16.0.0–172.31.255.255
192.168.0.0–192.168.255.255

firewall to provide an address translation capability between a large number of private Internet addresses used on the internal private network and a lesser number of assigned IP addresses. For example, an organization with a thousand workstations could assign one RFC Class B address internally and translate those addresses to one Class C-issued address, permitting up to 254 IP sessions at a time to be supported. In addition to enabling organizations to connect large internal networks to the Internet without having to obtain relatively scarce Class A or Class B and even Class C addresses, NAT hides internal addresses from the Internet community. This action results in a degree of security, as any hacker that attempts to attack a host cannot directly do so. Instead, he or she must attack an organization's router or proxy firewall, which hopefully is hardened by the manufacturer to resist such attacks.

3.6.3.5 Subnetting and the Subnet Mask   The use of IP addresses represents a precious resource. Recognizing the limited number of network addresses available for use as well as the need of organizations to create more manageable networks, the IETF approved subnetting in RFC 950 as a mechanism to share a single network address among two or more networks. To better understand the need for subnetting, consider a Class B address. That address permits up to 65,535 hosts. However, it would be both a performance and an administrative nightmare to have one network with that number of hosts. Thus subnetting provides users with the ability to subdivide a Class B network as well as Class A and Class C networks into more manageable entities.

Subnetting represents an extension of the network portion of a Class A, B, or C address internally to an organization. Through the process of subnetting, the two-level IPv4 address hierarchy of Class A, B, and C addresses is turned into a three-level hierarchy.

Figure 3.17 illustrates the creation of a subnet by the extension of the network address to the detriment of the host portion of an address. Note that the resulting action produces a subnet field and a reduced length host field, which reduces the number of hosts that can reside on each subnet.

Through the process of subnetting a Class A, B, or C network address can be extended, with the extension divided into different subnet numbers. Each subnet number can be used to identify a

Two-level Hierarchy

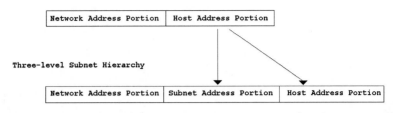

Figure 3.17   Comparing the two-level network class hierarchy to the three-level subnet hierarchy.

different network internal to an organization. However, because the network portion of the address does not change, all subnets appear externally to be located on the same network. This means that routing tables on devices that form the backbone of the Internet need to recognize a lesser number of network addresses, which in turn simplifies routing. This also means that routers within an organization must be able to differentiate between different subnets.

To illustrate the subnet process let's consider an organization that within a building operates five Ethernet networks, with between 20 and 30 stations on each network. Although the organization could apply for five Class C addresses and assign one address to each network, doing so would waste precious Class C address space since each Class C address supports a maximum of 254 devices. In addition, the assignment of five Class C addresses would result in configuring numerous routers on the Internet to note those addresses. This in turn would adversely affect bandwidth utilization on the Internet, as five router table entries would be transmitted each time routers broadcast the contents of their routing tables.

Because we need to support five networks at one location, we would extend the network portion of one Class C address by three bit positions. This is because 2^3 provides eight subnets, while 2^2 provides four, which is an insufficient number of subnets. Because a Class C address uses one 8-bit byte for host identification, this also means that a maximum of five bit positions $(8 - 3)$ can be used for the host number. This reduces the number of hosts that can reside on each subnet to $2^5 - 2$, or 30, which is sufficient for our example.

Let us assume we obtained the Class C network address 205.131.175.0 for our subnetting effort. To use that network we would extend its network prefix by three bit positions as illustrated in Figure 3.18. In

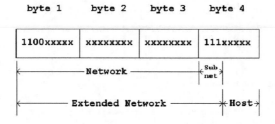

Figure 3.18 Creating a Class C three-level addressing scheme.

examining Figure 3.18 note that the top entry labeled "Network" represents the Class C network address with a host address byte field set to all zeros. Because we previously decided to use three bits from the host portion of the Class C IPv4 address, the entries below the base network indicate the use of three bits from the host position in the address to create extended prefixes to identify all possible distinct subnets.

For each subnet there are several addressing restrictions that reduce the number of hosts, or more correctly, interfaces that can be supported. First, you cannot use a base subnet of all 0s or all 1s. Thus for subnet 0 in Figure 3.18 valid host addresses would range from 1 to 30, while for subnet 1 valid host addresses would range from 33 to 61, and so on.

A second limitation on subnetting for Class A, B, and C addresses concerns the subdivision of the last byte of an IP address. Because a subnet must be able to have some hosts residing on it, you can only use up to six bits in the last byte when you create a subnet mask. Thus the maximum Class C subnet would be 6 bits, while the maximum Class A and B subnets would be 22 and 14 bits, respectively.

Although the use of a 3-bit subnet mask permits eight subnets to be defined, our requirement was to assign subnets to five LANs. Thus in the example shown in Figure 3.19, in which a base network of

```
Base Network:  11000110.01010000.00101110.00000000 = 198.78.46.0

Subnet #0:11000110.01010000.00101110.00000000 = 198.78.46.0
Subnet #1:11000110.01010000.00101110.00100000 = 198.78.46.32
Subnet #2:11000110.01010000.00101110.01000000 = 198.78.46.64
Subnet #3:11000110.01010000.00101110.01100000 = 198.78.46.96
Subnet #4:11000110.01010000.00101110.10000000 = 198.78.46.128
```

Figure 3.19 Creating extended network prefixes via subnetting.

198.78.46.0 is subnetted, for illustrative purposes we use subnets 0 through 4, although we could select any five of the eight subnets. To the router connecting the organization's network to the Internet, all five subnets we use would appear as the base network address, with the router of our organization being responsible for directing traffic to the appropriate subnet.

It is important to note that external to the organization there is no knowledge of the dotted decimal numbers shown in the right column of Figure 3.19, which represents distinct subnets. This results from the fact that routers external to the organization view the binary value of the first byte of each dotted decimal number, and note that the first two bits are set. This informs each router that the address is a Class C address and that the first three bytes represent the network portion of the IPv4 address, while the last byte represents the host address. Thus to the outside world the 198.78.46.32 address would not be recognized as subnet 1 on network 198.78.46.0. Thus routers external to the organization would interpret the address as network 198.78.46.0 with a host address of 32. Similarly, subnet 4 would be recognized as a Class C network address of 198.78.46.0 with a host address of 128. However, within the organization internally each of the IPv4 addresses listed in the right column in Figure 3.19 would be interpreted and recognized as a subnet. Figure 3.20 illustrates the difference between viewing the network internally and externally.

3.6.3.5.1 Host Addresses on Subnets   Although we briefly discussed some subnet addressing rules, we have yet to denote how we assign host addresses to devices connected to different subnets or how a

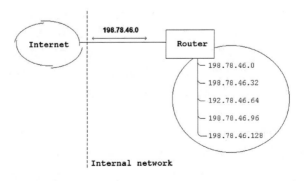

Figure 3.20   An internal versus external view of subnets.

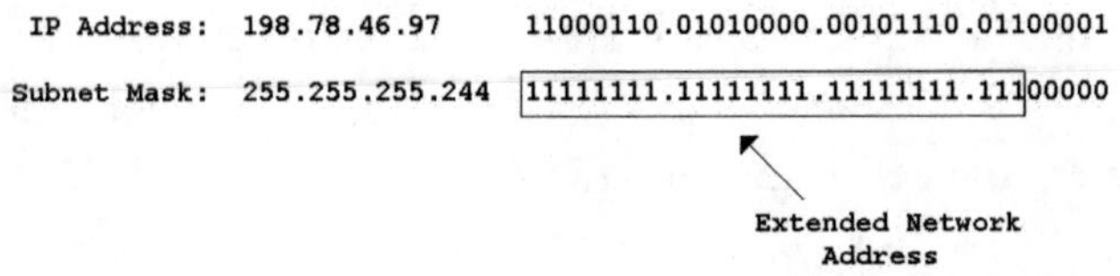

```
IP Address:   198.78.46.97     11000110.01010000.00101110.01100001

Subnet Mask:  255.255.255.244  11111111.11111111.11111111.11100000
```

Extended Network
Address

Figure 3.21   Examining the relationship between a Class C IPv4 address and a subnet mask.

router can examine an IPv4 address so it can correctly route traffic to an appropriate subnet. Thus let's turn our attention to these topics.

In Figure 3.18 we subdivided the host portion of the Class C address into a 3-bit subnet field and a 5-bit host field. Because we cannot use a host field address of all 0s or all 1s this means each subnet can support a maximum of $2^5 - 2$, or 30 addresses. Thus we could use host addresses 1 through 30 on subnet 0, 33 through 62 on subnet 1, and so on. Remembering the restriction that we cannot use all 0s or all 1s in the host portion of a subnet governs our ability to assign host addresses by subnet. This is illustrated in Figure 3.21, which indicates how we could assign host addresses to subnet 3, whose creation was previously indicated in Figure 3.19. In examining Figure 3.21 note that we commence our addressing operation with the subnet address 205.131.175.96, for which the first three bits in the fourth byte are used to indicate the subnet. Then we use the remaining five bits to define the host address on each subnet. Thus the address 198.78.46.97 represents the third subnet on the 198.78.46.0 network, while addresses 198.78.46.96 through 198.78.46.126 represent hosts 1 through 30 that can reside on subnet 3.

While the previously presented information explained how we can create subnets and host addresses on subnets, an unanswered question is how devices on a private network recognize subnet addressing. For example, assume an IP datagram with the destination address of 198.78.46.97 arrives at your organization's router. How does that router know to route the datagram onto subnet 3? The answer to this question is the use of a subnet mask, so let's turn our attention to this topic.

3.6.3.5.2 The Subnet Mask   The subnet mask is a sequence of binary 1s that indicates the length of the network address, to include any subnetting that has occurred. Thus the subnet mask provides a mechanism that enables communications devices on a network to determine the separation of an IPv4 address into its network, subnet, and host portions.

To illustrate the use of the subnet mask, let's assume our network address is 198.78.46.0 and we need to develop a subnet mask that can be used to identify the extended network as well as the subnet and host on the subnet. Because we previously extended the network by 3 bits the subnet would become:

11111111.11111111.11111111.11100000

Note that the above mask can be expressed in dotted decimal notation as 255.255.255.224.

The subnet mask tells a communications device which bits in an IP address should be treated as an extended network address consisting of network and subnet addresses. Then the remaining bits that are not set indicate the host on the extended network address. Because the first or first few bits in an IP address denote the address class, a communications device that examines those bits determines the number of bits in the network portion of the address. Subtracting that value from the number of bits in the subnet mask indicates the subnet field, allowing the device to note the subnet. For example, consider the IPv4 address 198.78.46.66 and the subnet mask 255.255.255.244. The address 198.78.46.66 has the first two bits in the address set, representing a Class C address that uses 3 bytes or 24 bits for the network address. Because the subnet mask represents 27 set bits, this indicates that the subnet is 27 − 24, or 3 bits in length, and occurs in bit positions 25 through 27 in the IPv4 address. Because bits 25 through 27 have the bit composition 010, this indicates the subnet is subnet 2. Because the last five bits have the value 00010, this indicates host 2 on subnet 2.

To facilitate the ability to work with subnets Table 3.8 contains a listing of the number of subnets that can be created for IPv4 Class B and C addresses, their subnet masks, the number of hosts that can reside on a network, and the total number of hosts capable of being supported by a particular subnet mask. Thus this table can be used as a guide for considering the extension of a network address internally to form a subnet. In examining the entries in Table 3.8 note that the total number of hosts can vary considerably based upon the use of

Table 3.8   Subnet Mask Reference

NUMBER OF SUBNET BITS	SUBNET MASK	NUMBER OF SUBNETWORKS	HOSTS/SUBNET	TOTAL NUMBER OF HOSTS
CLASS B				
1	—	—	—	—
2	255.255.192.0	2	16382	32764
3	255.255.224.0	6	8190	49140
4	255.255.240.0	14	4094	57316
5	255.255.248.0	30	2046	61380
6	255.255.252.0	62	1022	63364
7	255.255.254.0	126	510	64260
8	255.255.255.0	254	254	64516
9	255.255.255.128	510	126	64260
10	255.255.255.192	1022	62	63364
11	255.255.255.224	2046	30	61380
12	255.255.255.240	4094	14	57316
13	255.255.255.248	8190	6	49140
14	255.255.255.252	16382	2	32764
15	—	—	—	—
16	—	—	—	—
CLASS C				
1	—	—	—	—
2	255.255.255.192	2	62	124
3	255.255.255.224	6	30	180
4	255.255.255.240	14	14	196
5	255.255.255.248	30	6	170
6	255.255.255.252	62	2	124
7	—	—	—	—
8	—	—	—	—

different subnet masks and should be carefully considered prior to performing the subdivision of a network.

3.6.3.5.3 Configuration Examples   There is an old adage that states: "The proof of the pudding is in its eating." We can apply this adage to the information previously discussed about IPv4 addressing by turning our attention to the manner by which workstations and servers are configured to operate on a TCP/IP network.

When configuring a workstation or server to operate on a TCP/IP network, most operating systems will require you to enter a minimum of the IP addresses of the station and an optional subnet mask.

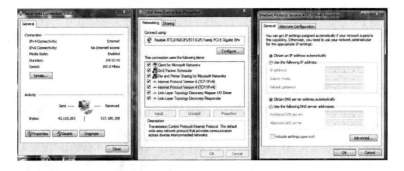

Figure 3.22   Configuring a station on a LAN under Windows 7.

In some operating systems a total of three IPv4 addresses may be required. The three IPv4 addresses you may have to configure include the IP address assigned to the interface of a workstation or server, the IP address of the gateway responsible for relaying packets with a destination address different from the local network and the address of a name resolver. The gateway represents an old term for the modern router. The resolver is a computer responsible for translating host addresses entered in a browser, FTP, or Telnet client applications, or another application, into its IP address, as routing in a TCP/IP environment is based upon IP addresses. The name resolver is also referred to as a Domain Name Service (DNS).

Figure 3.22 illustrates the first three configuration screens in a series of screens displayed by the modern Windows 7 Internet properties dialog box for configuring a station on a LAN. You can first go to Control Panel and enter "adapter" in the search bar. Next, you would select Network and Sharing Center, after which you would select View Network Connections. The first dialog box that will be displayed is on the left in Figure 3.22, titled Local Area Connection Status. Selecting Properties results in the display of the middle dialog box appropriately labeled Local Area Connection Properties, which indicates the software used by the selected adapter. By selecting IPv4 and Configure the dialog box in the right of Figure 3.22 is displayed. From this dialog box you can either obtain an IP address and DNS server address automatically or define the IP address, subnet mask, and default gateway as well as a preferred and alternate DNS server address. Note that selecting Automatically results in Windows using an automatic detection feature that uses the Dynamic Host Configuration Protocol (DHCP) to obtain required addresses.

3.6.3.6 Classless Networking Although the term *classless* normally refers to a person without taste, when applied to IPv4 addressing it represents a technique to more efficiently assign addresses to organizations. Classless networking obtains its name from representing a technique that does away with network classes, enabling the inefficiencies associated with allocating Class A, B, and C addresses to organizations that have a limited number of devices to be overcome.

Under classless networking an organization is assigned a number of bits for use as the local part of its address that best corresponds to the number of addresses it requires. For example, assume your organization requires 4000 IP addresses. Because 2^{12} provides 4096 distinct addresses that best correspond to your organization's requirements, you would be assigned 12 bits for use as the local portion of your organization's address. The remaining 20 bits in the 32-bit IPv4 address space are then used as a prefix to denote what is referred to as a supernetwork. Thus the format of a classless address is as follows:

Supernetwork address: network address

The forward slash is used to denote the network portion of a classless network. That character is then followed by the number of bits in the network address. Thus the previously described classless network would be denoted as /20.

Address allocations employed for classless networking are taken from available Class C addresses. This means that obtaining a 20-bit classless network prefix to support up to 4096 devices is equivalent to obtaining 16 continuous Class C addresses. Table 3.9 provides a list of classless network address assignments that can be assigned from available Class C address space.

Another key advantage of classless networking concerns the use of router tables and router performance. Under classless addressing a router becomes able to forward traffic to an organization using a single routing entry. This permits a reduction in router table entries, which in turn allows the router to perform lookup operations faster. Thus classless addressing provides a mechanism to both extend the availability of IP addresses in a more efficient

Table 3.9   Classless Address Blocks

NETWORK PART	LOCAL BITS	EQUIVALENT NUMBER	DISTINCT ADDRESSES OF CLASS C ADDRESSES
124	8	1	256
123	9	2	512
122	10	4	1024
121	11	8	2048
120	12	16	4096
119	13	32	8192
118	14	64	16284
117	15	128	32768

manner and enable routers to operate more efficiently until IPv6 is deployed.

3.7 The IPv6 Header

During 2011 the U.S. government directed all federal agencies to support IPv6 on their public websites by September 30, 2012, resulting in approximately 10,000 websites falling under this mandate. In April 2011 Asia depleted all of its IPv4 address space, while the European regional registry is expected to run out of IPv4 address space in 2012, quickly followed by North America, which is expected to deplete its IPv4 address space during 2013. Although IPv4 addresses are rapidly being depleted, this is only one of the several issues that was the driving force for the development of a replacement for that version of the Internet Protocol. Other issues include the need to improve support for extending the IP header to accommodate features and functions yet to be developed, simplify the header to reduce packet processing time, and enable the labeling of packets belonging to a flow as a mechanism to provide a quality of service capability. These issues resulted in a complete redesign of the IP header.

Figure 3.23 illustrates the format of an IPv6 header. Note that the resulting header is significantly simpler than the IPv4 header, consisting of only seven fields. Although the header is simpler than an IPv4 header, we will soon note that through the use of the Next Header field we can daisy-chain IPv6 headers, one after another, which considerably expands the capability of an IPv6 header, enabling such security

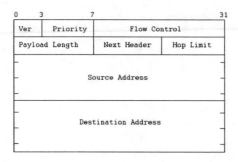

Figure 3.23   The IPv6 header.

options as authentication to be added. To obtain an appreciation of the IPv6 header, let's examine each field in the header.

3.7.1 Ver Field

The Ver field is 4 bits in length and functions in the same manner as its IPv4 cousin. That is, it identifies the version of the Internet Protocol. For IPv6 a binary value of 0110 is placed in this field. Because the Ver field in an IPv6 header like its IPv4 counterpart is located at the beginning of the header, it enables a communications device to rapidly distinguish an IPv4 packet from an IPv6 packet.

3.7.2 Priority Field

The Priority field enables a data originator to identify the desired delivery priority of a packet. Because this field is 4 bits, up to 16 priorities (0 to 15) can be specified. Table 3.10 lists presently defined Priority field values. In examining the recommended priority values

Table 3.10   Priority Field Value Assignments

PRIORITY FIELD VALUE	RECOMMENDED ASSIGNMENT
0	Uncharacterized traffic
1	Filler traffic
2	Unattended traffic
3	Reserved
4	Attended bulk transfer
5	Reserved
6	Interactive traffic
7	Internet control traffic

listed in Table 3.10, Netnews and email can be considered to represent applications that could be assigned priorities of filler and unattended data transfer, respectively. FTP could represent an example of an attended bulk transfer priority, while Telnet and SNMP could represent interactive traffic and Internet control traffic. Priority values of 8 through 15 are reserved for non-congestion-controlled traffic or traffic consisting of real-time packets that does not back off in response to network congestion. The lowest-priority value (8) should be used for packets the originator is most willing to have discarded when congestion effects data flow, while the highest value (15) should be assigned to packets the originator is least willing to have discarded.

3.7.3 Flow Label Field

The Flow Label field is 24 bits in length. This field enables a source to identify a sequence of related packets that require special handling by intermediate routers when the packets travel from source to destination. An example of a flow could be a real-time video conference. Through the identification of a traffic flow it becomes possible for a quality of service (QoS) protocol, such as the Resource Reservation Setup Protocol (RSVP), to use the Priority and Flow Label fields to provide special packet handling based upon the allocation of bandwidth.

3.7.4 Payload Length Field

The Payload Length field is 16 bits in length and its value indicates the payload carried by the packet after the header. Because an IPv6 header's length is fixed at 40 octets, the total length of the packet is the value of the Payload Length field plus 40.

3.7.5 Next Header Field

The Next Header field identifies the type of header that immediately follows the IPv6 header. Although the values used for this 8-bit field are the same values as used in the IPv4 Protocol field (refer to Table 3.4), the use of this field considerably differs from the IPv4 Protocol field. The latter simply indicates the protocol that follows

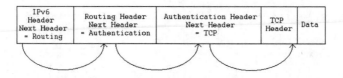

Figure 3.24 An example of an IPv6 packet with daisy-chained extension headers.

the IPv4 header. In comparison, the Next Header field can indicate an optional header, a higher-layer protocol, or no protocol above IP. This significantly expands the capability of IPv6 since it enables headers to be daisy-chained to support a particular function or series of functions.

Figure 3.24 illustrates an example of the extension of an IPv6 packet through the daisy chaining of headers. In this example a value of 43 in the IPv6 header indicates that the next header is a routing header. The routing header in turn would have a value of 51 in its Next Header field to indicate authentication follows, resulting in an authentication header following the routing header. The authentication header would then have a value in its Next Header field to indicate a TCP header follows.

3.7.6 Hop Limit Field

This 8-bit field indicates the maximum number of routers a packet can traverse prior to being discarded. This field acknowledges that the use of a time entry in the IPv4 TTL field was impractical and the earlier protocol's more practical use of a hop count is officially used by the newer protocol.

3.7.7 Source and Destination Address Fields

Both Source and Destination Address fields were extended to 128 bits from IPv4's 32-bit addresses. Because IPv6 is based upon the same architecture used in IPv4, each network interface still requires a distinct IP address. However, under IPv6 an interface can be identified by several types of addresses, each of which contains 128 bits or 96 more bits than an IPv4 address. In the remainder of this section we turn our attention to some of the address types supported under IPv6, their notation or representation, and the manner by which IPv6 address space is allocated.

3.7.7.1 Address Types   IPv6 defines three types of addresses—unicast, multicast, and anycast—with the latter representing a new address category that was not included in IPv4. An anycast address identifies a group of devices similar to a multicast address. However, a packet with a multicast address is delivered to only one host, usually the closest one to the source with "close" defined by the routing protocol. The use of anycast addressing can be expected to facilitate network restructuring while minimizing the amount of configuration changes required to support a new network topology. This can be accomplished since an anycast address could be used to reference a group of routers, and the alteration of a network when IPv6 is used with anycast addressing would allow the stations to continue to access the nearest router without having to change the station's address configuration in its TCP/IP protocol stack.

3.7.7.2 Address Notation   IPv6 addresses are written in dotted decimal notation similar to the manner by which they are used to specify an IPv4 address. However, because an IPv6 address consists of 128 bits or 32 decimals, the format by which dotted decimal numbers are used changed. Instead of a period or dot to separate individual numbers, under IPv6 a colon (:) is used to separate 16-bit or 4-hex-character address entities. Because IPv6 addresses will often have a long string of zeros, such as a 32-bit IPv4 address represented in a 128-bit IPv6 address field, a double colon (::) is used to represent contiguous multiple 16-bit (4-hex-character) blocks of zeros. To illustrate IPv6 address notation, let's examine the use of colons and double colons. For example, consider the following IPv6 address:

1ACD:4ABD:0003:0000:0000:0001:31BC:010A

To facilitate the entry of IPv6 addresses you can ignore or skip the leading zeros in each hexadecimal 4-byte component. This allows you to rewrite the previous IPv6 network address as:

1ACD:4ABD:3:0:0:1:31BC:10A

We can simplify the address further by replacing consecutive null 16-bit numbers by double colons. Doing so we obtain:

1ACD:4ABD:3::1:31BC:10A

Note that the double colon can only be used once inside an IPv6 address. This is because the reconstruction of the address requires the number of integer fields in the address to be subtracted from 8 to determine the number of consecutive fields of zero value the double colon represents. Otherwise, the use of two or more double colons would result in an ambiguity that would prevent the address from being correctly reconstructed.

3.7.7.3 Address Allocation The use of a 128-bit address space for IPv6 results in a much higher degree of address assignment flexibility than obtainable when using IPv4 addresses. For example, under IPv6 addressing Internet service providers can be identified. In addition, IPv6 addressing provides the ability to identify local and global multicast addresses, private site addresses for use within an organization, hierarchical global unicast addresses, and other types of addresses. In Table 3.11 you will note a list of the initial allocation of address space under IPv6.

Table 3.11   IPv6 Address Space Allocation

ALLOCATION	PREFIX (BINARY)	FRACTION OF ADDRESS SPACE
Reserved	0000 0000	1/256
Unassigned	0000 0001	1/256
Reserved for NSAP allocation	0000 001	1/128
Reserved for IPX allocation	0000 010	1/128
Unassigned	0000 1	1/128
Unassigned	0001	1/32
Unassigned	001	1/8
Provider-based unicast address	010	1/8
Unassigned	011	1/8
Reserved for geographic-based unicast addresses	100	1/8
Unassigned	101	1/8
Unassigned	110	1/8
Unassigned	1110	1/16
Unassigned	1111 0	1/32
Unassigned	1111 10	1/64
Unassigned	1111 110	1/128
Unassigned	1111 1110 0	1/512
Link-local use addresses	1111 1110 10	1/1024
Site-local use addresses	1111 1110 11	1/1024
Multicast addresses	1111 1111	1/256

IPv6 address space allocation was assigned to the Internet Assigned Numbers Authority (IANA). IANA distributes portions of IPv6 address space to regional registries, such as the InterNIC in North America, RIPE in Europe, APNIC in Asia, and similar organizations. To obtain an appreciation for the potential use of IPv6 addresses, let's examine several types of IPv6 addresses.

3.7.8 Provider-Based Unicast Addresses

A provider-based unicast address is assigned by an Internet service provider to a customer. Based upon the initial allocation of IPv6 addresses shown in Table 3.11, each provider-based unicast address has the 3-bit prefix 010. That prefix is followed by fields that identify the Internet address registry from which the ISP obtained the address (registry identifier), the address block assigned to the ISP by the registry authority, which identifies the ISP (provider identifier), the ISP's subscriber (subscriber identifier), and the subscriber address in the form of a 16-bit subnet identifier (subnet) and a 48-bit interface identifier (station). The latter can represent the MAC address of a station and, when used, also represents a unique address. Figure 3.25 illustrates the format of a provider-based unicast address.

3.7.9 Multicast Addresses

As indicated in Table 3.11, a multicast address begins with eight ones set (hex FF). This address is used in IPv6 to identify a group of nodes, with the term *node* used to indicate a device that supports the new version of the Internet Protocol and which replaces the term

Prefix	Registry ID	Provider ID	Subscriber ID	Subnet ID	Station ID

```
Legend:
        Prefix          three bits set to 010
        Registry        5 bits identifies organization that
                        allocated the address
        Provider        24 bits with 16 used to identify ISP and 8
                        used for future extensions
        Subscriber      32 bits with 24 used to identify the
                        subscriber and 8 for extension
        Subnet          16 bits to identify the subnetwork
        Station         48 bits to identify the station
```

Figure 3.25   IPv6 provider-based unicast address structure.

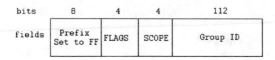

Figure 3.26   The IPv6 multicast address format.

interface used under IPv4. A node can belong to any number of multicast groups that allow the device to participate in multiple multicast sessions.

Figure 3.26 illustrates the IPv6 multicast address format. Note that after the first eight set bits the next four bits represent a set of flag bits. The first three flag bits are currently set to zero, while the fourth bit is used to indicate a permanently assigned (0) or transient (1) multicast address. The next field consists of 4 bits, which indicates the scope of the address. Here the Scope field denotes the portion of the network for which the multicast is relevant, in effect providing a mechanism to focus a multicast to a specific area. Scope values include node-local (0001), link-local (0010), site-local (0101), organization-local (1000), and global (1111). The remaining 112 bits in the 128-bit address represents a Group Identifier field, which identifies the multicast group for a permanent or transient application within a given scope.

3.7.10 Transporting IPv4 Addresses

In a mixed IPv4 and IPv6 environment communications devices that do not support IPv6 will have their addresses mapped using a special form of IPv6:

$$0:0:0:0:0:FFF:w.x.y.z$$

In the above format w.x.y.z represents the original 32-bit IPv4 address. Thus an organization with a considerable investment in time and effort in configuring hundreds or thousands of workstations and servers can migrate to IPv6 yet only need to upgrade the organization's router to support IPv6 addressing when it deploys the new version of IP. Then, if it wishes to do so, it can gradually convert existing IPv4 addresses to IPv6 addresses.

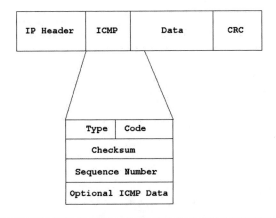

Figure 3.27   ICMP messages are transported via encapsulation within an IPv4 or IPv6 datagram.

3.8 ICMP and ARP

In concluding this chapter on the Internet Protocol we turn our attention to two special protocols that facilitate the operation of the Internet Protocol: the ICMP and the ARP.

3.8.1 ICMP

In this section we focus our attention upon the ICMP. ICMP represents an error reporting mechanism that is transported via IP datagrams.

The format of an ICMP message and its relationship to an IP datagram is illustrated in Figure 3.27. Note that although each ICMP message has its own format, they all begin with the same three fields: an 8-bit Type field, an 8-bit Code field, and 16-bit Checksum field.

Similar to IP, there are two versions of ICMP you should obtain familiarity with: ICMPv4 and ICMPv6. In this section we first examine the values of the Type and Code fields associated with ICMPv4. Once this is accomplished we turn our attention to the values of those fields when ICMPv6 is employed.

3.8.1.1 ICMPv4   When ICMPv4 is used to transport control messages, an IPv4 header precedes the ICMP header. This results in the use of 32-bit IPv4 addressing for the routing of datagrams.

3.8.1.1.1 Type Field   The ICMP Type field defines the meaning of the message as well as its format. Perhaps the two most familiar ICMP

Table 3.12 ICMP Type Field Values

TYPE	NAME
0	Echo reply
1	Unassigned
2	Unassigned
3	Destination unreachable
4	Source quench
5	Redirect
6	Alternate host address
7	Unassigned
8	Echo request
9	Router advertisement
10	Router selection
11	Time exceeded
12	Parameter problem
13	Timestamp
14	Timestamp reply
15	Information request
16	Information reply
17	Address mask request
18	Address mask reply
19	Reserved (for security)
20–29	Reserved (for robustness experiment)
30	Traceroute
31	Datagram conversion error
32	Mobile host redirect
33	IPv6 where-are-you
34	IPv6 I-am-here
35	Mobile registration request
36	Mobile registration reply
37	Domain name request
38	Domain name reply
39	SKIP
40	Photuris
41–255	Reserved

messages are type 0 and type 8. A Type field value of 8 represents an echo request, while a Type 0 ICMP message denotes an echo reply. Although their official names are echo reply and echo request, most persons are more familiar with the term *ping*, which is used to reference both an ICMP echo request and an ICMP echo reply. Table 3.12

lists the values of the ICMP Type fields that identify specific types of ICMP messages.

3.8.1.1.2 Code Field The second field common to each ICMP header is the Code field. The Code field provides additional information about the message and may not be meaningful for certain messages. For example, both Type field values of 0 and 8 always have a Code field value of 0. In comparison, a Type field value of 3 (destination unreachable) can have one of 16 possible Code field values, which further defines the reason why the destination was unreachable.

Table 3.13 lists the Code field values presently assigned to ICMPv4 based upon their Type field values. As we will note when we discuss security issues later in this book, many firewalls and routers provide administrators with the ability to filter all or selected ICMP messages. You could use this feature to prevent malicious pinging either as an attempt by a hacker to learn the devices on your organization's internal network or as a mechanism to deny service to a host by flooding it with pings.

3.8.1.2 ICMPv6 ICMPv6 is functionally very similar to ICMPv4, using a similar message format that results in the message being transported within an IP datagram. However, ICMPv6 is transported within an IPv6 datagram and the IPv6 header uses a Next Header field value of 58 to indicate that an ICMPv6 header follows.

3.8.1.2.1 Type Field In comparison to ICMPv4 the universe of ICMPv6 Type field values is considerably reduced. Table 3.14 lists presently defined ICMPv6 Type field values. In examining the entries in Table 3.14 note that only four types of error messages are defined. A Destination Unreachable error message indicates a packet cannot be delivered to its destination address other than due to congestion causing the packet to be discarded. A Packet Too Big error message is transmitted from a router to the packet originator when the packet exceeds the MTU of the outgoing link and cannot be forwarded.

The third message, Time Exceeded, is sent by a router when a packet's Hop Limit value reaches zero or if all fragments of a datagram are not received within the fragment reassembly time. The fourth error message, Parameter Problem, is generated by a device that notes a problem in a field in the packet header that makes it impossible to

Table 3.13 ICMP Code Field Values Based on Message Type

MESSAGE TYPE	CODE FIELD VALUES
3 DESTINATION UNREACHABLE CODES	
0	Net unreachable
1	Host unreachable
2	Protocol unreachable
3	Port unreachable
4	Fragmentation needed and don't fragment were set
5	Source route failed
6	Destination network unknown
7	Destination host unknown
8	Source host isolated
9	Communication with destination network is administratively prohibited
10	Communication with destination host is administratively prohibited
11	Destination network unreachable for type of service
12	Destination host unreachable for type of service
13	Destination host unreachable for type of service
14	Communication administratively prohibited
15	Precedence cutoff in effect
5 REDIRECT CODES	
0	Redirect datagram for the network (or subnet)
1	Redirect datagram for the host
2	Redirect datagram for the type of service and network
3	Redirect datagram for the type of service and host
6 ALTERNATE HOST ADDRESS CODES	
0	Alternate address for host
11 TIME EXCEEDED CODES	
0	Time to live exceeded in transit
1	Fragment reassembly time exceeded
12 PARAMETER PROBLEM CODES	
0	Point indicates the error
1	Missing a required option
2	Bad length
40 PHOTURIS CODES	
0	Reserved
1	Unknown security parameters index
2	Valid security parameters, but authentication failed
3	Valid security parameters, but decryption failed

Table 3.14 ICMPv6 Type Field Values

TYPE	NAME
1	Destination unreachable
2	Packet too big
3	Time exceeded
4	Parameter problem
128	Echo request
129	Echo reply
130	Group membership query
131	Group membership report
132	Group membership reduction
133	Router solicitation
134	Router advertisement
135	Neighbor solicitation
136	Neighbor advertisement
137	Redirect message
138	Router renumbering

process the header. Thus by observing the type of ICMPv6 error messages you can obtain an appreciation for the cause of several common types of network-related problems.

In addition to four error messages, the ICMPv6 Type field currently defines 11 informational messages. The first two listed in Table 3.14, echo request and echo reply, are used for diagnostic purposes, while the three "group" messages are used to convey information about multicast group membership from IPv6 nodes to their neighboring routers.

3.8.2 ARP

In concluding this chapter, we turn our attention to the manner by which datagrams with layer 3 IPv4 and IPv6 addresses can be routed to adapter cards built to recognize layer 2 MAC addresses.

3.8.2.1 LAN Delivery When an IP datagram arrives at a LAN, it contains a 32-bit destination address. To deliver the datagram to its destination, the router must create a LAN frame with an appropriate MAC destination address. Thus the router needs a mechanism to resolve or convert the IP address into the MAC address of the workstation configured with the destination IP address. In the opposite direction, a workstation may need to transmit an IP datagram to another workstation. In this situation, the workstation must be able to convert a MAC address into an IP address. Both of these address translation requirements are handled by protocols specifically developed to provide an address resolution capability. One protocol referred to as the ARP translates an IP address into a hardware address. A second protocol referred to as the Reverse Address Resolution Protocol (RARP) performs a reverse translation process, converting a hardware layer address into an IP address.

3.8.2.1.1 Address Resolution Operation   The address resolution operation begins when a device needs to transmit a datagram. First, the device checks its memory to determine if it previously learned the MAC address associated with a particular destination IP address. This memory location is referred to as an ARP cache. Because the first occurrence of an IP address means its associated MAC address will not be in the ARP cache, it must learn the MAC address. To do so, the device will broadcast an ARP packet to all devices on the LAN. Figure 3.28 illustrates the format of an ARP packet. Note that the numbers shown in some fields in the ARP packet indicate the byte numbers in a field when a field spans a 4-byte boundary.

3.8.2.1.2 ARP Packet Fields   To illustrate the operation of ARP, let us examine the fields in the ARP packet. The 16-bit Hardware Type field indicates the type of network adapter, such as 10 Mbps Ethernet (value = 1), IEEE 802 network (value = 6), and so on. The 16-bit

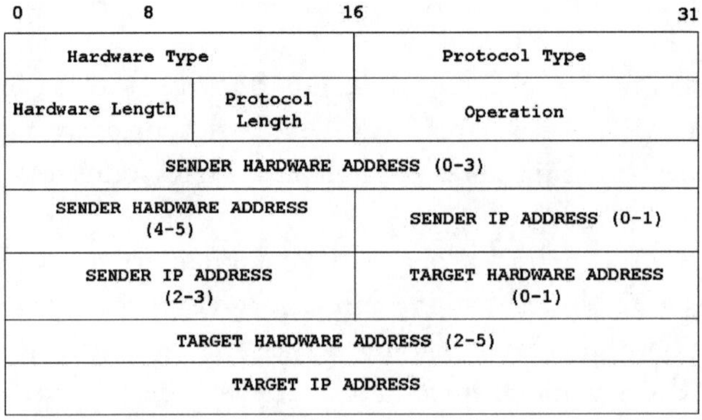

Figure 3.28   The IPv4 ARP packet format.

Protocol Type field indicates the protocol for which an address resolution process is being performed. For IPv4 the Protocol Type field has a value of hex 0800.

The Hardware Length field defines the number of bytes in the hardware address. Thus the ARP packet format can be varied to accommodate different types of address resolutions beyond IP and MAC addresses. Because Ethernet and Token-Ring have the same MAC length, the value of this field is 6 for both.

The Protocol Length field indicates the length of the address for the protocol to be resolved. For IPv4 the value of this field is set to 4. The Operation field indicates the operation to be performed. This field has a value of 1 for an ARP request. When a target station responds, the value of this field is changed to Z to denote an ARP reply.

The Sender Hardware Address field indicates the hardware addresses of the station generating the ARP request or ARP reply. This field is 6 bytes in length and is followed by a 4-byte Sender IP Address field. The latter indicates the IP address of the originator of the datagram.

The next-to-last field is the Target Hardware Address field. Because the ARP process must discover its value, this field is originally set to all zeros in an ARP request. Once a station receives the request and notes it has the same IP address as that in the Target IP Address field, it places its MAC address in the Target Hardware Address field. Thus the last field, Target IP Address, is set to the IP address the originator needs for a hardware address.

3.8.2.1.3 Locating the Required Address To put the pieces together, let us assume a router receives a datagram from the Internet with the destination address of 205.131.175.5. Let us further assume that the router has a connection to an Ethernet network, and one station on that network has that IP address. The router needs to determine the MAC address associated with the IP address so it can construct a frame to deliver the datagram. Assuming there is no entry in its ARP cache, the router creates an ARP frame and transmits the frame using a MAC broadcast address of FFFFFFFFFFFF. Because the frame was broadcast to all stations on the network, each device reads the frame. The station that has its protocol stack configured to the same

IP address as that of the Target IP Address field in the ARP frame would respond to the ARP request. When it does, it will transmit an ARP reply in which its physical MAC address is inserted into the ARP Target Hardware Address field that was previously set to zero.

The ARP standard includes provisions for devices on a network to update their ARP table with the MAC and IP address pair of the sender of the ARP request. Thus as ARP requests flow on a LAN, they contribute to the building of tables that reduce the necessity of additional broadcasts.

3.8.2.1.4 Gratuitous ARP   There is a special type of ARP referred to as a gratuitous ARP that deserves mention. When a TCP/IP stack is initialized, it issues a gratuitous ARP, which represents an ARP request for its own IP address. If the station receives a reply containing a MAC address that differs from its address, this indicates that another device on the network is using its assigned IP address. If this situation occurs, an error message warning you of an address conflict will be displayed.

3.8.2.1.5 Proxy ARP   Another type of ARP that deserves mention is a proxy ARP. A proxy is a device that works on the behalf of another. Thus a proxy ARP represents a mechanism that enables a device to answer an ARP request on behalf of another device.

The rationale for the development of proxy ARP, which is also referred to as ARP hack, dates to the early use of subnetting when a LAN could be subdivided into two or more segments. If a station on one segment required the MAC address of a station on another subnet, the router would block the ARP request since it is a layer 2 broadcast, and routers operate at layer 3. Because the router is aware of both subnets, it could answer an ARP request on one subnet on behalf of other devices on the second subnet by supplying its own MAC address. The originating device will then enter the router's MAC address in its ARP cache and will correctly transmit packets destined for the end host to the router.

3.8.3 RARP

The RARP was at one time quite popular when diskless workstations were commonly used in corporations. In such situations, the workstation would know its MAC address, but be forced to learn its IP address from a server on the network. Thus the RARP protocol would be used by the client to access a server on the local network and would provide the client's IP address. Similar to ARP, RARP is a layer 2 protocol that cannot normally cross router boundaries. Some router manufacturers implemented RARP, which allows requests and responses to flow between networks.

The RARP frame format is the same as ARP. The key difference between the two is the setting of field values. The RARP protocol fills in the sender's hardware address and sets the IP Address field to zeros. Upon receipt of the RARP frame, the RARP server fills in the IP Address field and transmits the frame back to the client, reversing the ARP process.

4

TRANSPORT LAYER PROTOCOLS

The purpose of this chapter is to acquaint you with the two key transport layer protocols supported by the TCP/IP suite. Those protocols are the Transmission Control Protocol (TCP) and the User Datagram Protocol (UDP).

As indicated in Chapter 3, when we discussed the IP protocol, either TCP or UDP can be identified by the setting of an applicable value in the IP header under both IPv4 and IPv6. Although the use of either transport layer protocol results in the placement of the appropriate transport layer header behind the IP header, there are significant differences between the functionality of each transport protocol. Those differences make one protocol more suitable for certain applications than the other protocol, and vice versa.

4.1 TCP

The Transmission Control Protocol is a connection-oriented protocol. This means that the protocol will not forward data until a session is established in which the destination acknowledges that it is ready to receive data. This also means that the TCP setup process requires more time than when UDP is used as the transport layer protocol. However, because you would not wish to commence certain operations, such as dialing a telephone number, performing a remote log-on, or a file transfer, unless you knew the destination was ready to support the appropriate application, the use of TCP is more suitable for certain applications than UDP. Conversely, when we examine UDP, we note that this transport layer protocol similarly supports certain applications better than other applications. Because the best way to become familiar with TCP is by first examining the fields in its header, we do so.

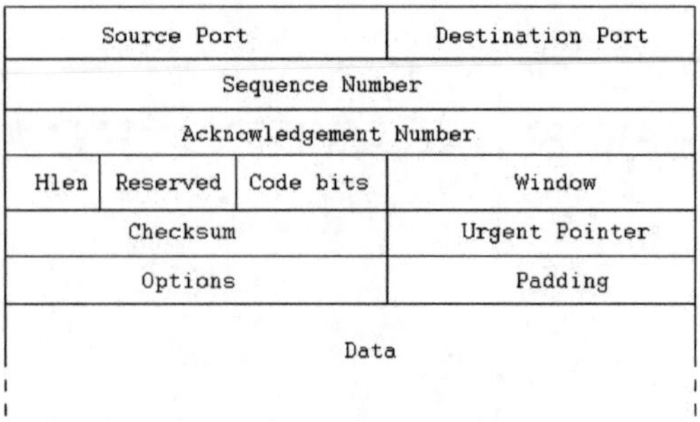

Source Port			Destination Port
Sequence Number			
Acknowledgement Number			
Hlen	Reserved	Code bits	Window
Checksum			Urgent Pointer
Options			Padding
Data			

Figure 4.1   TCP header.

4.1.1 TCP Header

The TCP header consists of 12 fields, as illustrated in Figure 4.1. When we examine the UDP header later in the chapter we note by comparing the two that the TCP header is far more complex. The reason for this additional complexity results from the fact that TCP is not only a connection-oriented protocol, but in addition, it supports error detection and correction as well as packet sequencing, with the latter used to note the ordering of packets, to include determining if one or more packets are lost.

4.1.1.1 Source and Destination Port Fields   The Source and Destination Port fields are each 16 bits in length. Each field denotes a particular process or application. In actuality, most applications use the destination port number to denote a particular process or application, and either set the Source Port field value to a random number greater than 1023 or to zero. The reason the destination port number defines the process or application results from the fact that an application operating at the receiver normally operates acquiescently, waiting for requests, looking for a specific destination port number to determine the request.

The reason the originator sets the source port to zero or a value above 1023 is due to the fact that the first 1023 out of 65,536 available port numbers are standardized with respect to the type of traffic transported via the use of specific numeric values. To illustrate the use of port numbers, let us assume one station wishes to open a Telnet connection with a distant server. Because Telnet is defined as port 23, the application will set the destination port value to that numeric. The source port will normally be set to a random value above 1023, and an IP header will then add the destination and source IP addresses for routing the datagram from the client to the server. In some literature you may encounter the term *socket*, sometimes incorrectly used as a synonym for *port*. In actuality, the destination port in the TCP or UDP header plus the destination IP address cumulatively identify a unique process or an application on a host. The combination of port number and IP address is correctly referenced as a socket. Note that while in the past the term *host* usually meant a computer, today it can be any intelligent device, ranging from a smart phone to even a refrigerator.

Returning to our example, at the server the destination port value of 23 identifies the application as Telnet. When the server forms a response, it first reverses source and destination IP addresses. Similarly, the server places the source port number in the Destination Port field, which enables the Telnet originator's application to correctly identify the response to its initial datagram.

4.1.1.1.1 Multiplexing and Demultiplexing   Port numbers play an important role in TCP/IP, as they enable multiple applications to flow between the same pair of stations or from multiple non-related stations to a common station. This flow of multiple applications to a common address is referred to as multiplexing. Upon receipt of a datagram, the removal of the IP and TCP headers requires the remaining portion of the packet to be routed to its correct process or application based upon the destination port number in the TCP header. This process is referred to as demultiplexing.

Both TCP and UDP use port numbers to support the multiplexing of different processes or applications to a common IP address. An example of this multiplexing and demultiplexing of packets is illustrated in Figure 4.2.

The top portion of Figure 4.2 illustrates how both Telnet and FTP, representing two TCP applications, could be multiplexed into a stream of IP datagrams that flow to a common IP address. In comparison, the middle portion of Figure 4.2 illustrates how through port numbering UDP ports permit a similar method of multiplexing of applications. Finally, in the bottom of Figure 4.2 a mixture of TCP and UDP is shown that can be multiplexed over a common serial circuit.

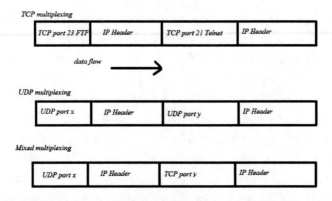

Figure 4.2   Port numbers permit applications to be multiplexed via serial communications flowing to a common IP address.

4.1.1.1.2 Port Numbers   The universe of both TCP and UDP port numbers can vary from a value of 0 to 65535, resulting in a total of 65,535 ports capable of being used by each transport protocol. This so-called port universe is divided into three ranges referred to as well-known ports, registered ports, and dynamic or private ports.

4.1.1.1.3 Well-Known Ports   Well-known ports are the most commonly used port values as they represent assigned numbers that identify specific processes or applications. Ports 0 through 1023 represent the range of well-known ports. These port numbers are assigned by the Internet Assigned Numbers Authority (IANA) and are used to indicate the transportation of standardized processes. Where possible, the same well-known port number assignments are used with TCP and UDP. Ports used with TCP are normally used to provide connections that transport long-term conversations. In some literature, you may encounter well-known port numbers being specified as in the range of value from 0 to 255. While this range was correct many years ago, the modern range for assigned ports managed by the IANA was expanded to cover the first 1024 port values from 0 to 1023. Table 4.1 provides a summary of the port value assignments from 0 through 255 for well-known ports, to include the service supported by a particular port and the type of port, TCP or UDP, for which the port number is primarily used. A good source for the full list of assigned port numbers is RFC 1700.

Table 4.1 Well-Known TCP and UDP Services and Port Use

KEYWORD	SERVICE	PORT TYPE	PORT NUMBER
TCPMUX	TCP Port Service Multiplexer	TCP	1
RJE	Remote Job Entry	TCP	5
ECHO	Echo	TCP and UDP	7
DAYTIME	Daytime	TCP and UDP	13
QOTD	Quote of the Day	TCP	17
CHARGEN	Character Generator	TCP	19
FTD-DATA	File Transfer (Default Data)	TCP	20
FTP	File Transfer (Control)	TCP	21
TELNET	Telnet	TCP	23
SMTP	Simple Mail Transfer Protocol	TCP	25
MSG-AUTH	Message Authentication	TCP	31
TIME	Time	TCP	37
NAMESERVER	Host Name Server	TCP and UDP	42
NICNAME	Who Is	TCP	43
DOMAIN	Domain Name Server	TCP and UDP	53
BOOTPS	Bootstrap Protocol Server	TCP	67
BOOTPC	Bootstrap Protocol Client	TCP	68
TFTP	Trivial File Transfer Protocol	UDP	69
FINGER	Finger	TCP	79
HTTP	World Wide Web	TCP	80
KERBEROS	Kerberos	TCP	88
RTELNET	Remote Telnet Service	TCP	107
POP2	Post Office Protocol Version 2	TCP	109
POP3	Post Office Protocol Version 3	TCP	110
NNTP	Network News Transfer Protocol	TCP	119
NTP	Network Time Protocol	TCP and UDP	123
NETBIOS-NS	NetBIOS Name Server	UDP	137
NETBIOS-DGM	NetBIOS Datagram Service	UDP	138
NETBIOS-SSN	NetBIOS Session Service	UDP	139
NEWS	News	TCP	144
SNMP	Simple Network Management Protocol	UDP	161
SNMTTRAP	Simple Network Management Protocol Traps	UDP	162
BGP	Border Gateway Protocol	TCP	179
HTTPS	Secure HTTP	TDP	413
RLOGIN	Remote Login	TCP	513
TALK	Talk	TCP and UDP	517

4.1.1.1.4 Registered Port Numbers   Registered ports are ones whose values range from 1024 to 49151. Although all ports above 1023 can be used freely, the IANA requests vendors to register their application port numbers with it. Although an application or process may be registered, its registration does not hold legal implications and is primarily to enable other vendors to develop compatible products as well as to enable end users to appropriately set up equipment. For example, if a new application uses a registered port number it is a relatively easy process to adjust a router's access list or firewall to enable data to flow through those devices. Although developers can use any port number beyond 1023, many respect registered port numbers.

4.1.1.1.5 Dynamic or Private Ports   The third range of port numbers is from 49152 to 65535. This port number range is associated with dynamic or private ports. This port range is usually used by new applications that remain to be standardized, such as many Internet video applications as well as a variety of text messaging services.

4.1.1.2 Sequence and Acknowledgment Number Fields   TCP is a byte-oriented sequencing protocol. Thus a Sequence field is necessary to ensure that missing or misordered packets are noted or identified. That field is 32 bits in length and provides the mechanism for ensuring that missing or misordered packets are noted or identified.

The actual entry in the Sequence Number field is based upon the number of bytes in the TCP Data field. That is, because TCP was developed as a byte-oriented protocol, each byte in each packet is assigned a sequence number. Because it would be most inefficient for TCP to transmit 1 byte at a time, groups of bytes, typically 512 or 536, are placed in a segment and one sequence number is assigned to the segment and placed in the Sequence field. That number is based upon the number of bytes in the current segment as well as previous segments, as the Sequence field value increments its count until all 16-bit positions are used and then continues via a rollover through zero. For example, assume the first TCP segment contains 512 bytes and a second segment will have the sequence number 1024.

The Acknowledgment Number field, which is also 32 bits in length, is used to verify the receipt of data. The number in this field also reflects bytes. For example, returning to our sequence of two 512-byte segments, when the first segment is received the receiver expects the next sequence number to be 513. Therefore if the receiver were acknowledging each segment, it would first return an acknowledgment with a value of 513 in the Acknowledgment Number field. When it acknowledges the next segment, the receiver would set the value in the Acknowledgment Number field to 1025, and so on.

Because it would be inefficient to have to acknowledge each datagram, a variable or sliding window is supported by the TCP protocol. That is, returning an Acknowledgment Number field value of $n + 1$ would indicate the receipt of all bytes through byte n. If the receiver has the ability to process a series of multiple segments and each is received without error, it would be less efficient to acknowledge each datagram. Thus, a TCP receiver can process a variable number of segments prior to returning an acknowledgment that informs the transmitter that n bytes were received correctly. To ensure lost datagrams or lost acknowledgments do not place the TCP protocol in an infinite waiting period, the originator sets a timer and will retransmit data if it does not receive a response within a predefined period of time.

The previously described use of the Acknowledgment Number field is referred to as Positive Acknowledgment and Retransmission (PAR). Under PAR, each unit of data must be either implicit (sending a value of $n + 1$ to acknowledge receipt of n bytes) or explicit. If a unit of data is not acknowledged by the time the originator's time-out period is reached, the previous transmission is retransmitted. When the Acknowledgment Number field is in use a flag bit, referred to as the ACK flag in the Code field, will be set. We will shortly discuss the six bit positions in the Code Bit field.

4.1.1.3 Hlen Field   The Header Length (Hlen) field is 4 bits in length. This field, which is also referred to as the Offset field, contains a value that indicates where the TCP header ends and the Data field begins. This value is specified as a number of 32-bit words. It is required due to the fact that the inclusion of options can result in a variable-length header. Because the minimum length of the TCP header is 20 bytes, the minimum value of the Hlen field would be five, denoting five 32-bit words, which equals 20 bytes.

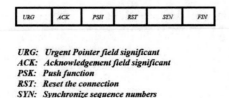

URG: *Urgent Pointer field significant*
ACK: *Acknowledgement field significant*
PSK: *Push function*
RST: *Reset the connection*
SYN: *Synchronize sequence numbers*
FIN: *Release the connection*

Figure 4.3   The six bits in the code bit field.

4.1.1.4 Code Bit Field   As indicated in Figure 4.1, there are six individual 1-bit fields within the Code Bit field. Each bit position functions as a flag to indicate whether or not a function is enabled or disabled. Figure 4.3 illustrates the position of the individual bits in the Code Bit field. To obtain an appreciation for the use of the Code Bit field we need to examine each bit position in that field—which we will now do.

4.1.1.4.1 URG Bit   The urgent (URG) bit or flag is used to denote an urgent or priority activity. When such a situation occurs, an application will set the URG bit position, which acts as a flag and results in TCP immediately transmitting everything it has for the connection instead of waiting for additional characters. An example of an action that could result in an application setting the urgent flag would be a user pressing the CTRL-BREAK key combination.

A second meaning resulting from the setting of the urgent bit or flag is that it also indicates the Urgent Pointer field is in use. Here the Urgent Pointer field indicates the offset in bytes from the current sequence number where the urgent data are located.

4.1.1.4.2 ACK Bit   The setting of the ACK bit indicates that the segment contains an acknowledgment to a previously transmitted datagram or series of datagrams. Then the value in the Acknowledgment Number field indicates the correct receipt of all bytes through byte n by having the byte number $n + 1$ in the field.

4.1.1.4.3 PSH Bit   The third bit position in the Code Bit field is the push (PSH) bit. This 1-bit field is set to request the receiver to immediately deliver data to the application and flags any buffering.

Normally the delivery of urgent information would result in the setting of both the URG and PSH bits in the Code Bit field.

4.1.1.4.4 RST Bit   The fourth bit position in the Code Bit field is the reset (RST) bit. This bit position is set to reset a connection. By responding to a connection request with the RST bit set, this bit position can also be used as a mechanism to decline a connection request.

4.1.1.4.5 SYN Bit   The fifth bit in the Code Bit field is the synchronization (SYN) bit. This bit position is set at start-up during what is referred to as a three-way handshake, which we will cover below.

4.1.1.4.6 FIN Bit   The sixth and last bit position in the Code Bit field is the finish (FIN) bit. This bit position is set by the sender to indicate that it has no additional data, and the connection should be released.

4.1.1.5 Window Field   The Window field is 16 bits in length and provides TCP with the ability to regulate the flow of data between source and destination. Thus this field indirectly performs flow control.

The Window field indicates the maximum number of bytes that the receiving device can accept. Thus, it indirectly indicates the available buffer memory of the receiver. Here a large value can significantly improve TCP performance, as it permits the originator to transmit a number of segments without having to wait for an acknowledgment, while permitting the receiver to acknowledge the receipt of multiple segments with one acknowledgment.

Because TCP is a full-duplex transmission protocol, both the originator and recipient can insert values in the Window field to control the flow of data in each direction. By reducing the value in the Window field, one end of a session in effect informs the other end to transmit less data. Thus the use of the Window field provides a bidirectional flow control capability.

4.1.1.6 Checksum Field   The Checksum field is 16 bits or 2 bytes in length. The function of this field is to provide an error detection capability for TCP. To do so, this field is primarily concerned with ensuring that key fields are validated instead of protecting the entire header. Thus the checksum calculation occurs over what is referred to as a 12-byte pseudo-header. This pseudo-header includes the 32-bit Source and Destination Address fields in the IP header, the 8-bit Protocol field, and a Length field that indicates the length of the TCP header and data transported within the TCP segment. Thus, the primary purpose of the Checksum field is to ensure data arrived at their correct destination, and the receiver has no doubt about the address of the originator or the length of the header and the type of application data transported.

4.1.1.7 Urgent Pointer Field   The Urgent Pointer field is 1 byte in length. The value in this field acts as a pointer to the sequence number of the byte following the urgent data. As previously noted, the URG bit position in the Code field must be set for the data in the Urgent Pointer field to be interpreted.

4.1.1.8 Options Field   The Options field, if present, can be variable in length. The purpose of this field is to enable TCP to support various options, with maximum segment size (MSS) representing a popular TCP option. Because the header must end on a 32-bit boundary, any option that does not do so is extended via pad characters that in some literature are referred to as a Padding field.

4.1.1.9 Padding Field   The Padding field is optional and is included only when the Options field does not end on a 32-bit boundary. Thus the purpose of the Padding field is to ensure that the TCP header, when extended, falls on a 32-bit boundary. Now that we have an appreciation for the composition of the TCP header, let us turn our attention to the manner by which this protocol operates. In doing so we examine how TCP establishes a connection with a distant device and its initial handshaking process, its use of sequence and acknowledgment numbers, how flow control is supported by the protocol, and how the protocol terminates a session.

4.1.2 Connection Establishment

As mentioned above, TCP is a connection-oriented protocol that requires a connection between two stations to be established prior to the actual transfer of data occurring. The actual manner by which an

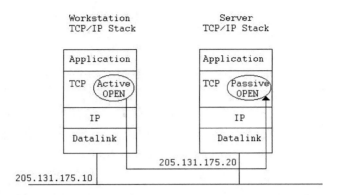

Figure 4.4 Using function calls to establish a TCP connection.

application communicates with TCP is through a series of function calls. In order to obtain an appreciation for the manner by which TCP establishes a session we must first examine connection function calls used by applications, for example, Telnet and FTP.

4.1.2.1 Connection Function Calls   Figure 4.4 illustrates the use of the OPEN connection function calls during the TCP connection establishment process. This process commences when an application requires a connection to a remote station. At that time the application will request TCP to place an OPEN function call. There are two types of OPEN function calls, passive and active. A passive OPEN function call represents a call to allow connections to be accepted from a remote station. This type of call is normally issued upon application start-up, informing TCP that, for example, FTP or Telnet is active and ready to accept connections originating from other stations. TCP will then note that the application is active and will also note its port assignment. The TCP protocol will then allow connections on that port number.

4.1.2.2 Port Hiding   One of the little known aspects of TCP is that some organizations attempt to hide their applications by configuring applications for ports other than well-known ones. For example, assigning web services to port 2080 instead of port 80 is an example of port hiding. Although a person with port scanning software would be able to easily discover that port 2080 is being used, the theory behind port hiding is that it reduces the ability of lay personnel to easily discover applications at different network addresses and then attempt to use those applications.

4.1.2.3 Passive OPEN   Returning to the use of a passive OPEN function call, its use governs the number of connections allowed. That is, while a client would usually issue one passive OPEN, a server would issue multiple OPENs since it is designed to service multiple sessions. Another term used for the passive end of the TCP action is responder or TCP responder. Thus a TCP responder can be thought of as an opening up of connection slots to accept any inbound connection request without waiting for any particular station request. Because each OPEN requires a buffer area on a server, a hacking method that dates back to the beginning of the Internet is still successfully employed. That hacking method is referred to as a denial of service (DOS) attack that can take one of several forms, ranging from a single computer used for an attack to a distributed denial of attack method (DDOS) where remote computers are infected with so-called zombie programs. The goal of the denial of service attack is to make a server inoperative. That is, because a server has a finite number of OPENs and buffer area it can support, a denial of service attack involves flooding the server with requests until all of its OPENs and reserved buffer area are in play, in effect precluding legitimate users from accessing its facilities.

4.1.2.4 Active OPEN   A station that needs to initiate a connection to a remote station issues the second type of OPEN call. This type of function call is referred to as an active OPEN. In the example in Figure 4.4, station X would issue an active OPEN call to station Y. For the connection to be serviced by station Y, that station must have previously issued a passive OPEN request, which as previously explained allows incoming connections to be established. To successfully connect, station X's active OPEN must use the same port number that the passive OPEN used on station Y. In addition to active and passive OPEN calls, other calls include CLOSE (to close a connection), SEND and RECEIVE (to transfer information), and STATUS (to receive information for a previously established connection).

Now that we have an appreciation for the use of active and passive OPEN calls to establish a TCP connection, let us turn our attention to the manner by which TCP segments are exchanged. As we will note, the exchange of segments enables a session to occur. The initial exchange of datagrams that transport TCP segments is referred to as a three-way handshake. It is important to note how and why this process occurs, as it has been used in modified form as a mechanism to create a DOS attack or allow a person in the middle to gain access to data flowing between the entities within a handshake, referred to as a man-in-the-middle wireless TCP attack.

4.1.3 The Three-Way Handshake

To ensure that the sender and receiver are ready to commence the exchange of data requires both parties to the exchange to be synchronized. Thus during the TCP initialization process sender and receiver exchange a few control packets for synchronization purposes. This exchange is referred to as a three-way handshake. This functions as a mechanism to synchronize each endpoint at the beginning of a TCP connection with a sequence number and an acknowledgment number.

4.1.3.1 Overview   As we will soon note, a three-way handshake begins with the originator sending a segment with its SYN bit in the Code Bit field set. The receiving station will respond with a similar segment with its ACK bit in the Code Bit field set. Thus an alternate name for the three-way handshake is an initial SYN-SYN-ACK sequence.

4.1.3.2 Operation   To illustrate the three-way handshake, let us continue from our prior example shown in Figure 4.4, in which station X placed an active OPEN call to TCP to request a connection to a remote station and an application on that station. Once the TCP/IP protocol stack receives an active OPEN call, it will construct a TCP header with the SYN bit in the Code Bit field set. The stack will also assign an initial sequence number and place that number in the Sequence Number field in the TCP header. Other fields in the header, such as the destination port number, are also set and the

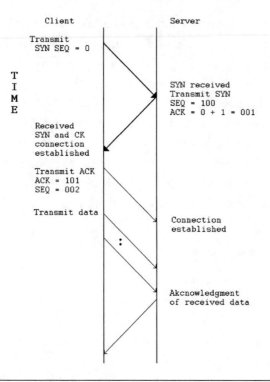

Figure 4.5   The TCP three-way handshake.

segment is then transferred to IP for the formation of a datagram for transmission onto the network.

To illustrate the operation of the three-way handshake, consider Figure 4.5, which illustrates the process between stations X and Y. Because the initial sequence number does not have to start at zero, we will assume it commenced at 1000 and then further assume that the value was placed in the Sequence Number field. Thus the TCP header flowing from station X to station Y is shown with SYN = 1 and SEQ = 1000.

Because the IP header results in the routing of a datagram to station Y, that station strips the IP header and notes that the setting of the SYN bit in the TCP header represents a connection request. Assuming station Y can accept a new connection, it will acknowledge the connection request by building a TCP segment. That segment will have its SYN and ACK bits in its Code Bit field set. In addition, station Y will place its own initial sequence number in the Sequence Number field of the TCP header it is forming. Because the connection request had a sequence number of 1000, station Y will acknowledge receipt by setting its Acknowledgment field value to 1001 (station X sequence number plus 1), which indicates the next expected sequence number.

Once station Y forms its TCP segment, the segment has an IP header added to form a datagram. The datagram flows to station X. Station X receives the datagram, removes the IP header, and notes via the setting of the XYN and ACK bits and Sequence Number field value that it is a response to its previously issued connection request. To complete the connection request, station X must in effect acknowledge the acknowledgment. To do so, station X will construct a new TCP segment in which the ACK bit will be set and the sequence number will be incremented by 1 to 1001. Station X will also set the acknowledgment number to 2001 and form a datagram that is transmitted to station Y. Once station Y examines the TCP header and confirms the correct values for the Acknowledgment and Sequence Number fields, the connection becomes active. At this point, both data and commands can flow between the two endpoints. As this occurs, each side of the connection maintains its own set of tables for transmitted and received sequence numbers. Those numbers are always in ascending order. When the applicable 16-bit field reaches its maximum value, the settings wrap to 0.

In examining the three-way handshake in Figure 4.5, note that after the originating station establishes a connection with the receiver, it transmits a second TCP initialization segment to the receivers and follows that segment with one or more IP datagrams that transport the actual data. In Figure 4.5, a sequence of three datagrams is shown being transmitted prior to station Y generating an acknowledgment to the three segments transported in the three datagrams. The actual number of outstanding segments depends upon the TCP window, so let us turn our attention to this topic.

4.1.3.2 The TCP Window TCP is a connection-oriented protocol that includes a built-in capability to regulate the flow of information, a function referred to as flow control. TCP manages the flow of information by increasing or decreasing the number of segments that can be outstanding at any point in time. For example, under periods of congestion when a station is running out of available buffer space, the receiver may indicate it can only accept one segment at a time and

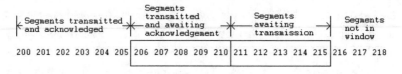

Segments transmitted and acknowledged	Segments transmitted and awaiting acknowledgement	Segments awaiting transmission	Segments not in window
200 201 202 203 204 205	206 207 208 209 210	211 212 213 214 215	216 217 218

Figure 4.6   Flow control and the TCP sliding window.

delay its acknowledgment to ensure it can service the next segment without losing data. Conversely, if a receiver has free and available buffer space, it may allow multiple segments to be transmitted to it and quickly acknowledge the segments.

TCP forms segments sequentially in memory. Each segment of memory waits for an IP header to be added to form a datagram for transmission. A window is placed over this series of datagrams that structures three types of data: data transmitted and acknowledged, data transmitted but not yet acknowledged, and data waiting to be transmitted. Because this window slides over the three types of data, it is referred to as a sliding window.

Figure 4.6 illustrates the use of the TCP sliding window for flow control purposes. Although the actual TCP segments' size is normally 512 bytes, for simplicity of illustration a condensed sequence of segments with sequence numbers varying by unity is shown. In this example, we assume that sequence numbers 10 through 15 have been transmitted to the destination station. The remote station acknowledges receipt of those segments. Datagrams containing segment sequence numbers 16 through 20 were transmitted by the source station, but at this particular point in time have not received an acknowledgment. Thus those data represent the second type of data covered by a sliding window. Note that this window will slide up the segments as each datagram is transmitted. The third type of data covered by the sliding window is segments. In Figure 4.6 segments 21 through 24 are in the source station awaiting transmission, while segments 25 through 28 are awaiting coverage by the sliding window.

If we return to Figure 4.1, which illustrated the TCP header, we will note a field labeled "Window." That field value indirectly governs the length of the sliding window. In addition, the setting of that field provides a flow control mechanism. For example, the Window field transmitted by a receiver to a sender indicates the range of sequence number, which equates to bytes that the receiver is willing to accept.

If a remote station cannot accept additional data, it would then set the Window field value to zero. The receiving station continues to transmit TCP segments with the Window field set to zero until its buffer is emptied a bit (no pun intended), in effect allowing the resumption of transmission conveying data by the originator. That is, when the transmitting station receives a response with a Window field value of zero, it replies to the response with an ACK (Code field ACK bit set to one) and its Window field set to a value of zero. This inhibits the flow of data. When sufficient buffer space becomes available at the receiver, it will form a segment with its Window field set to a non-zero value, an indication that it can again receive data. At this point, the transmitting of data goes to the receiver.

4.1.3.3 Avoiding Congestion   One of the initial problems associated with TCP is that a connection could commence with the originator transmitting multiple segments, up to the Window field value, returned by the receiver during the previously described three-way handshake. If there are slow-speed wide area network (WAN) connections between originator and recipient, it is possible that routers could become saturated when a series of transmissions originated at the same time. In such a situation, the router would discard datagrams, causing retransmissions that continued the abnormal situation. The solution developed to avoid this situation is referred to as a TCP slow-start process.

4.1.3.3.1 TCP Slow Start   Slow start represents an algorithm procedure added to TCP that implicitly uses a new window, referred to as the congestion window. This window is not contained as a field in the TCP header. Instead it becomes active through the algorithm that defined the slow-start process. That is, when a new connection is established the congestion window is initialized to a size of one segment, typically 512 or 536 bytes. Each time an ACK is received the congestion window's length is increased by one segment. The originator can transmit any number of segments up to the minimum value of the congestion window or the Window field value (advertised window). Note that flow control is imposed by the transmitter in one direction through the congestion window, while it is imposed in the other direction by the receiver's advertised Window field value.

Although slow start commences with a congestion window of one segment, it builds up exponentially until it reaches the advertised window size. That is, it is incremented by subsequent ACKs from 1 to 2, then it is increased to 4, 8, 16, and so on, until it reaches the advertised window size. Once this occurs segments are transferred using the advertised window size for congestion control and the slow-start process is terminated.

4.1.3.3.2 Slow-Start Threshold   In addition to working at initiation, slow start will return upon the occurrence of one of two conditions: duplicate ACKs or a time-out condition where a response is not received within a predefined period. When either situation occurs, the originator commences another algorithm referred to as the congestion control algorithm.

When congestion occurs, a comparison is initiated between the congestion window size and the current advertised window size. The smaller number is halved and saved in a variable referred to as a slow-start threshold. The minimum value of the slow-start threshold is 2 segments unless congestion occurred via a time-out, with the congestion window then set to a value of 1, the same as a slow-start process. The TCP originator has the option of using the slow-start start-up or congestion avoidance. To determine which method to use, the originator compares the congestion value to the value of the slow-start threshold. If the congestion value matches the value of the slow-start threshold the congestion avoidance algorithm will be used. Otherwise, the originator will use the slow-start method. Since we previously described the slow-start method, let us turn our attention to the congestion avoidance method and the algorithm it uses.

Upon the receipt of ACKs, the congestion window will be increased until its value matches the value saved in the slow-start threshold. When this occurs, the slow-start algorithm terminates and the congestion avoidance algorithm starts. This algorithm multiplies the segment size by 2, divides that value by the congestion window size, and then continually increases its value based on the previously described algorithm each time an ACK is received. The result of this algorithm is a more linear growth in the number of segments that can be transmitted in comparison to the exponential growth of the slow-start algorithm.

4.1.4 TCP Retransmissions

While it is obvious that the negative acknowledgment of a segment by the receiver returning the same segment number expected indicates a retransmission request, what happens if a datagram is delayed? Since delays across a TCP/IP network depend upon the activity of other routers in the network, the number of hops in the path between source and destination, and other factors, it is relatively impossible to have an exact expected delay prior to a station assuming data are lost and retransmitting. Recognizing this situation, the developers of TCP included an adaptive retransmission algorithm in the protocol. Under this algorithm, when TCP submits a segment for transmission, the protocol records the segment sequence number and time. When an acknowledgment is received to that segment, TCP also records the time, obtaining a round-trip delay. The TCP protocol uses such timing information to construct an average round-trip delay that is used by a timer to denote, when the timer expires, that a retransmission should occur. When a new transmit-response sequence occurs, another round-trip delay is computed that slightly changes the average. Thus this technique slowly changes the timer value that governs the acceptable delay for waiting for an ACK. Now that we have an appreciation for the manner by which TCP determines when to retransmit a segment, let us conclude our coverage of this protocol by turning our attention to the manner by which it gracefully terminates a session.

4.1.5 Session Termination

If we remember the components of the Code Bit field, we previously noted that field has a FIN bit. The purpose of this bit is to enable TCP to gracefully terminate a session. Before TCP supports full-duplex communication, each party to the session must close the session. This means that both the originator and recipient must exchange segments with the FIN bit set in each segment.

Figure 4.7 illustrates the exchange of segments to gracefully terminate a TCP connection. In this example assume station X has completed its transmission and indicates this fact by sending a segment to station Y with the FIN bit set. Station Y will acknowledge the

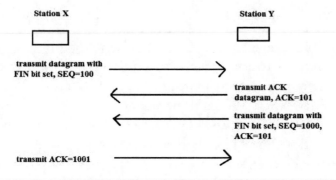

Figure 4.7   Terminating a TCP connection.

segment with an ACK. At this point, station Y will no longer accept data from station X. Station Y can continue to accept data from its application to transmit to station X. If station Y does not have any more data to transmit, it will then completely close the connection by transmitting a segment to station X with the FIN bit set in the segment. Station X will then ACK that segment and terminate the connection. If an ACK should be lost in transit, segments with FIN are transmitted and a timer is set. Then either an ACK is received or a time-out occurs, which serves to close the connection.

4.2 UDP

The UDP is the second transport layer protocol supported by the TCP/IP protocol suite. UDP is a connectionless protocol. This means that an application using UDP can have its data transported in the form of IP datagrams without first having to establish a connection to the destination. This also means that when transmission occurs via UDP, there is no need to release a connection, simplifying the communication's process. Other features of UDP include the fact that this protocol has no ordering capability, nor does it provide an error detection and correction capability. This in turn results in a header that is greatly simplified and is much smaller than TCPs.

4.2.1 UDP Header

Figure 4.8 illustrates the composition of the UDP header. This header consists of 64 bytes followed by actual user data. In comparing the TCP

| 0 | 16 | 31 |

Source Port	Destination Port
Length	Checksum

Figure 4.8 UDP header.

and UDP headers, it is easy to note the relative simplicity of the latter since it lacks many of the features of the former. For example, because it does not require the acknowledgment of datagrams or sequence datagrams, there is no need for Sequence and Acknowledgment fields. Similarly, since UDP does not provide a flow control mechanism, the TCP Window field is removed. The result of UDP performing a best-effort delivery mechanism is a relatively small transport layer protocol header, with the protocol relatively simple in comparison to TCP. The best way to understand the operation of UDP is via an examination of its header. Before we do so, as a reminder, note that similar to TCP, an IP header will prefix the UDP header, with the resulting message consisting of the IP header, UDP header, and user data referred to as a UDP datagram.

4.2.1.1 Source and Destination Port Fields The Source and Destination Port fields are each 16 bits or 2 bytes in length and function in a manner similar to their counterparts in the TCP header. That is, the Source Port field is optionally used, with a value either randomly selected or filled in with zeros when not in use, while the destination port contains a numeric that identifies the destination application or process.

4.2.1.2 Length Field The Length field indicates the length of the UDP datagram, to include header and user data that follow the header. This 2-byte field has a minimum value of eight, which represents a UDP header without data.

4.2.1.3 Checksum Field The Checksum field is 2 bytes in length. The use of this field is optional and its value is set to 0 if the application does not require a checksum. If a checksum is required, it is calculated on what is referred to as a pseudo-header. The pseudo-header is a logically formed header that consists of the source and destination addresses and the Protocol field from the IP header. By verifying the contents of the two address fields through its checksum computation, the pseudo-header ensures that the UDP datagram is delivered to the correct destination network and host on the network. This does not verify the contents of the datagram.

4.2.2 Operation

Because the UDP header does not include within the protocol an acknowledgment capability or a sequence numbering capability, it is up to the application layer to provide this capability. This enables some applications to add this capability, whereas other applications that run on top of UDP may elect not to include one or both. As previously described, a UDP header and its data are prefixed with an IP header to form a data frame. Upon receipt of the datagram, the IP layer strips off that header and submits the remainder to UDP software at the transport layer. The UDP layer reads the destination port number as a mechanism to demultiplex the data and send them to their appropriate applications.

4.2.3 Applications

The UDP protocol is primarily used by applications that transmit relatively short segments and for which the use of TCP would result in a high level of overhead in comparison to UDP. Common examples of applications that use UDP as a transport protocol include the Simple Network Management Protocol (SNMP), Domain Name Service (DNS), and the newly emerging series of applications from numerous vendors that transport digitized voice over the Internet and are collectively referred to as Internet telephony. Expanding upon the transport of voice, many organizations now offer video, to include a voice capability. Concerning the transport of voice or video, most implementations of Internet telephony and video applications use both TCP and UDP. TCP is used for call setup, whereas UDP is used to transport digitized voice and data once the setup operation is completed. Because real-time voice cannot tolerate more than a fraction of a second of delay, Internet applications do not implement error detection and correction, as retransmissions would add delays that would make reconstructed voice sound awkward. Instead, because voice does not rapidly change, applications may either smooth an error or drop the datagram and generate a small period of noise that cannot affect the human ear. This is because most Internet telephony applications transmit 10 or 20 ms slices of digitized voice, making the error or even the loss of one of a few datagrams transmitting such slices of a conversation most difficult to notice. When video is transmitted you can probably easily view transmission problems, as most video implementations employ a form of data compression in which blocks of pixels that are nearly similar are considered to be one and the same, allowing bandwidth to be significantly reduced. When a router discards a datagram due to heavy traffic the end result may be a second or two of blocks appearing on your screen or a frozen image, as a delay will occur until the next datagram arrives.

5

WORKING WITH THE COMMAND PROMPT

Our focus in this chapter is on the use of the Windows built-in Command Prompt. This chapter can be considered a review for "old timers" who were brought up in the use of the Disk Operating System (DOS), which when Windows appeared was essentially regulated to the Command Prompt box and little used by most persons due to the ability to mouse around.

The rationale for including this chapter is based upon the fact that the use of Windows built-in networking tools can be facilitated by knowledge of such functions as where the Command Prompt resides, how to use function keys, and what piping is and how to take advantage of its use. For those who have no experience in DOS, we discuss piping in this chapter as well as other Command Prompt actions that will facilitate our use of built-in networking tools. The Command Prompt allows you to work in an environment that is like a traditional operating system as opposed to the icon-based Windows environment. When working in the Command Prompt you will use your keyboard as it predates the use of a mouse, which then becomes a useless device. The Command Prompt operates at a lower level than Windows, which means that you will have more control over the computer; however, if you're used to a point-and-click environment it is certainly less user-friendly.

5.1 The Command Prompt Location

There are several methods you can use to locate the Command Prompt. Perhaps one of the easiest methods is to use the search tool from the Start Menu in Windows. Figure 5.1 illustrates the use of Windows after this author entered "Co" into the search bar. Note that at this point the second entry from searching is the Command

Figure 5.1   Using the Windows search bar to locate the Command Prompt.

Prompt. As you continue entering your search the Command Prompt entry will eventually rise to the top. The reason that the Command Prompt entry is shown shaded results from the action of this author to highlight the entry.

If you simply click on the start button or globe at the lower left corner of your screen you will see the entry All Programs directly above the search bar. Clicking on this entry will result in a display of all the programs on your computer, which depending upon the use of your machine may be a considerable list. If you locate the entry Accessories, clicking on that entry will result in the display of the Command Prompt, as shown in Figure 5.2. Then selecting the Command Prompt entry will activate the Command Prompt. As an alternative, you can simply enter "cmd" at the Start Menu, which will automatically invoke the Command Prompt

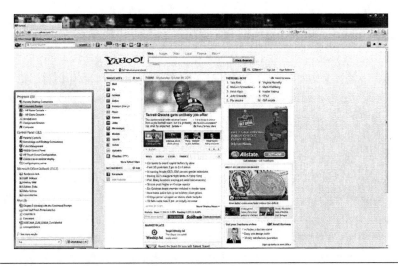

Figure 5.2   From Accessories you can also select the Command Prompt.

on your screen. Thus within a short period of time we have noted three methods by which the Command Prompt can be invoked. Once invoked, it will appear as an entry in a list of recent programs when you return to the Start Menu, allowing you to simply select it.

Figure 5.3 illustrates how once activated the Command Prompt will be displayed both as a small window as well as an icon at the bottom of your screen. In Figure 5.3 we see the Command Prompt

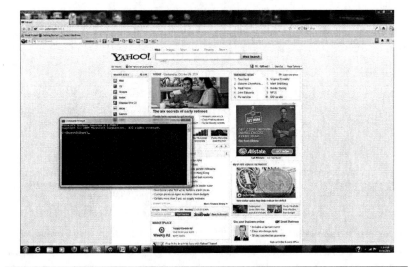

Figure 5.3   The Command Prompt window can be placed in the forefront by clicking on its icon on the taskbar.

window, which by default will appear on top of the browser this author was using as well as an icon at the bottom of the screen. Notice that the Command Prompt window has a black background by default with white lettering. As you examine the window you will note that it has the conventional minimize, restore, and close icons at the top right of the window; however, unlike most conventional windows in Windows, you can right-click on the top bar to obtain the ability to control how the Command Prompt window and its contents will appear. In addition, unlike a normal Windows window, selecting the restore icon at the top of the window by default will toggle you between the small rectangular window and a larger rectangular window. It should be noted that as you work with a variety of windows on your computer the Command Prompt window may become covered with other windows. To place the Command Prompt in the forefront for viewing you can simply click on the Command Prompt icon on the taskbar at the bottom of your screen.

The Command Prompt window is where you type commands and program names. The Command Prompt is case insensitive, which means that it does not care if you use upper- or lowercase. This means that command cd is the same as CD.

5.1.1 Options

If you right-click on the Command Prompt displayed from the Start Menu six options will be displayed from which you can select. The top option, Open, as the name implies will result in the execution of the command CD as it opens the Command Prompt window. The second option, "run as administrator," requires you to have administrative privileges. Assuming you do, selecting this option results in the Command Prompt dialog box labeled Administrative Command Prompt and will enable you to execute certain commands that require administrative privileges. The third option, Pin to Taskbar, results in the Command Prompt being pinned to the Taskbar, while the fourth option, Pin to Start Menu, pins the Command Prompt to the Start Menu. The fifth option, "remove from this list," results in the unpinning of the Command Prompt, while the sixth option, Properties, results in the display of the Command Prompt Properties dialog box that contains 10 tabs, of which the tab labeled Shortcut is shown by default in the foreground.

5.1.2 Positioning upon Opening

If you focus on the Command Prompt window shown in Figure 5.3, you will note that after the version of the Command Prompt and copyright information are displayed, you are positioned by default on the C drive under the applicable user, in this example gilbert. To reposition the Command Prompt you would enter the Change Directory (CD) command followed by the backward slash (CD\) followed by where you want to go, which in effect represents the position you require. For example, to position yourself to the root directory you would enter CD\. As you enter commands you will note that the contents of the Command Prompt window scroll up and eventually disappear from the screen. You can use the scroll bar on the right of the window, use your up arrow key, or expand the window to view data that scrolled off the screen. The actual amount of data available for backward scrolling will depend upon the buffer size associated with the Command Prompt. You can easily view the buffer size by right-clicking on the top of the console window and selecting either Defaults or Properties. Selecting either option will result in the display of a dialog box with four tabs, with the one labeled Options in the foreground that will show you the cursor size, buffer size, and number of buffers, as well as allow you to adjust one or more entries. Since this addition method to view information is associated with changing the size of the Command Prompt window, let's turn our attention to that topic.

5.1.3 Controlling the Command Prompt Window

Right-clicking on the top bar of the Command Prompt window and selecting either Defaults or Properties will result in the display of a dialog box that allows you to view various parameters associated with the Command Prompt as well as change one or more values. Assuming you selected the entry labeled Properties, doing so will result in a dialog box labeled Command Prompt Properties that will have four tabs. Those tabs are shown in Figure 5.4, where by default the tab labeled Options is selected, with the other tabs

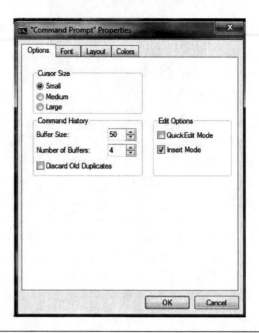

Figure 5.4 The default Command Prompt Properties dial box.

labeled Font, Layout, and Colors. The Options tab, which is shown in the foreground of Figure 5.4, enables you to select the cursor size, adjust the buffer size, which when increased allows an extended amount of past operations to be viewed, as well as perform other options. The Font tab allows you to specify the type and size of fonts as well as preview results of the selection process. The third tab, Layout, as its name implies, allows you to adjust the default position of the Command Prompt window, and adjust the screen buffer size and the window size based upon width and height character entries. The fourth tab, Colors, enables you to select screen and pop-up text and background colors as well as preview your selection. As we proceed through this chapter we adjust certain features of the Command Prompt Properties tabs to enable additional information to be viewed as well as captured for display in this book.

5.2 Working with Function Keys and Commands

In this section we focus our attention upon obtaining an appreciation of the use of several Command Prompt commands that will

Table 5.1 Function Key Operations When in the Command Prompt Mode

FUNCTION KEY	ACTION
F2	Enter char to copy up to
F3	Repeats previously entered characters
F4	Enter char to delete up to
F5	Change uppercase to lowercase
F6	Adds a Ctrl-Z to a line
F7	Lists commands by number previously entered in a dialog box, allowing easy selection
F8	Toggle through previously entered commands
F9	Allows entry of command by number (see F7)

facilitate our use of networking-related commands we cover later in this book. Since several function keys have special meanings when in the Command Prompt, and their use can facilitate our use of various networking program commands, let's briefly note their use.

5.2.1 Function Key Use

Table 5.1 lists eight function keys and the result obtained by pressing them when you are in the Command Prompt. Note that each key results in a particular action, such as copying a previously entered line up to a defined character (F2) or changing uppercase to lowercase (F5). By becoming familiar with their use, you should be able to simplify entering commands. For example, this author frequently uses the F3 key when he needs to reenter a command or simply change a few characters at the end of a previously entered command.

5.2.2 Repertoire of Commands

Because this author wants to show readers a near-complete repertoire of Command Prompt commands, he will stretch the window vertically by positioning his cursor at the bottom of the window and dragging it to the bottom of his computer screen. Similarly, he will then use his cursor and position it in the top middle of the window and drag it vertically toward the top of his screen. Once this is accomplished he will use the Help command, which lists the commands available in alphabetical order. The result obtained from modifying

Figure 5.5 Viewing the commands supported by the Command Prompt.

the Command Prompt window and then using the Help command is a list of commands supported, shown in Figure 5.5.

In examining Figure 5.5, note that because the list is extensive, it was too long to be displayed on this author's large monitor. Instead, you would have to use the scroll bar to be able to view a few commands. When this author used the VER command to determine the Windows version of the Command Prompt he received an interesting result.

The Windows version of the Command Prompt was 6.1.7601, while this author had upgraded his computer to Windows 7 Premium. Thus it appears that Microsoft's latest version of the Windows Command Prompt is a bit older than the version of Windows used by this author.

In Table 5.2 the commands supported by the version of the Command Prompt used by this author are listed. While we will discuss several commands in the referenced table, this author will leave it to the inquisitiveness of readers to obtain an understanding of how each command operates.

5.2.2.1 The Help Command The Help command is a very powerful tool for obtaining information about how one or more attributes are required by certain commands. For example, you can obtain additional information about how a command operates by entering "help" followed by the name of the command. When we do so we observe that certain commands can be operated in a variety of ways. Since we want to better understand how we can navigate directories, let's use the Help command followed by CD to determine our options in using the Change Directory command. As we note below, entering the command Help followed by a specific command, such as CD, results in the display of a description of what the command does, which in the case of CD results in a directory change. In addition, the use of the Help command in this manner will provide one or more examples of its use as well as display alternative examples of the command, which in the case of CD includes the alternative command entry of CHDIR.

Figure 5.6 illustrates the use of the Help command to determine how to use the CD command. In examining Figure 5.6 note that after we enter the Help command followed by CD, we are told that CD is used to display the name of or change the current directory. Next, because both CD and CHDIR are the same commands, our display shows two examples of the format of each command, with the double dot (..) noted as a mechanism to change to the parent directory. Depending upon where you are currently located in the directory structure you can use one or more CD.. commands to change to the root directory of the drive you are located on. For example, if you are presently located at c:\users\gilbert on the C drive, entering CD.. would result in you being repositioned to c:\users. Then,

Table 5.2   Command Prompt Commands Supported under Windows Version 6.1.7601

ASSOC	Displays or modifies file extension associations
ATTRIB	Displays or changes file attributes
BREAK	Sets or clears extended CTRL+C checking
BCDEDIT	Sets properties in boot database to control boot loading
CACLS	Displays or modifies access control lists (ACLs) of files
CALL	Calls one batch program from another
CD	Displays the name of or changes the current directory
CHCP	Displays or sets the active code page number
CHDIR	Displays the name of or changes the current directory
CHKDSK	Checks a disk and displays a status report
CHKNTFS	Displays or modifies the checking of disk at boot time
CLS	Clears the screen
CMD	Starts a new instance of the Windows command interpreter
COLOR	Sets the default console foreground and background colors
COMP	Compares the contents of two files or sets of files
COMPACT	Displays or alters the compression of files on NTFS partitions
CONVERT	Converts FAT volumes to NTFS; note you cannot convert the current drive
COPY	Copies one or more files to another location
DATE	Displays or sets the date
DEL	Deletes one or more files
DIR	Displays a list of files and subdirectories in a directory
DISKCOMP	Compares the contents of two floppy disks
DISKCOPY	Copies the contents of one floppy disk to another
DISKPART	Displays or configures disk partition properties
DOSKEY	Edits command lines, recalls Windows commands, and creates macros
DRIVERQUERY	Displays current device driver status and properties
ECHO	Displays messages, or turns command echoing on or off
ENDLOCAL	Ends localization of environment changes in a batch file
ERASE	Deletes one or more files
EXIT	Quits the cmd.exe program (command interpreter)
FC	Compares two files or sets of files, and displays the differences between them
FIND	Searches for a text string in a file or files
FINDSTR	Searches for strings in files
FOR	Runs a specified command for each file in a set of files
FORMAT	Formats a disk for use with Windows
FSUTIL	Displays or configures the file system properties
FTYPE	Displays or modifies file types used in file extension associations
GOTO	Directs the Windows command interpreter to a labeled line in a batch program
GPRESULT	Displays Group Policy information for machine or user
GRAFTABL	Enables Windows to display an extended character set in graphics mode
HELP	Provides Help information for Windows commands

(continued)

Table 5.2 Command Prompt Commands Supported under Windows Version 6.1.7601 (continued)

ICACLS	Displays, modifies, backs up, or restores ACLs for files and directories
IF	Performs conditional processing in batch programs
LABEL	Creates, changes, or deletes the volume label of a disk
MD	Creates a directory
MKDIR	Creates a directory
MKLINK	Creates symbolic links and hard links
MODE	Configures a system device
MORE	Displays output one screen at a time
MOVE	Moves one or more files from one directory to another directory
OPENFILES	Displays files opened by remote users for a file share
PATH	Displays or sets a search path for executable files
PAUSE	Suspends processing of a batch file and displays a message
POPD	Restores the previous value of the current directory saved by PUSHD command
PRINT	Prints a text file
PROMPT	Changes the Windows Command Prompt
PUSHD	Saves the current directory then changes it
RD	Removes a directory
RECOVER	Recovers readable information from a bad or defective disk
REM	Records comments (remarks) in batch files or config.sys
REN	Renames a file or files
RENAME	Renames a file or files
REPLACE	Replaces files
RMDIR	Removes a directory
ROBOCOPY	Advanced utility to copy files and directory trees
SET	Displays, sets, or removes Windows environment variables
SETLOCAL	Begins localization of environment changes in a batch file
SC	Displays or configures services (background processes)
SCHTASKS	Schedules commands and programs to run on a computer
SHIFT	Shifts the position of replaceable parameters in batch files
SHUTDOWN	Allows proper local or remote shutdown of machine
SORT	Sorts input
START	Starts a separate window to run a specified program or command
SUBST	Associates a path with a drive letter
SYSTEMINFO	Displays machine-specific properties and configuration
TASKLIST	Displays all currently running tasks, including services
TASKKILL	Kill or stop a running process or application
TIME	Displays or sets the system time
TITLE	Sets the window title for a cmd.exe session
TREE	Graphically displays the directory structure of a drive or path
TYPE	Displays the contents of a text file

(continued)

Table 5.2   Command Prompt Commands Supported under Windows Version 6.1.7601 (continued)

VER	Displays the Windows version
VERIFY	Tells Windows whether to verify that your files are written correctly to a disk
VOL	Displays a disk volume label and serial number
XCOPY	Copies files and directory trees
WMIC	Displays WMI information inside interactive command shell

entering CD.. again would position you at c:\, or the root directory on the c drive. Of course, simply entering CD followed by a backslash (\) or CD\ would take you directly to the root directory. This illustrates an important concept. That is, when working in Command Prompt mode there are usually several methods you can use to achieve the same results, although sometimes a certain method used can save you several steps. Another important concept is that commands are case insensitive. That is, you could enter CD, cd, or even Cd to change a directory through the use of the CD command.

5.2.2.2 The CLS Command   One of the more valuable commands is the Clear Screen command, which is entered by typing CLS. Note that similar to all Command Prompt commands, you can enter a command as all

Figure 5.6   Using the Help command to obtain information on the use of the CD command.

capitals, all lowercase, or even a mixture of uppercase and lowercase letters, as commands are case insensitive. Thus you could enter CLS, cls, or even Cls to clear the screen and obtain a more visually appealing display.

5.2.3 Controlling Output and Additional Commands

Although we have only covered two commands so far, let's digress a bit and cover a very important topic: controlling output. This topic will also enable us to discuss some additional commands.

When in Command Prompt mode there are several methods you can use to control the flow of data. Collectively these methods are referred to as piping, and the end result is similar to the manner by which pipes are used to control the flow of liquids; however, instead of liquids you can redirect the flow of information. By default DOS commands send output to the screen and require input from the keyboard. Through the use of a redirection capability the output of a command can be sent to another device, such as a printer, to another program, or even to a file.

5.2.3.1 Redirection Methods   When working in the Command Prompt there are four redirection functions you can use. Those functions are listed in Table 5.3. To illustrate the use of redirection functions we need to know the available device names to use in a command entry as well as the syntax or format of a redirection command. We can kill two birds with one stone by first examining the syntax used for redirection. The syntax employed for redirection is as follows:

```
Command > Device
```

where Device can be the monitor (COM), a printer (PRN or LPT1 through LPT3), a serial port (COM1 through COM4), a file name, to include its location in the directory structure, or NUL, an electronic

Table 5.3   Command Prompt Redirection Functions

Greater than (>)	Redirect output
Two greater thans (>>)	Append
Less than (<)	Redirect input
Vertical bar (I)	Pipe

void sometimes referred to as the deep dark hole that is typically used for testing. It should be noted that by default output is generated to your display or monitor.

5.2.3.1.1 Printing One of the problems associated with the use of the Command Prompt is that it dates to the era where parallel printers were predominant and the use of PRN and LPTR1 through LPT4 was associated with parallel printers. Today just about all printers are USB based, which results in an interesting quandary concerning printing. That is, how can you redirect output to a USB printer? Prior to answering that question, let's slightly digress and illustrate how we can redirect data to a file. Then once we have generated data onto a file, we can easily use a number of tools to print the results on a USB-based printer.

To illustrate the use of the redirection facility as well as a few DOS commands let's create a directory called Junk, change to that directory, and take a directory listing that will be stored on the file list.txt. Afterwards we will take a directory listing and discuss how we can use different tools to view the resulting file.

5.2.3.1.2 The CD, MD, and DIR Commands Figure 5.7 illustrates an example of the redirection process. First, the CD\ command was used to position ourselves under the root directory. Next, the MD command was used to make the directory called Junk, after which the

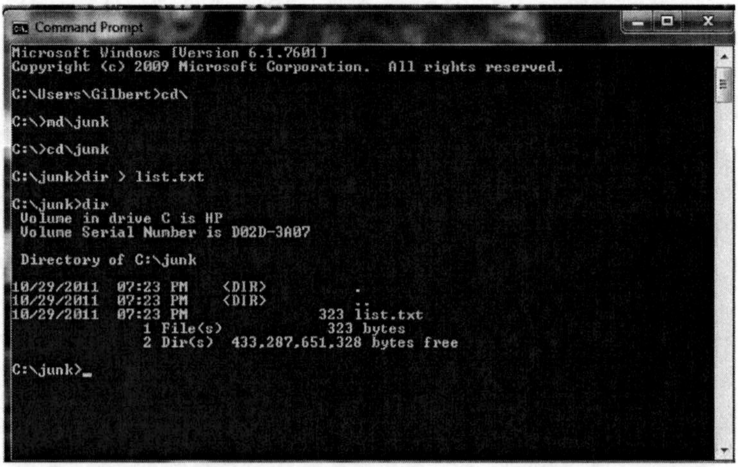

Figure 5.7 An example of the redirection process.

CD command was used to position ourselves in that directory. This was followed by the fourth entry, which through the use of the DIR (Directory) command creates the directory on the file named list.txt. Note that you have to be careful when using file redirection because if you specify an existing file name, it will be overwritten without any warnings. Also note that if you wanted to append data to an existing file you would use two greater than (>>) signs, resulting in the command DIR >> list.txt.

While there are some programs that allow the direct use of the Command Prompt with USB printers, they are usually restricted to certain versions of Windows, such as XP and Vista. Instead of focusing on those programs, let's turn our attention to how we can view the results of a redirection to a file. Those methods include the use of the Type and More commands, as well as several built-in applications common to each version of Windows.

5.2.3.1.3 Using the Type and More Commands   You can use the Type command to display the contents of a text file or group of files specified with a wildcard. The format of this command is:

```
TYPE [drive:] [path] filename
```

Through the use of the More command you can display the contents one screen at a time. The format of the More command is as follows:

```
MORE [/E] [/C] [/P] [/S] [/Tn] [+n] ] < [drive:] [path] filename
command-name | MORE [/E [/C] [/P] [/S] [/Tn] [+n] ]
MORE/E [/C] [/P] [/S] [/Tn] [+n] [files]
```

where the entry of [drive:][path]filename specifies a file to display one screen at a time, and the command name specifies a command whose output will be displayed. This command supports a variety of optional switches whose functions are listed below:

- /E   Enable extended features
- /C   Clear screen before displaying page
- /P   Expand FormFeed characters
- /S   Squeeze multiple blank lines into a single line
- /Tn   Expand tabs to n spaces (default 8)

+n   Start displaying the first file at line n

files List of files to be displayed; files in the list are separated
by blanks

If extended features are enabled, the following commands can be used at the — More— prompt:

P n	Display next n lines
S n	Skip next n lines
F	Display next file
Q	Quit
=	Show line number
?	Show help line
<space>	Display next page
<ret>	Display next line

One of the most common uses of the More command is as a pipe to accept the output of another command, such as the DIR (Directory) command. As an illustration of its use you would enter the following commands to display a screen and generate — More— at the bottom left corner of the Command Prompt window.

```
dir | more
```

Then you can scroll through the contents of the directory not shown by pressing Return to display each additional line from the directory.

5.2.3.1.4 Viewing Files Every version of Windows includes an application called Notepad that can be used to read text files. You can either locate the Notepad program in the Accessories folder or simply type its name into the search bar above the Start Menu. Another method of viewing the resulting text file under Windows includes going to the Start Menu and accessing Computer and then searching for and double-clicking on the file once it is located, which will automatically invoke the Notepad program. However, if you have Office, Word Perfect, or a similar program, those programs can also be used to view text files. In addition, if you have a USB printer, you can simply print the viewed text file instead of worrying about finding and installing applicable drivers for your version of Windows that will allow redirection to a USB printer.

For example, to view a sorted directory listing of all files in the root directory you would enter the following command:

```
dir c:\/o
```

where the /o switch is used to sort the output of the command in alphabetical order. By the way, at any time you can type "help" followed by a command such as DIR to determine the available options and their meanings.

Depending upon the number of files in your directory being viewed and the size of your Command Prompt window, entering the above command can result in you being forced to use the scroll bar to view some of the files. In fact, if the directory listing is very extensive you may lose the ability to view some files as the directory exceeds available buffer space allocated to the Command Prompt window. To compensate for this potential problem as well as use a USB printer we can first output the directory listing to a file we will call output.txt located in the directory named Datadirectory as follows:

```
dir c:\/o >c:\datadirectory\output.txt
```

Note that if the file output.txt previously existed it will be overwritten. Also note that if the file named does not exist using the double greater than sign (>>) for append will result in the creation of the file.

Once you create or append data to the file you can then use Windows built-in Notepad or a word processing program to view and, if necessary, print the data, without having to consider how you might need to upgrade software to allow redirection to a USB printer.

A third redirection method available from the Command Prompt results from the use of the less than sign (<). The use of the < directs input to a command from a source other than the default, which is usually the keyboard. The format of this redirection within a Command Prompt command is simply as follows:

```
Command < data-source
```

where the data-source by default is the keyboard but is commonly used to input a previously generated file. For example, to sort the lines in the text file named list.txt located on the C: drive in the directory \Data on the 20th character in the file you would enter the following:

```
sort/+20 <c:\data list.txt
```

By now you probably have begun to appreciate some of the capability associated with the text-based Command Prompt. To become even more impressed with its capability let's turn our attention to piping within the Command Prompt.

5.2.3.1.5 Piping   Previously we noted that piping is specified using the vertical bar (|), which is located over the backslash (\) character on your keyboard. When specified piping redirects the output of a command or program to a second command or program. Thus its format is as follows:

```
command or program1 | command or program2
```

To illustrate the use of piping let's assume a sort directory listing based on the time the files were last modified. To do so we need to ascertain where in the directory listing is the time position. If we count character positions from the left we will note that the first 10 positions result in the display of the date of creation or modification of the file, after which two spaces are used to separate the date from the time. Thus the timestamp begins in the 13th character position.

We can use the DIR command followed by the directory we want sorted and pipe the results into the Sort command so that sorting occurs on the 13th character position. Some examples of the use of piping follow:

```
dir c: | sort+13  Sorts the root directory by time of
creation
dir c:\wills |sort/+13 Sorts the contents of the
directory Wills by time of creation
```

Thus if we want to sort the file docs located in the directory Data on the C drive beginning in the 39th position we would enter the following command:

```
DIR c:\data\docs | SORT/+39
```

5.2.3.2 Other Useful Commands While the old expression "one person's passion is another person's pleasure" holds true for a discussion of Command Prompt commands, we will review the use of a handful of additional commands in this chapter that will provide readers with an appreciation of working within the Command Prompt window. Some commands in Table 5.1 will not be covered, and readers are referred to the use of the Help command to determine how they work and the use of a variety of switches supported by some commands. To begin our journey let's start with the previously covered CD command, which we will use as a basis for other directory manipulation commands.

5.2.3.1.1 Returning to the CD Command To change directories, you would use the CD command with the name of a directory:

```
C:\> cd directory-name
```

This results in the Command Prompt

```
C:\directory-name>
```

To view what is in this directory you would type:

```
C:\directory-name> dir
Volume in drive C is xxx.
Volume Serial Number is yyyy-zzzz
Directory of C:\directory-name
07/11/2012 09:18 AM <DIR> .
07/11/2012 09:18 AM <DIR> ..
08/11/2012 10:41 AM <DIR> Desktop
01/17/2005 10:42 AM <DIR> Documents
. . . . .. .. .. ..
  xxxx File(s)      yyyy bytes
  yyyy Dir(s) zzzzzzz bytes free
```

where xxxx, yyyy, and zzzz represent either alphanumerics or numerics, depending upon where used.

5.2.3.2.2 Reviewing the MD and MKDIR Commands   To create a new directory you can use either the MD or MKDIR command followed by the directory name. Thus the syntax or format of this command is:

```
[md][mkdir] [path]directory-name
```

To illustrate the use of the MD command let's create the directory named Training under the root directory. To do so we could first enter CD\ to change to the root directory, and then use the MD version of the make directory command as follows:

```
C:\> mkdir training
```

To verify that this command worked, you can use the DIR command.

5.2.3.2.3 The Copy Command   The Copy command can be quite useful when you need a backup copy of a file. This command has a large number of switches that can be employed that allow you to copy ASCII or binary files, suppress or enable prompting prior to overwriting a file, and even verifying file copying.

In its most basic form the Copy command syntax or format is as follows:

```
copy [path]source [path]destination
```

The following command creates a backup copy of the file training. txt in the Training directory.

```
C:>copy \training\training.txt c:\training\training.
bak
```

5.2.3.2.4 The Del and Erase Commands   You can use either the Del or the Erase command to delete a file. The format of this command is:

```
[del][erase] [path]filename
```

is case insensitive) that have the file extension .doc. If there are no matches the error message "file not found" will be returned.

One of the more frequent uses of the asterisk wildcard is to clean out a directory. For example, entering the following command removes all files from the directory named Temp.

```
C:\temp\>delete *.*
```

In the above example the first asterisk covers every file name, while the second asterisk covers every extension; hence all files in the directory except for any hidden files are deleted.

5.2.3.3.2 The Question Mark Wildcard   The question mark (?) is used as a wildcard character to represent exactly one character, which can be any single character. Thus two question marks in succession would represent any two characters in succession, while three question marks in succession would represent any string consisting of three characters, and so on. To illustrate the use of the question mark wildcard character let's assume you want to delete a large number of files that begin with payxxxx.doc, where xxxx represents a four-digit code with the first two digits representing the month and the last two digits the year since the turn of the current century. Thus to delete all pay files with the extension .doc you could enter:

```
delete pay*.doc
```

However, suppose we only wanted to delete the 12 pay files that have the extension .doc from 2000. To do so we would enter:

```
delete pay??00.doc
```

Note that in the prior example we used two question marks so that all months from the year 2000 will be deleted.

Some words of caution are warranted when using the Delete command with a wildcard. As indicated in our example concerning the asterisk, it's very easy to erase a directory. Another caution concerns the use of the question mark character with Delete or Erase as well as Copy and Move commands, to name a few. Remember that the use of the question mark character is positional. Thus the command:

```
C:\>del ?.doc
```

would only delete files that had a single-character file name and a *.doc* extension from the root directory. So a file named a.doc or files 1.doc through 9.doc would be sent to the great bit bucket in the sky; however, a file named 10.doc, because it has two characters in the file name, would not be affected by the previous command, which may not have been your intention.

5.2.3.3.3 Combining Wildcards   Wildcards can be combined with other characters to represent parts of strings. In doing so you have to be careful, or the result may not meet your intention. For example, consider the following command:

```
C:\temp\>delete *abcd?.doc
```

This command represents a very selective method of deleting files. First, this command would look in the directory named Temp for files that had anywhere from one to three beginning characters, followed by the letters abcd, followed by any one character, and which had an extension of doc.

The command would then delete any such files as matched. Because DOS worked with file names of up to eight characters and three-character extensions, the asterisk represents one to three beginning characters and abcd? represents five characters. Thus subtracting five from eight results in up to three positions represented by the asterisk. Examples of matching files could include: xyzabc5.doc, 123abcd2.doc, and even payabcd1.doc. To make matters more interesting, if you used the asterisk for the file extension position you could wind up deleting not only .doc files but also .exe files, as well as other extensions, which may not be your intention. Thus be careful when you use wildcards and ensure you have backup to prevent the situation where a distraction could result in the entry of a command whose results you did not anticipate.

6
WINDOWS BUILT-IN NETWORKING TOOLS

Now that we have a sound base of knowledge concerning TCP/IP, which includes IP addressing as well as the use of the Command Prompt and how data flow on a network, we are ready to focus on Windows built-in networking tools. In this chapter we cover in detail the operation and utilization of a variety of Windows built-in networking tools that can be used to perform different functions as well as ascertain if current networking conditions would enable you to perform future operations in a reasonable manner, such as integrating Video over IP. While we commence our review of built-in networking tools with the often used ping and tracert programs, we also analyze how we can use these tools in numerous situations beyond simply finding out if a workstation is reachable or about the route to a particular workstation.

6.1 Ping

Since each built-in networking tool is accessed through the Command Prompt, as a quick refresher, you can type cmd or Command Prompt in your search bar to access the Command Prompt window. As an alternative, if you previously used the Command Prompt it can be simply selected from an entry in the list of recently used programs accessible from the Start Menu. Once accessed, simply enter either the command ping by itself or ping/ to obtain information about the format of the command. Although ping by itself does not require administrative privileges, you should consider running the Command Prompt as the administrator if you have such privileges, as its use will support all programs covered in this chapter. When you enter either version of the command you will obtain a display similar to the one shown in Figure 6.1.

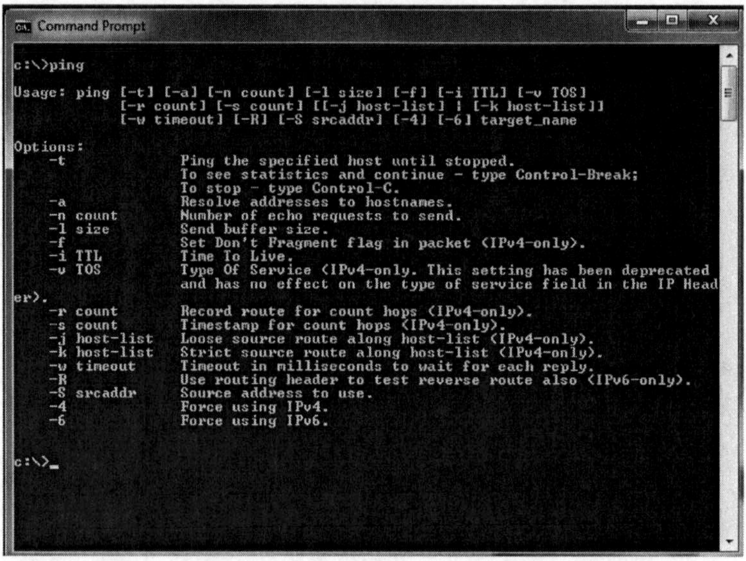

Figure 6.1   Viewing ping options in the Command Prompt window.

Ping operates by transmitting a series of Internet Control Message Protocol (ICMP) echo request packets to the destination host, waiting for ICMP responses. This program measures the time from transmission to reception to obtain the round-trip time, which is referred to in many texts as the round-trip delay. In addition, the use of ping records any packet loss. The results of the test are displayed in the form of a statistical summary of the response packets received, including the minimum, maximum, and mean round-trip times. The ping program can be run using various options, referred to as command line switches, that enable special operational modes, such as to specify the packet size used for transmission, the number of repeated operations, timestamping options, or to perform a ping flood by continuously issuing pings. The latter can be considered a simple form of a denial of service attack, in which the attacker overwhelms the victim with ICMP echo request packets.

As you will note from Figure 6.1 there are a large number of switches that can be used with the ping program. However, prior to examining switches it's a good idea to use our knowledge of TCP/IP by pinging the address 127.0.0.1, which is the loopback address associated with every TCP/IP interface. By first using this loopback address within ping we can literally kill two birds with one operation—determining

Figure 6.2 Pinging the loopback address.

if our interface is operating correctly as well as examining how the program operates without using switches.

Figure 6.2 illustrates the pinging of the loopback address on the TCP/IP interface used by this author. Note that by default ping transmits 32 bytes of data four times to the destination address. That address, by the way, does not have to be an IP address. For example, you can use a host name, such as yahoo.com, and that name will be resolved into an appropriate IP address by the Domain Name Service (DNS) that is an integral part of the TCP/IP protocol.

Continuing our examination of Figure 6.2, note that ping will receive any of four responses from the pinged address, which may include one or more "request timed out" messages. These messages can indicate one of two conditions: Either the host or IP address is not active or the destination is protected by a firewall or router programmed not to respond to certain ICMP messages, such as ping. Thus by itself the use of the ping program does not indicate if a destination is active on a TCP/IP network. However, when a destination is active it responds to the sequence of four messages with responses or replies indicating the round-trip time, which is shown in Figure 6.2 as less than 1 ms since we are pinging the loopback address.

At the lower portion of Figure 6.2 note that statistics concerning the use of ping are summarized, with the number of packets sent, received, and lost summarized by quantity and percentage. Concerning lost packets, when routers are congested they drop packets, so indirectly a high percentage of lost packets will indicate that somewhere between source and destination one or more routers are dropping packets due to congestion. While this information can be used to indicate if Voice or Video over IP is practical, it doesn't indicate where a bottleneck may be occurring. To obtain specific information about where congestion may be occurring we need to use a different networking tool called tracert, which is short for traceroute.

6.1.1 Discovery via Ping

In the days prior to security being a key issue, as well as today when some company employees forget to configure protection, the use of ping is employed to determine what computers are on a network. In fact, the IP address of 192.168.2.1, which represents a Class C private IP address, is used by several router manufacturers as the default address for their routers. As a result of this default assignment the IP address of 192.168.2.1 is usually set as the default gateway on computers connected to the router. In addition, the port 80 address obtained via http://192.168.2.1 usually contains a web interface that controls the router's configuration. Unfortunately, many users leave the default password as is, which means that anyone can access documentation via the web to ascertain the default password and use that password if they are located on the same network to gain access and eventually gain control of the gateway, to the detriment of valid users. Sometimes it's also possible for a third party located outside the network to use the Internet and gain control of the gateway. Thus one of the first things users setting up a gateway should do is to change the default password of the device.

6.1.2 Ping Options

When you type the command ping by itself or with a suffix of a slash (/) you will display a Command Prompt screen that illustrates the options available for selection. Those options include pinging the specified host until stopped (-t), which then allows Control-Break to view statistics, while Control-C stops continuous pinging, pinging a specified number of times (-n count); transmitting a specified buffer size (-l size); inhibiting the Don't Fragment flag setting in IPv4 packets (-f); resolving addresses to host names (-a); setting the Time to Live (-i TTL); recording the route for count of hops in IPv4 (-r count); timestamping for count of hops in IPv4 (-s); losing the source route for IPv4 (-j host-list); strict source routing along the host list again for IPv4 only (-k); a time-out value in milliseconds to wait for each reply (-w time-out); specifying a source address to use (-S srcaddr); and forcing the use of IPv4 (-4) or IPv6 (-6). To illustrate a few of these options let's start with the -t option. For example, suppose you want to determine the round-trip delay to yahoo.com over a period of time. You could enter

```
ping yahoo.com -t
```

to continuously ping Yahoo and then enter Ctrl-C to abort the action and receive a summary of statistics, or you could use the -n option followed by a specific number of pings you want to issue as ICMP echoes. If the destination is barely reachable or not reachable you may want to alter the time-out via the use of the -w option. For example, again using yahoo.com, you could enter the following to wait up to 500 ms for a response:

```
ping yahoo.com -w 500
```

6.1.3 *Using the Round-Trip Delay*

If your organization has local area networks at two or more disparate locations, one technique to enhance efficiency is to implement Voice and Video over IP. However, prior to rushing ahead it's a good idea to consider if the networks to be interconnected have a round-trip delay time that will enable the application to work without modifying access to the Internet. Otherwise, you may need to upgrade one or more network access locations or even ask your Internet service provider (ISP) to enhance the capability of one or more routers between networks. For example, assume the round-trip delay is 1.5 s according to the use of ping and one of the connections to be interconnected has a 56 kbps Internet connection, while the other location is connected to the Internet via a T1 line operating at 1.544 Mbps. Because the ratio of the T1 line to the 56 kbps connection is approximately 27 to 1, you might assume that the 56 kbps connection is the cause of the bottleneck. In communications first appearances can be deceiving and you would have to know the traffic load on each connection as well as through the Internet. While the ping round-trip delay can be used to determine if the networks can be interconnected without modification, by itself ping will not indicate where bottlenecks exist. Thus we need a better tool that can be obtained from the use of the built-in tracert command.

6.2 Tracert

Where the use of ping allows you to verify connectivity between devices, the tracert (traceroute) command can be used to discover the paths packets take to a remote destination, as well as if and where routing breaks down.

The purpose behind the tracert command is to record the source of each ICMP "time exceeded" message in order to provide a trace of the path the packet took to reach the destination. To do so, the device that executes the tracert command sends out a sequence of User Datagram Protocol (UDP) datagrams, each with incrementing Time to Live (TTL) values, which are also referred to as hop count values, to an invalid port address at the remote host, typically using port 33434. The use of the TTL value as a hop count was designed to prevent packets from continuously circulating the Internet. Since packets have a TTL value that is decremented by each router, when the value is zero a router will then discard the packet. Thus in addition to ensuring that packets do not wander the Internet forever, the TTL is used by the tracert program to trace a route from source to destination. Initially, three datagrams are transmitted by the source, each with a TTL field value set to 1. The TTL value of 1 causes the datagram to time out as soon as it hits the first router in the path. This router decrements the value of the TTL field to zero and then responds with an ICMP "time exceeded" message, which indicates that the datagram has expired. Next, three additional UDP messages are transmitted, each with the TTL value set to 2. This causes the second router in the path to the destination to return ICMP "time exceeded" messages. This process continues until the packets reach the destination and the host that originated the tracert receives ICMP "time exceeded" messages from every router in the path to the destination. Since these datagrams try to access an invalid port at the destination host, the host responds with ICMP "port unreachable" messages that indicate an unreachable port that signals the tracert program to finish.

Similar to ping, information about the tracert command can be obtained by entering the command name in the Command Prompt window. Like ping, there are a number of options associated with the use of the command, which we will soon cover. While called tracert due to the limitations of DOS, on other operating systems different names may be used for this networking tool. By default the Windows tracert program will trace a route over a maximum of 30 hops; however, you can alter the maximum hops through the use of the -h switch to a higher number if necessary.

Figure 6.3 illustrates the optional switches available by the use of the tracert program. Note that you can elect not to resolve addresses to host names through the use of the -d switch, use the -h switch to specify a maximum number of hops, use the -j switch followed by a host list to employ a loose source route that is applicable to IPv4, use the -w switch to control the wait time for a response in milliseconds, use the -R switch to trace a round-trip, and the -S switch to specify

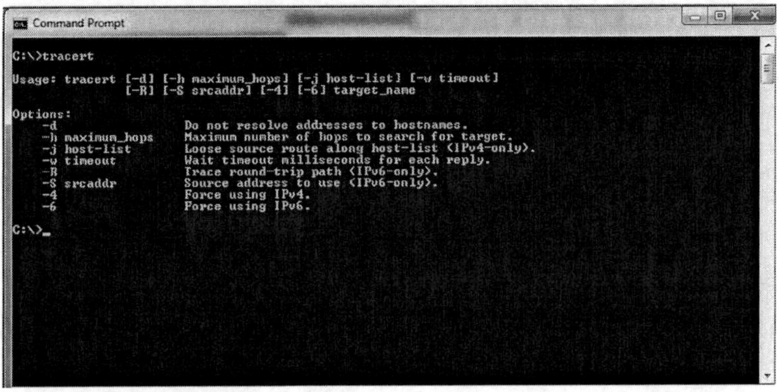

Figure 6.3 Tracert program switches.

a source address to use in IPv6, as well as use the -4 or -6 switches to specify the use of either IPv4 or IPv6, respectively. Note that loose source routing specified by the -j switch followed by a host list uses a source routing option within IP that results in the use of a set of addresses (host names) that a packet must visit. Note that the name *loose source routing* results from the fact that only a portion of the path is set in advance. In comparison, in strict source routing each and every step of the route is determined in advance when data are transmitted from source to destination.

The use of tracert results in a series of one or more returned ICMP messages that will display a list of routers that the packets traversed. Along with the response in the form of three timestamped values routers along the path may be programmed to identify them. To illustrate this the author used tracert to determine the path to the website logtel.com, an Israeli-based company from Hilton Head Island, South Carolina. The top portion of Figure 6.4 shows the results of the use of tracert, indicating the server hosting logtel.com was located 16 hops from this author. As a side note, this tracert was performed using IPv4 since specifying IPv4 provided a similar result in the middle of

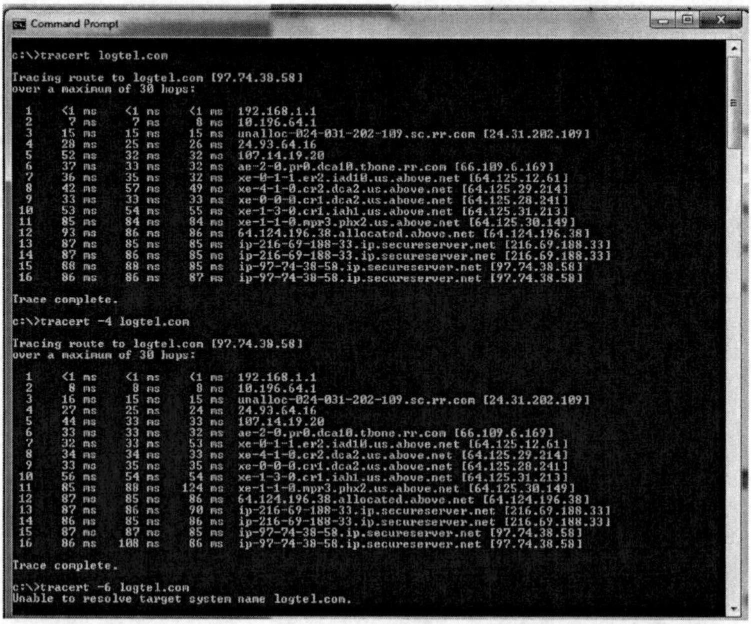

Figure 6.4   Using tracert to determine the path to logtel.com from Hilton Head, South Carolina.

the referenced figure. However, an attempt to force the use of IPv6 was not successful, as the ISP used by this author did not operate an IPv6 name resolution process, as indicated at the bottom of the referenced figure.

Let's examine the results of Figure 6.4. First note that each hop or TTL increment resulted in three timestamped values for each router along the path. Also note that some of the routers not only return their IP address but also a short description, such as us.above.net, which helps identify the device. It should be noted that the description returned, if any, depends upon how the router operator configured the device. Once this author encountered a path that included "smersh" in the name during the premier of a James Bond movie, which indicated that the operator may have been a bit deceitful.

If you use the -d switch the result will be a list of three timestamped values for each hop, which will be indicated solely in terms of their IP addresses. Thus you will lose your host names and the ability to observe what to some users is a more meaningful path.

6.2.1 Using Tracert

If the use of ping indicates a timing problem the next step is to locate where the problem is occurring. Thus a natural turn to the use of tracert is in order. Tracert can be used to indicate if your network access to the Internet is a problem, if transmission through the Internet is a problem, or if the transmission line connecting a distant device to a network is causing an inordinate delay. Thus while ping can be used to determine if Voice or Video over IP is possible, the use of tracert can be used to determine where one or more bottlenecks occur when ping indicates there is a problem. Now that we have an appreciation for the use of tracert, let's move forward and discuss one of the favorite tools used by the help desk of ISPs.

6.3 The Pathping Command

Although ping and tracert can be used individually, with the introduction of Windows NT Microsoft combined the functionality of both commands, resulting in the introduction of the Pathping command. The use of Pathping results in the display of ping-like statistics for each node in a path based on samples taken over a time period, depending on how many nodes are between the start and end host. Two key advantages associated with the use of Pathping are that each node is pinged as the result of a single command and that the behavior of nodes is examined over an extended time period instead of the default ping sample of four messages or the default traceroute occurring over a single route trace.

The format or syntax of the Pathping command is shown below:

```
pathping [-g host-list] [-h maximum_hops] [-i
address] [-n]
  [-p period] [-q num_queries] [-w timeout]
  [-4] [-6] target_name
```

where the following switches result in the indicated actions:

-g host-list	Loose source route along host list
-h maximum_hops target	Maximum number of hops to search for
-i address	Use the specified source address
-n	Do not resolve addresses to host names
-p period	Wait period milliseconds between pings
-q num_queries	Number of queries per hop
-w timeout	Wait time-out milliseconds for each reply
-4	Force using IPv4
-6	Force using IPv6

If you use the Pathping command only with a specified address and without any additional parameters, it will first trace the route to the address and then compute and display statistics for 300 s or 5 min. This is shown in the following example in which the Pathping command was used to trace the route to logtel.com and display the default statistics of 300 s and 100 queries for each hop. Note that you can adjust the default time by the use of the -p parameter and the number of queries per hop through the use of the -q parameter, as well as use other parameters in the command to satisfy different conditions applicable to your circumstances.

```
C:\Users\Gil>pathping logtel.com
Tracing route to logtel.com [97.74.38.58]
```

over a maximum of 30 hops:
0 Gil-PC [192.168.1.6]
1 192.168.1.1
2 10.196.64.1
3 unalloc-024-031-202-109.sc.rr.com [24.31.202.109]
4 xe-7-0-0.rlghncpop-rtr1.southeast.rr.com [24.93.64.40]
5 ae-3-0.cr0.dca10.tbone.rr.com [66.109.6.80]
6 107.14.19.133
7 TeG1-4.ar4.DCA3.gblx.net [208.49.195.129]
8 64.210.13.110
9 ip-216-69-188-45.ip.secureserver.net [216.69.188.45]
10 ip-216-69-188-45.ip.secureserver.net [216.69.188.45]
11 ip-97-74-38-58.ip.secureserver.net [97.74.38.58]
12 ip-97-74-38-58.ip.secureserver.net [97.74.38.58]
Computing statistics for 300 seconds...
  Source to Here This Node/Link
Hop RTT Lost/Sent = Pct Lost/Sent = Pct Address
0 Gil-PC [192.168.1.6]
   0/100 = 0% |
1 0ms 0/100 = 0% 0/100 = 0% 192.168.1.1
   0/100 = 0% |
2— - 100/100 = 100% 100/100 = 100% 10.196.64.1
   0/100 = 0% |
3 14ms 0/100 = 0% 0/100 = 0% unalloc-024-031-202-109.
sc.rr.com [24.31.202.109]
   0/100 = 0% |
4 24ms 0/100 = 0% 0/100 = 0% xe-7-0-0.rlghncpop-rtr1.
southeast.rr.com [24.93.64.40]
   0/100 = 0% |
5 32ms 0/100 = 0% 0/100 = 0% ae-3-0.cr0.dca10.tbone.
rr.com [66.109.6.80]
   0/100 = 0% |
6 36ms 0/100 = 0% 0/100 = 0% 107.14.19.133
   0/100 = 0% |
7 55ms 0/100 = 0% 0/100 = 0% TeG1-4.ar4.DCA3.gblx.
net [208.49.195.129]
   0/100 = 0% |
8 59ms 0/100 = 0% 0/100 = 0% 64.210.13.110
   0/100 = 0% |
9 96ms 0/100 = 0% 0/100 = 0% ip-216-69-188-45.
ip.secureserver.net [216.69.188.45]
   0/100 = 0% |
10 92ms 0/100 = 0% 0/100 = 0% ip-216-69-188-45.
ip.secureserver.net [216.69.188.45]
   0/100 = 0% |

```
11 87ms 0/100 = 0% 0/100 = 0% ip-97-74-38-58.
ip.secureserver.net [97.74.38.58]
   0/100 = 0% |
12 87ms 0/100 = 0% 0/100 = 0% ip-97-74-38-58.
ip.secureserver.net [97.74.38.58]
Trace complete.
```

6.4 The ipconfig Command

Both ping and tracert are interesting programs for which you can determine allowable switches by simply entering the name of each command in the Command Prompt window. Unlike those commands, you need to enter ipconfig followed by the slash (/) and question mark (?) characters to ascertain the options available for the use of this command as well as examples of its use. It should be noted that you can also enter ping/? and tracert/? to determine available switches. In addition, you can also enter either command without the slash and question mark.

Ipconfig represents a commmand line utility available for all versions of Microsoft Windows operating TCP/IP beginning with Windows NT. The ipconfig command is the command line equivalent to the winipcfg command, which was available in Windows Millennium Edition, Windows 98, and Windows 95. Since those versions of Windows represent a rapidly decreasing share of the Windows market we will not cover the use of that utility.

Through the use of the ipconfig utility you can obtain IP and Media Access Control (MAC) address information associated with a Windows computer. It also provides a degree of control over active TCP/IP connections and can be used to display current TCP/IP network configuration values, refresh the Dynamic Host Configuration Protocol (DHCP), which assigns IP addresses automatically, as well as DNS settings. When used without parameters where IPv4 is used, ipconfig displays the IP address, subnet mask, and default gateway for all adapters. When the ISP also utilizes IPv6 via tuneling the use of ipconfig will add additional information to the display, such as the name of the tunnel adapter, its IPv6 address, the link-local IPv6 address, which represents an address intended only for communications within the segment of a local network or link, or a

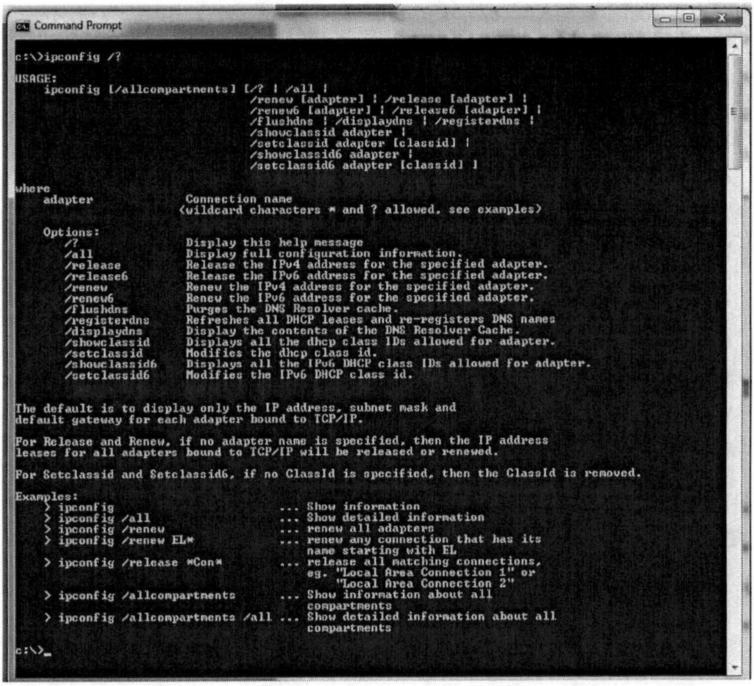

Figure 6.5   Examining the use of ipconfig.

point-to-point connection that a host is connected to. Note that routers do not forward packets with link-local addresses. Under IPv6 link-local addresses are assigned using the prefix fe80::/64. It should also be noted that link-local addresses are available under IPv4 defined in the address block 169.254.0.0/16 and are typically used to assign IP addresses to network interfaces when no external stateful mechanism of configuring addressing exists, such as DHCP. Since most ISPs use DHCP link-local addressing is rarely used under IPv4.

Figure 6.5 illustrates the display of information about ipconfig through the use of the command followed the /? characters. Note that after displaying information about the available switches the display continues by describing the options, which are then followed by examples of their use.

To better understand the use of ipconfig and some of the techniques a help desk will put you through let's first examine the format or syntax associated with the use of this command. Table 6.1 lists the 13 options available for the use of ipconfig.

Table 6.1   Ipconfig Options

IPCONFIG/?	Display the Help message for this utility
IPCONFIG/all	Display full configuration information
IPCONFIG/release [adapter]	Release the IPv4 address for the specified adapter
IPCONFIG/release6 [adapter]	Release the IPv6 address for the specified adapter
IPCONFIG/renew [adapter]	Renew the IPv4 address for the specified adapter
IPCONFIG/renew6 [adapter]	Renew the IPv6 address for the specified adapter
IPCONFIG/flushdns	Purge the DNS resolver cache
IPCONFIG/registerdns	Refresh all DHCP leases and reregister DNS names
IPCONFIG/displaydns	Display the contents of the DNS resolver cache
IPCONFIG/showclassid adapter	Display the DHCP class IDs allowed for adapter
IPCONFIG/setclassid adapter [classid]	Modify the DHCP class ID
IPCONFIG/showclassid6 adapter	Display all the IPv6 DHCP class IDs allowed for the adapter
IPCONFIG/setclassid6	Modify the IPv6 DHCP class ID

Note that if an adapter name contains one or more spaces you should use quotes (") around the name. You can also use wildcards, such as the asterisk (*) and question mark (?) characters, as we below ascertain via an example. Concerning the use of release and renew options, if no adapter name is specified, then the IP address leases for all adapters bound to TCP/IP on the host are affected and will be released or renewed. Let's illustrate an example of the use of ipconfig as follows:

```
ipconfig/all
```

One of the first things that happens when you call a help desk to report a connectivity problem is being asked to enter the command ipconfig or ipconfig/all. Usually the help desk employee will assume you know absolutely nothing about the Command Prompt and walk you through accessing it and entering the ipconfigf command. Depending upon several variables, to include the configuration of your computer and its name, use of a wireless network connection, and incorporation of Bluetooth and other variables, the result of this program will be the display of a description of each adapter, its physical address, whether or not DHCP is enabled, and if enabled, when the lease was obtained and when it expires, the IP address (IPv4 usually but eventually migrating to IPv6), the subnet mask and default gateway address, and DHCP address

Table 6.2   Using Ipconfig/all to View Data about the Author's Ethernet Adapter

Ethernet adapter Local Area Connection	
Connection-specific DNS Suffix	
Description	Realtek RTL8168C(P)/8111C(P) Family PCI-E Gigabit Ethernet NIC (NDIS 6.20)
Physical Address	00-22-15-08-05-D0
DHCP Enabled	Yes
Autoconfiguration Enabled	Yes
Link-local IPv6 Address	fe80::4cf5:611c:ad21:fbed%11(Preferred)
IPv4 Address	192.168.1.2(Preferred)
Subnet Mask	255.255.255.0
Lease Obtained	Sunday, November 06, 2011 1:53:37 PM
Lease Expires	Monday, November 07, 2011 11:32:31 AM
Default Gateway	192.168.1.1
DHCP Server	192.168.1.1
DHCPv6 IAID	285221397
DHCPv6 Client DUID	00-01-00-01-14-78-A2-A6-00-22-15-08-05-D0
DNS Servers	192.168.1.1
NetBIOS over Tcpip	Enabled

information. Because Windows, like other software operating systems, has tens of thousands of lines of code, it's possible that once in a while things can go wrong, from an unexpected shutdown to a hacker or a friend who doesn't exactly know what he or she is doing when trying to fix your computer. The end result is probably an inability to log on to the Internet and a call to a help desk that asks you to enter either the command ipconfig or ipconfig/all. By verifying the settings resulting from the use of ipconfig the person at the help desk will decide if you need a release and renew series of operations to clean a DHCP lease. Table 6.2 shows a portion of the result obtained from ipconfig/all for this author's Ethernet adapter, which was connected to a cable modem that in turn was connected to the Internet via Time Warner's network in Hilton Head, South Carolina.

6.4.2 The Release and Renew Options

The transmission of a dhcprelease message to the DHCP server will, as its name implies, result in the release of the current DHCP configuration, to include discarding the IP address configuration for either all adapters (if an adapter is not specified) or a specific adapter if the parameter is included. The use of the release parameter disables TCP/IP for adapters configured to obtain an IP address automatically. Normally this action is followed by the use of a renew option to clear one or more problems that may have occurred. For example, to release and then renew local area connections we could enter the following two ipconfig commands:

```
c:>ipconfig/release *Local*
c:>ipconfig/renew *Local*
```

In the previous two examples we used wildcards to define the adapter connection that we wanted to release and then renew. It is quite common when you call your cable or DSL subscriber for the called party representing a level 1 service that they ask you to enter ipconfig/release followed by an ipconfig/renew command in an attempt to clear a glitch adversely affecting the computer.

6.4.3 The Flushdns Option

The use of the /flushdns option flushes and resets the contents of the DNS client resolver cache. During DNS troubleshooting, this procedure is commonly used to discard negative cache entries from the cache, as well as any other entries that have been added dynamically. In response to the use of this option you should receive a "successfully flushed DNS resolver cache" message.

6.4.4 The Displaydns Option

The use of the /displaydns option results in the display of the contents of the DNS client resolver cache, which includes both entries preloaded from the local Hosts file and any recently obtained resource records for name queries resolved by the computer. The Hosts file is a plaintext computer file named Hosts used by an operating system to map host names to IP addresses. In a Windows 7 environment the Hosts file is located in the System32 directory under the subdirectories Drivers and Etc. That is, its location is C:\Windows\System32\drivers\etc\hosts. Note that the Hosts file has no extension. You can view the contents of the Hosts file by typing the command Type Hosts after you change your location to C:\Windows\System32\drivers\etc\hosts.

The DNS client service uses the information provided by the displaydns option to resolve frequently queried names quickly, before querying its configured DNS servers. When using the displaydns option you may wish to consider piping the output to a file and then viewing the contents of the file. This results from the fact that there are six entries for each item in the cache, to include record name, record type, time to live, data length, section, and record type. Thus the displayed information can quickly scroll through the Command Prompt screen, to include any buffer area allocated.

6.5 ARP

TCP/IP operates at layer 3 of the International Organization for Standardization (ISO) Open Systems Interconnection (OSI) Reference Model, while local area networks, cable modems, and DSL modems connect to computers at layer 2 of the model. This means that the layer 3 IP address must be converted into a layer 2 address. The mechanism used for this conversion is the Address Resolution Protocol (ARP). As you might expect, Microsoft Windows includes an ARP program that allows you to display and, if desired, modify entries in the ARP cache, an area of memory that contains one or more tables that are used to store IP addresses and their resolved physical addresses. Note that separate tables are used for each Ethernet or Token-Ring network adapter that is installed on your computer as well as wireless Ethernet adapters installed on tablets and other devices.

You can enter either arp by itself or arp/? to display a Help screen that provides information about the use of the ARP command, to include its switches. Figure 6.6 illustrates the display of the ARP Help screen in response to this author entering the command arp/?.

The format or syntax of the ARP command is as follows:

```
arp [-a [inet_addr] [-N if_addr]] [-g [inet_addr]
[-N iface_addr]] [-d inet_addr [iface_addr]]
[-s inet-addr ethe_addr [iface_addr]]
```

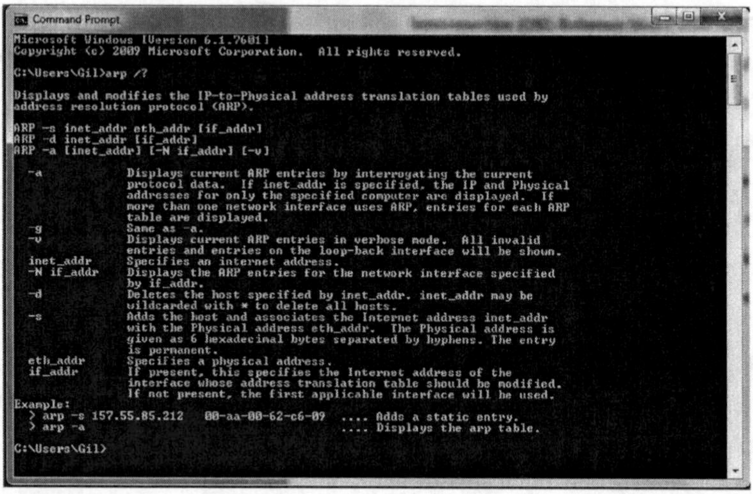

Figure 6.6   The ARP Help display.

where the IP addresses for inet_addr and iface_addr are expressed in dotted decimal notation, while the physical address for ether_address consists of 6 bytes that are expressed in hexadecimal notation, with each byte separated by hyphens.

To display the ARP cache tables for all interfaces, type the command followed by the -a switch as follows:

```
arp -a
```

The result of this operation on the author's computer was as follows:

```
Interface: 192.168.1.3— - 0xb
Internet Address Physical Address      Type
192.168.1.1  00-22-3f-09-75-db   dynamic
192.168.1.255        ff-ff-ff-ff-ff-ff   static
224.0.0.22           01-00-5e-00-00-16   static
224.0.0.252  01-00-5e-00-00-fc   static
224.0.0.253  01-00-5e-00-00-fd   static
239.255.255.250 01-00-5e-7f-ff-fa       static
255.255.255.255 ff-ff-ff-ff-ff-ff       static
```

Note that in the above example IP addresses are in dotted decimal notation, while layer 2 MAC addresses are expressed in hexadecimal notation. Also note that the IP address 192.168.1.1 represents the gateway or router used by the ISP, while the IP address

224.0.0.22 represents a multicast IPv4 address for igmp.mcast.net, which supports the Internet Group Management Protocol (IGMP) used by hosts and adjacent routers to establish multicast group memberships on IP networks for streaming videos, gaming, and similar activities where one stream of data goes to multiple persons in place of multiple streams transmitted to multiple people. This system is used to allow for one stream of data to go to multiple people, rather than the normal method of multiple streams of the same data transmitted to multiple people. Similarly, the 239.255.255.250 address represents an administratively scoped multicast address. Note that while some firewalls may automatically block the use of such addresses, other firewalls will ask you to deny or permit the use of those addresses.

To display the ARP cache table for the interface that is assigned the IP address 192.168.1.1, type:

```
arp -a 192.168.1.1
```

which would result in the following display:

```
Interface: 192.168.1.3- - 0xb
Internet Address Physical Address Type
192.168.1.1          00-22-3f-09-75-db dynamic
```

If you look at the switches available for ARP that are listed in Figure 6.6 you will note that the -g switch is identical to −a; thus we will not discuss its use. If you want to delete an entry in the ARP table you would specify either the IP address with the inet_addr parameter or a specific interface using the iface-addr after the use of the -d switch. Similarly, you can use the -N switch to display the ARP cache table for a specific IP address or the -s switch to add a static entry for either a specific interface or an IP address assigned to the interface.

To illustrate the assignment of a static ARP cache entry let's assume you wish to add an entry that resolves the IP address 192.168.1.4 to the physical address 00-AA-00-4F-2A-9C. To do so you would type:

```
arp -s 192.168.1.4 00-22-3f-09-75-db
```

Depending how you initialized the Command Prompt window you may receive the message "the requested operation requires elevation." If you received this message you need to run Command Prompt as an administrator. To do so you would right-click on the Command Prompt icon and select "run as administrator."

6.5.1 Reverse ARP (RARP) and ARP and IPv6

Prior to concluding our discussion of ARP a few words about the reverse ARP (RARP) is warranted, as well as a discussion of ARP and IPv6.

RARP represents a TCP/IP protocol that was used by diskless devices to obtain an IP address. Upon start-up, the client station sends out a RARP request in an Ethernet frame to the RARP server, which returns the layer 3 address for a layer 2 address, essentially performing the opposite function of ARP. As an obsolete computer program RARP is not directly supported by Microsoft; however, there are some reasons you might consider the use of third-party products or an alternative. For example, in a wireless environment it may be relatively simple to turn an access point upside down and read its MAC address, but you might also need its IP address. One method you can consider is simply pinging the broadcast address (ping -b (broadcast address)) on your subnet, which is often.255, and then dumping your ARP table by entering arp -a, which will provide the MAC address of the access point as well as its IP address.

Under IPv6 the ARP protocol goes the way of the dodo bird. Its replacement consists of the ICMPv6 Neighbor Discovery (ND) and ICMPv6 Neighbor Solicitation (NS) protocols. Neighbor Discovery allows an IPv6 host to discover the link-local and auto-configured addresses of all other IPv6 systems on the local network, while Neighbor Solicitation is employed to determine if a given IPv6 address exists on the local subnet. The link-local address is guaranteed to be unique per host, per link, by picking an address generated by the EUI-64 algorithm. This algorithm uses the network adapter MAC address to generate a unique IPv6 address. For example, a system with a hardware MAC of 01:02:03:04:05:06 would use a link-local address of fe80::0102:03FF:FE04:0506. An 8-byte prefix is created by taking the first three bytes of the MAC, appending FF:FE, and then the next three bytes of the MAC. In addition to link-local addresses, IPv6 also supports stateless autoconfiguration. Stateless autoconfigured addresses use the 2000:: prefix. Additional information about Neighbor Discovery can be found in RFC 2461.

6.6 The Getmac Command

Once you determine the IP address associated with a physical address you might consider doing a Ronald Reagan. That is, trust but verify, which is one of the uses for the getmac command. The use of this command allows you to display the MAC address associated with network adapters on a system. Figure 6.7 illustrates the format or syntax of this command as well as its switches and a few examples of its use. The use of this command can be extremely helpful when you do not know the physical address of an adapter, such as when you call the help desk of an organization and the person on the other end of the connection begins to ask you questions about the Ethernet adapter in the computer you are working at, such as its physical address. Note that if you have administrator privileges you can obtain the MAC address of other devices on your network as long as you know their names.

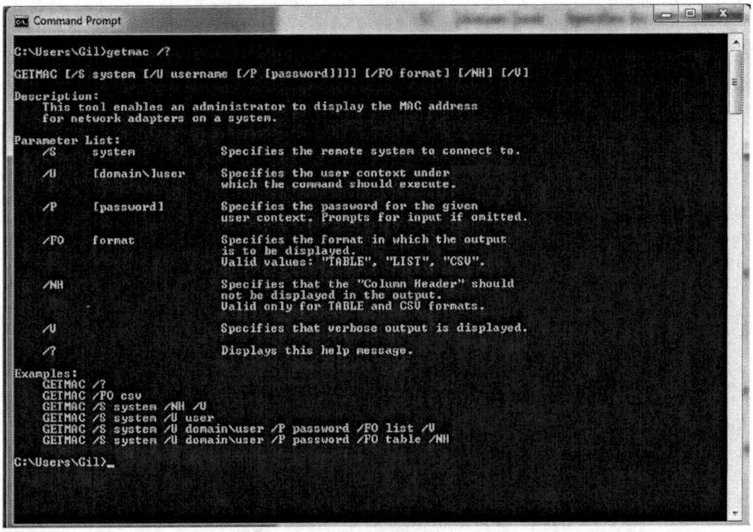

Figure 6.7 Displaying the menu associated with the getmac command.

The format or syntax of the getmac command is shown below:

```
GETMAC [/S system [/U username [/P [password]]]] [/FO
format] [/NH] [/V]
```

where the parameter values or switches are as follows:

/S system	Specifies the remote system to connect to
/U [domain\]user	Specifies the user context under which the command should execute
/P [password]	Specifies the password for the given user context; prompts for input if omitted
/FO format	Specifies the format in which the output is to be displayed; valid values: table, list, csv
/NH	Specifies that the column header should not be displayed in the output; this option is only valid for table and csv formats
/V	Specifies that verbose output is displayed
/?	Displays this Help message

A common use of the getmac command is to determine the physical adapter(s) associated with a given computer, such as this author's computer named gil-pc. To determine its physical address this author would enter the following command:

```
getmac/s gil-pc
```

As a result of the above command entry a list of physical addresses and transport names associated with the physical addresses would be displayed. Note that you could append /fo followed by "table," "list," or "cvs" to refine the display. For example, you could enter:

```
getmac/s gil-pc/fo table
```

Entering the preceding command would result in the same tabular display as if you did not use the /fo option.

6.7 The Netstat Command

The netstat command can be used to obtain a wealth of information concerning your TCP/IP network connection. Because it's relatively easy to have a lot of TCP/IP applications running on your computer, it's possible for those applications to open a large number of valid TCP connections. For example, web browsers commonly initiate parallel threads to download portions of a page that contain data and pictures, resulting in a large number of established connections appearing as a result of a netstat command display. Thus sometimes you may wish to consider piping the results to a printer or file and printing the latter. If you have a large number of established connections as a result of the use of the netstat command and you're not running any applications that need IP connectivity, it's quite possible that this indicates that something may not be right on your system, such as a Trojan or other virus, which will then warrant further investigation.

6.7.1 Command Format

The netstat tool allows you to see what sort of network services are running on your machine (these will be in the LISTENING state), as well as seeing what sort of connections you have active (these are TCP connections in the ESTABLISHED state). Figure 6.8 illustrates the Help screen obtained for netstat by entering the command followed by the slash and question mark characters. The general format or syntax of this command is as follows:

```
NETSTAT [-a] [-b] [-e] [-f] [-n] [-o] [-p proto] [-r]
[-s] [-t] [interval]
```

While it may appear that the switches are self-explanatory, let's turn our attention to how those switches operate.

6.7.1.1 The -a Switch Perhaps one of the more interesting switches associated with this command is its -a switch. The use of the command netstat -a results in a list of all connections and listening ports, which at a glance can be used to determine if any suspicious activity is occurring that may require additional software, such as the failure of certain products to correctly identify threats to a computer.

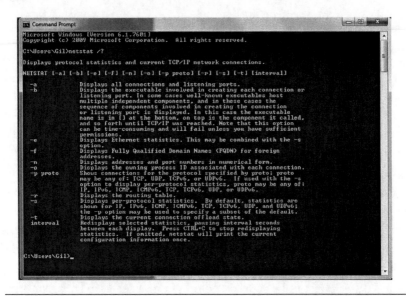

Figure 6.8   Viewing netstat switches.

When you use the netstat -a switch your display will generate a list or table with four entries. Those entries include the protocol (TCP or UDP); the local IP address that specifies the name of your computer on the network; the port number you are using to receive connections, which is randomly generated; the foreign address, which is the IP address or host name using that port for a connection; and the state of the connection. Each of these TCP states is defined in detail in RFC 793 and summarized in Table 6.3. If you're browsing bing.com, for example, and quickly do a netstat -a, you should see an entry ending in a bing.com address followed by :http or :80. Note that ports

Table 6.3   Netstat Connection States

ESTABLISHED	Indicates that both hosts are connected
CLOSED	Indicates that the remote host has received an ACK and closed its connection
LISTENING	Indicates that the computer is waiting to handle an incoming connection
SYN_RECEIVED	Indicates a remote host has received a SYN to start a connection
SYN_SENT	Indicates that this particular connection is open and active
LAST_ACK	Your computer needs to obliterate the packets before closing the connection
TIMED_WAIT	Indicates that the client recognizes the connection is still active but not in use
CLOSE_WAIT	The remote host is closing its connection with your computer
FIN_WAIT 1	Indicates that the client is closing its connection
FIN_WAIT 2	Indicates that both hosts have agreed to close the connection

are indicated for both local and foreign addresses, appearing after a colon (:).

6.7.1.2 The –b Switch   As indicated in Figure 6.8, the -b switch results in the display of executable programs involved in creating each connection or listening port. To use this option you need to have administrative permission, which should represent the manner by which you use the Command Prompt if you have this capability. As indicated in the program display, it is possible that some executables can be involved in creating multiple listening ports. As a result of using the -b switch, the executable name is displayed in brackets ([]) at the bottom, while the calling component is displayed above the component called. This is illustrated in Figure 6.9, where the command netstat -b was used.

Similar to the use of the -a switch, the -b switch results in a four-column display. This display shows the protocol, abbreviated Proto, the local address, foreign address, and state. While readers may not be familiar with some of the executables shown in Figure 6.9, most should be familiar with skype.exe, which is the popular phone and video service bought by Microsoft Corporation in 2011, and iexplore. exe, the Internet Explorer browser.

If you look carefully at the upper left portion of Figure 6.9 you first note that this author ran the Command Prompt as an administrator. Then, after entering the netstat -b command the display indicated

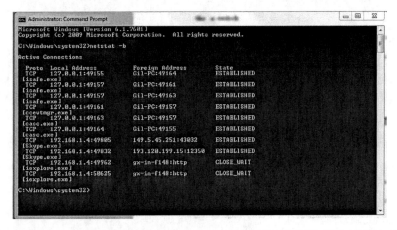

Figure 6.9   Viewing the use of the netstat -b switch.

that there were five executables running on this author's computer: isafe.exe, ccevtmgr.exe, casc.exe, skype.exe, and iexplore.exe. Isafe. exe is a part of Computer Associates eTrust Antivirus program, which was provided by this author's ISP as an Internet security product. Ccevtmgr.exe is a process belonging to the Norton Internet Security Suite that is also known as the Common Client Event Manager Service and provides logging events as well as enables scheduled scans and automatic updates. Casc.exe represents another program from Computer Associates, which is part of the CA Security Suite. While it's possible for malware to name a file to correspond to what you think is a valid process, you can check the file size and date of creation as one mechanism to verify if it is kosher.

6.7.1.3 The -e and -s Switches   The use of the -s switch results in the display of Ethernet statistics concerning bytes and packets sent (transmitted) and received, to include unicast and non-unicast packets, discards, errors, and unknown protocols. By looking at the sent and receive errors you can easily determine if you have a layer 2 problem, as normally the errors should be zero. You can also consider using the -e switch along with the -s switch, which will add IPv4 and IPv6 statistics that will provide information on layer 3 packets, to include packets discarded as well as packets in error. In addition, routing discards can be used as an indication of whether or not the router is capable of handling the packet flow. Note that the use of the -s switch will result in the display of TCP and UDP statistical information, to include data concerning datagrams received and received errors. While TCP is a connection-oriented protocol with error detection and correction, UDP is not. This means that while a low error rate for TCP can be tolerated and corrected by retransmissions, UDP may be a different story. Because UDP is used to transport digitized voice, typically in 20 ms segments, as the number of UDP errors increase voice will become more choppy since errors are not corrected and the 20 ms segment of digitized voice is simply dropped.

To use both switches you would enter the following command:

```
netstat -e -s
```

Note that regardless of the position of -s and -e switches the Command Prompt display will first provide Ethernet statistics, which will be followed by IPv4 and IPv6 statistics and TCP and UDP statistics.

6.7.1.4 The -f Switch   The use of the -f switch results in the display of a table of active connections in a manner similar to that obtained from the use of the -a switch, but only for active connection, which results in the display of fully qualified domain names (FQDNs) for foreign addresses. In addition to FQDNs for foreign addresses, the table displayed for active connections shows the protocol, local address, and state of the connection.

6.7.1.5 The -n Switch   The -n switch provides a display of active connection similar to that of the use of the -f switch. The only difference is that addresses and port numbers are displayed in numerical format. The top portion of Figure 6.10 illustrates the use of the -f switch, while the lower portion of that figure shows the use of the netstat -n switch. In comparing the two you will note that the only difference is in the foreign address, which went from being expressed as FQDN

Figure 6.10   Comparing the use of the -f and -n nstat switches.

to a numerical format. Also note that the IP address of 127.0.0.1 represents a loopback address.

6.7.1.6 The -o Switch The -o parameter is an addition applicable to Windows XP and beyond but requires a hot fix to Windows 2000. Through the use of the -o switch you obtain the ability to audit and troubleshoot ports that are being used. When you use the netstat command with the -o parameter, the command displays the owning process ID (PID) that is associated with each active connection. You can find the application based on the PID on the Processes tab in Windows Task Manager. Note that this parameter can be combined with -a, -n, and -p switches.

6.7.1.7 The -p Switch and Interval Use The nstat command with the -p switch allows you to specify a protocol that can be TCP, UDP, TCPv6, or UDPv6. Thus it is often referred to as the protocol switch. When used with the -s switch (-ps or -sp) you can display per protocol statistics where the protocol can include IP, IPv6, ICMP, ICMPv6, TCP, TCPv6, UDP, or UDPv6. For example, to obtain a display of IPv4 statistics you could enter:

```
netstat -ps ip
```

or

```
netstat -sp ip
```

If you wanted to obtain statistics for TCP you could enter:

```
netstat -ps tcp
```

or

```
netstat -sp tcp
```

Similarly, you can replace the above TCP with UDP or any of the previously mentioned protocols.

One key use of the -ps set of switches is obtained by using the interval to generate a repeating display of a protocol at a predefined period. For example, to display active TCP connections every 10 s you would enter the following command:

```
netstat -ps tcp 10
```

Note that if you do not require summary IP statistic you could simply enter:

```
netstat -o 10
```

To stop the repetitive nature of including an interval, simply enter Ctrl+C, which functions as a break. Also note that instead of increasing the buffer area of the Command Prompt you should consider piping the output of the command to a file. For example, entering

c:>netstat -o 10 >example.txt

would result in the creation of the file example.txt, for which you can use either Notepad or a word processor to observe and print, or you can simply enter the Type command followed by the drive and path to the file to observe your output. If you stored too much information that would result in the rapid display of more lines than capable of being displayed, you might consider using the More command to display the contents of a text file one screen at a time. For example, to display the file example.txt on your display you could enter either of the following commands:

```
more < example.txt
type example.txt | more
```

The More command has a number of options. As a refresher, simply enter the command More followed by the slash question mark (/?) to display a list of the switches associated with this command.

6.7.1.8 The -r Switch   The use of the -r switch results in a display of the routing table associated with your computer. This table is separated into three parts, as illustrated in Figure 6.11, as this author was running a dual stack of IPv4 and IPv6. The top portion of the display shown in Figure 6.11 results in an interface list of adapters present in the host, ranging from any Wi-Fi and Bluetooth adapters to Ethernet

Figure 6.11   Using the netstat -r switch to display the routing table.

and several Microsoft virtual adapters. Note that the Microsoft Intra-Site Automatic Tunnel Addressing Protocol (ISATAP) represents a method that allows ISPs and enterprises to gradually transition to an IPv6 environment. This IPv6 transition mechanism is employed to transmit IPv6 packets between dual-stack nodes on top of an IPv4 network. This means that ISATAP provides a mechanism for generating a local-link IPv6 address from an IPv4 address. Also in the interface list you will note Teredo Tunneling Pseudo-Interface. This was also developed at Microsoft and provides full IPv6 connectivity for IPv6-capable computers that are located on an IPv4 network that has no direct native connection to an IPv6 network. Teredo functions via the use of a tunneling protocol by encapsulating IPv6 datagrams within IPv4 UDP packets. The UDP packets can then be routed on a IPv4 network as well as through network address translation (NAT) devices.

The middle portion of Figure 6.11 illustrates the IPv4 routing table, while the lower portion displays the contents of the IPv6 routing table. Both routing tables represent data tables that list the routes to particular network destinations. In the case of the IPv4 routing table information is also displayed concerning the distances (metrics) associated with each route.

Observing the contents of the routing table provides an indication of the structure or topology of the network immediately around it. As you examine Figure 6.11 note five columns are displayed for the IPv4 routing table labeled Network Destination, Network Mask, Gateway, Interface, and Metric. If the destination host is on the local network, the data are delivered to the destination host. In comparison, if the destination host is on a remote network, the data are forwarded to a local gateway. The gateway's main function in life is to route data between all network devices. Since routing is based upon the network, IP makes routing decisions based upon the network portion of addresses, with the IP module determining the network portion of the destination address by applying the network mask to the address. To ensure readers are knowledgeable in the columns, let's discuss each of the columns shown in the middle of Figure 6.11.

The Network Destination column defines the destination host, subnet address, network address, or default route. The destination for a default route is 0.0.0.0. If the destination network is the local network, the mask that is applied may be the local subnet mask. If no mask is provided with the address, the address class determines the network portion of the address.

The column labeled Netmask indicates the subnet mask that is applied to the destination IP address when matching it to the value in the network destination. The subnet mask is used in conjunction with the destination to determine when a route is used.

The column labeled Gateway indicates the IP address that the local host uses to forward IP datagrams to other IP networks. Remember that the term *gateway* actually references a router. Thus this is either the IP address of a local network adapter or the IP address of an IP router, such as a default gateway router on the local network.

The column labeled Interface indicates the network IP address that is configured on the local computer for the local network adapter that is to be used to reach the next router when an IP datagram is forwarded on the network.

The last column is labeled Metric. Entries in this column indicate the cost of using a route. This cost is typically expressed as the number of hops or the number of routers to cross to reach the IP destination. Any station on the local subnet is one hop, and each router crossed after that is an additional hop. If there are multiple routes to the same destination with different metrics, the route with the lowest metric represents the best route selected.

Returning our attention to the routing table, the first entry represents the default route to the gateway located at 192.168.1.1. The default route is the reserved network number mentioned earlier in this chapter: 0.0.0.0. The default gateway is used whenever there is no specific route in the table for a destination network address. For example, this routing table has no entry for network 192.198.1.5. If IP receives any datagrams addressed to this network, it will send the datagram via the default gateway 192.168.1.1.

The first two columns labeled Network Destination and Netmask together describe the Network ID. For example, destination 192.168.1.1 and netmask 255.255.255.0 can be written as network ID 192.168.1.1/24. Next, the column labeled Gateway contains the same information as would a next hop, as it points to the gateway through which the network can be reached. The Interface column indicates what locally available interface is responsible for reaching the gateway. In this example, gateway 192.168.1.1, which is the Internet router, can be reached through the local network card whose IP address is 192.168.1.5. The fifth column, which is labeled Metric, indicates the associated cost of using the indicated route. This is useful for determining the efficiency of a route from two points in a network. In this example, it is more efficient based upon the column labeled Metric to communicate with the computer itself through the use of address 127.0.0.1 than it would be through 192.168.1.50, which is the IP address of the local network card.

The series of 127 dot addresses represent the *loopback route* for the local host. This is the loopback address mentioned previously in Chapter 3 as a reserved network number. Because every system uses the loopback route to send datagrams to itself, this entry is in every host's routing table.

6.7.1.9 The -s Switch   The use of the -s switch by default provides statistics for IPv4, IPv6, ICMPv4, ICMPv6, TCP, TCPv6, UDP, and UDPv6. Note that you can add the -p (protocol) option to specify a subset of the default. For example, to display TCP statistics for IPv4 you would enter the following command:

```
netstat -sp tcp
```

6.7.1.10 The -t Switch   The last netstat parameter or switch that we will cover is the -t switch, which is used to display the current connection offload state. However, prior to using this switch a few words about offloading are warranted. Essentially offloading represents a technology used in high-speed network interface cards that results in the offload processing of the TCP/IP stack to the network controller. Thus cyclic redundancy check (CRC) computations as well as other functions are no longer performed in the computer. As a result of offloading CPU cycles are freed up while the efficiency of the computer's bus is increased.

To use the -t switch simply enter the following command:

```
netstat -t
```

This would result in a list of active connections and their offload states. The offload state will say "InHost," which means it's not being used. Otherwise, it will say "Offloaded."

6.8 The Route Command

Since we previously discussed the netstat command a logical follow-on is to discuss the Route command. You can use this command to display and, if desired, modify the entries in the local IP routing table. Used without parameters, Route, as well as Route/?, displays a Help screen concerning the use of this command. Figure 6.12 illustrates the use of the Route/? command to display data about the use of this Windows networking tool as well as a few examples of its use.

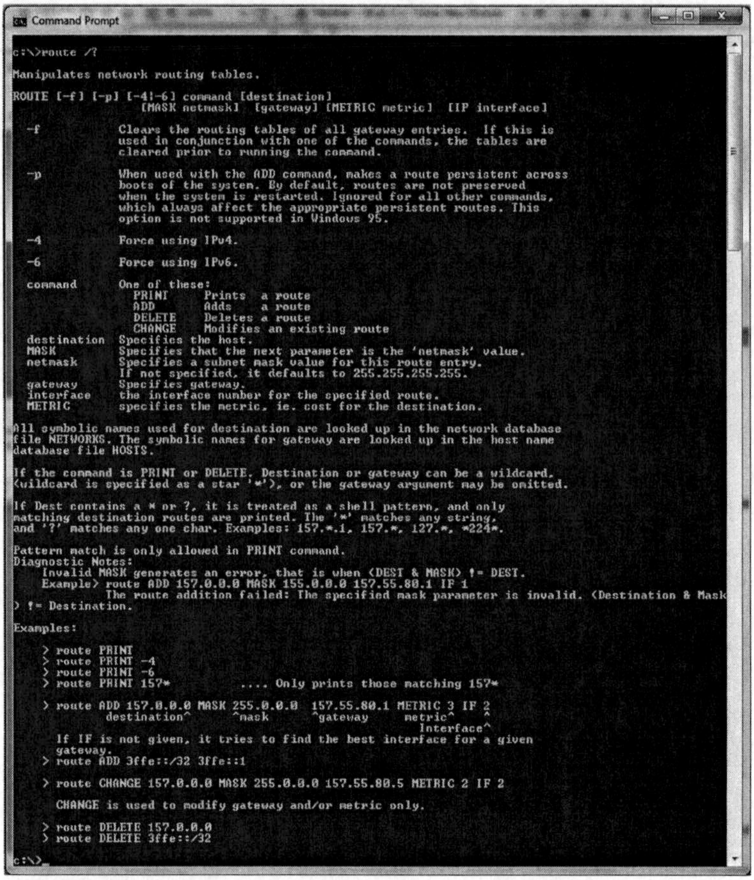

Figure 6.12 Displaying the route Help screen.

6.8.1 Command Format

The format or syntax of the Route command is:

```
route [-f] [-p] [4|6][Command [Destination]
[Mask Netmask] [Gateway] [Metric metric]]
[If Interface]]
```

In the following paragraphs we examine the use of different route switches and commands. However, prior to doing so note that you need administrative privileges to use options associated with this command that change values in the routing table.

6.8.1.1 -f Switch The -f switch is used to clear the routing table of all entries that include a host route (routes with a netmask of 255.255.255.255), a loopback network route (routes with a destination of 127.0.0.0 and a netmask of 255.0.0.0), or a multicast route (routes with a destination of 224.0.0.0 and a netmask of 240.0.0.0). If this switch is used in conjunction with one of the commands, such as Add, Change, or Delete, the table will be cleared prior to running the command.

6.8.1.2 -p Switch When used with the Add command, the specified route is added to the registry and is used to make a route persistent. This occurs by initializing the IP routing table whenever the TCP/IP protocol is started. By default, added routes are not preserved when the TCP/IP protocol is started. When used with the Print command, the list of persistent routes is displayed. This parameter is ignored for all other commands. Note that persistent routes are stored in the registry location HKEY_LOCAL_MACHINE\SYSTEM\CurrentControlSet\Services\Tcpip\Parameters\PersistentRoutes.

A word of caution is in order prior to using the -p switch as well as commands that modify or delete entries in the routing table. Doing so improperly can result in the inability to use your Internet connection. Fortunately, unless you initiate a persistent change and save the results, any damage can be rectified by a simple restart of your computer.

6.8.1.3 -4 Switch The -4 switch, as you might expect, forces the use of IPv4.

6.8.1.4 -6 Switch The -6 switch is employed to force the use of IPv6.

6.8.2 Commands Supported

There are four commands supported by route. The currently supported commands include Add, Change, Delete, and Print. Add results in the addition of a route, while Change allows you to modify an existing route. The use of Delete removes one or more routes, while Print displays a route or routes.

6.8.3 The Destination Option

The destination is used to specify the network destination of the route. The destination can be an IP network address where the host bits of the network address are set to 0, an IP address for a host route, or 0.0.0.0 for the default route.

6.8.4 Mask and Netmask

The mask is used to specify that the next parameter represents the netmask. The netmask is the term used to reference the subnet mask associated with the network destination. The subnet mask can be the appropriate subnet mask for an IP network address, 255.255.255.255 for a host route or 0.0.0.0 for the default route. If omitted, the subnet mask 255.255.255.255 is used. The relationship between the destination and the subnet mask in defining routes means that the destination cannot be more specific than its corresponding subnet mask. This means that there cannot be a bit set to 1 in the destination if the corresponding bit in the subnet mask is 0.

6.8.5 The Gateway Option

The gateway represents the forwarding or next-hop IP address over which the addresses defined by the network destination and subnet mask are reachable. For each locally attached subnet route the gateway address is the IP address assigned to the interface that is attached to the subnet. For remote routes that are reachable via one or more routers, the gateway address represents a directly reachable IP address that is assigned to a neighboring router.

6.8.6 The Metric Option

The metric option is used to specify an integer cost that can be set from 1 to 9999 for the route. This value is used when selecting from multiple routes in the routing table that closely match the destination address of a packet being forwarded. The route with the lowest metric is chosen. The metric can be used to define such variables as the number of hops to the destination, the speed of the path, path reliability, path throughput, or even administrative properties.

6.8.7 The If Interface Option

The If interface switch is used to specify the interface index for the interface over which the destination is reachable. You can obtain a list of interfaces and their corresponding interface indexes through the use of the Route Print command. You can use either decimal or hexadecimal values for the interface index. For hexadecimal values you need to precede the hexadecimal number with 0x, such as 0xFFFF. When the If parameter is omitted, the interface is determined from the gateway address.

6.8.8 Working with Route

When you use the Route Print command, depending upon the number of interfaces and routes, your output may scroll off your display. Even if it doesn't, some persons prefer to work with a hardcopy, so the question arises on how to obtain that hardcopy. Perhaps the easiest way is to direct the output of the command to a file and then print the file. For example, to direct the output of the Route Print command to the file myroute.txt you would enter the following in the Command Prompt window:

```
route print >myroute.txt
```

Note that when you direct the output to a file you will not have the output directly displayed on your screen. Thus you could follow the creation of the file for printing by entering the Route Print command a second time without sending it to a file. To obtain an appreciation of the display of the Route Print command let's examine its output obtained on this author's computer. Figure 6.13 illustrates the execution of Route Print in the Command Prompt window.

In turning our focus to Figure 6.13, note that the resulting display can be considered to be grouped into three areas: an interface list, an IPv4 routing table, and an IPv6 routing table. Because we previously described the interface list entries, let's turn our attention to the

Figure 6.13 Using the Route Print command.

routing tables. Note that for both tables there are no persistent routes. Since IPv4 is still predominantly used, let's concentrate our focus on this area of Figure 6.13.

6.8.8.1 The IPv4 Routing Table There are five columns in the IPv4 routing table. Those columns are labeled Network Destination, Netmask, Gateway, Interface, and Metric. The Network Destination represents the address where packets are to be delivered, while the Netmask is the dotted decimal version of the binary code used to determine the network and the host portions of the IP address. The Gateway is the address used by the local computer to get to the remote Network Destination indicated in the first column, while the Interface is the address of the physical interface. The fifth column, Metric, indicates the cost of using a route and can be set from 1 to 99,999.

Turning our attention to the first column, Network Destination, the first entry in the IPv4 routing table, 0.0.0.0, represents the wire address or default route, which is where the computer starts addressing from. Next, the 127 address represents the loopback interface, which is used mainly for testing. The 192.168.1.0 is the network address. The IP address of 192.168.1.2 represents the address of the local computer. In comparison, the IP address of 192.168.0.255 represents the network broadcast address, which when used transmits messages to all computers on the 192.168.0.x network. Moving down the IPv4 Network Destination column, 224.0.0.0 is a Class D address that represents a base multicast address. Last but not least, 255.255.255.255 represents the IP address for a limited broadcast address.

Note that the routing table is built automatically, based upon the current TCP/IP configuration associated with your computer. Each route will occupy a single line in the displayed table, with your computer searching the routing table for an entry that most closely matches the destination IP address. If no other host or network route matches the destination address included in an IP datagram, the default route will be used. The default route typically forwards an IP datagram for which there is no matching or explicit local route to the default gateway address for a router on the local subnet. In Figure 6.13 the default route forwards the datagram to a router with a gateway address of 192.168.1.1. The router that corresponds to the default gateway contains information about the network IDs of other IP subnets within the larger TCP/IP Internet. Thus it will forward datagrams to other routers until the datagram is eventually delivered to an IP router that is connected to the specified destination host or subnet within a larger network.

6.8.8.2 The IPv6 Routing Table   Now that we are familiar with the IPv4 routing table, let's turn our attention to the IPv6 routing table. This table is shown as a result of the Route Print command in the lower portion of Figure 6.13 on this author's Hilton Head computer. Every computer that operates IPv6 either by itself or as a dual stack with IPv4 will use the IPv6 routing table to determine how to forward packets based on the contents of that table. Entries in the IPv6 routing table consist of four columns. Those columns include the interface over which packets matching the address prefix are sent, using the heading If, a Metric column, a third column labeled Network Destination, and a fourth column under the heading Gateway. Prior to discussing the Network Destination column entries a brief refresher concerning IPv6 addressing is in order. Under IPv6, where addressing is extended to 128 bits, one or more consecutive groups of zero value may be replaced with a single empty group using two consecutive colons (::). Thus the first entry in the Network Destination IPv6 routing table with the address ::/0 is the same as the default or wire route to the gateway. The next entry in the column, ::1/128, represents the local host loopback address, 0:0:0:0:0:0:0:1. The next two entries in the column, which begin with 2001, are used for Teredo Tunneling by Microsoft and represent special purpose addresses. This is followed by four IPv6 addresses that begin with the prefix fe80. Under IPv4 link-local addresses are defined in the address block 169.254.0.0/16. In IPv6 link-local addresses are assigned using the fe80::/64 prefix. The ff00::/8 is the IPv6 address block for multicast applications.

Similar to IPv4, IPv6 hosts use routing tables to maintain information about other IPv6 networks and IPv6 hosts, providing data concerning how to communicate with remote networks and hosts. Each device that uses IPv6 determines how to forward packets based on the contents of the IPv6 routing table. When forwarding IPv6 packets, your computer searches the routing table for an entry that is the most specific match to the destination IPv6 address.

The default route with a prefix of ::/0 is used to forward an IPv6 packet to a default gateway or router on the local link. Because the router that corresponds to the default router contains information about the network prefixes of the other IPv6 subnets within the larger IPv6 internetwork, it forwards the packet to other routers until the packet is eventually delivered to the destination. Based upon the preceding as well as our knowledge of IP, we can summarize the IPv6 routing process as follows.

First, prior to transmitting an IPv6 packet, a computer forms an IPv6 packet by inserting its source IPv6 address and the destination IPv6 address into the IPv6 header. Next, the computer examines the destination IPv6 address and compares it to a locally maintained IPv6 routing table, and based upon the contents of the table, it passes the packet to a protocol layer above IPv6 on the local host, forwards the packet through one of its attached network interfaces, or it discards the packet. When forwarding the packet IPv6 searches the routing table for the route that is the closest match to the destination IPv6 address. The most specific to the least specific route is determined in the following order:

A route that matches the destination IPv6 address (a host route with a 128-bit prefix length)
A route that matches the destination with the longest prefix length
The default route (the network prefix ::/0)

If a matching route is not found, the destination is determined to be an on-link destination.

6.9 The Nslookup Command

Nslookup (name server lookup) represents a command line administrative tool for testing and troubleshooting DNS servers. The use of nslookup.exe obviously requires the TCP/IP protocol to be installed on the computer running nslookup.exe, and at least one DNS server must be specified when you run the IPCONFIG/ALL command from a Command Prompt. The nslookup command operates in both interactive and non-interactive modes of operation. When used interactively, you can issue parameter configurations or requests when presented with the nslookup prompt ('>') in a line-by-line manner. When used in a non-interactive mode the queries are specified as command line arguments in the invocation of the program.

The general command format or syntax of the nslookup command is:

```
nslookup [-option] [host name | -] [server]
```

Note that not specifying a host name or a host name using a specified server results in a non-interactive mode of operation. Otherwise, the absence of a host name results in the command being used interactively and generating a prompt (>) in a line-by-line manner. You should consider using nslookup in a non-interactive mode when you only need to look up one item, as the interactive mode allows you to continuously look up items.

The following example queries the Domain Name Service for the IP address of the domain name harvard.edu by issuing the command nslookup harvard.edu:

```
c:\nslookup harvard.edu
Server: unknown
Address: 192.168.1.1
Non-authoritative answer:
Name: harvard.edu
Address: 69.172.200.24
```

If you look at the above example, which shows the use of nslookup, this result means that the DNS server at 192.168.1.1 queried an external DNS server in order to resolve the IP address associated with harvard.edu; thus the answer is non-authoritative. Also note that if multiple IP addresses were used by the server they would then be listed instead of just one address.

You can also use nslookup in interactive mode by entering the command by itself or with the address or name of a host and waiting for the prompt (>) to enter one or more commands. Once completed you can type "exit" or enter a Ctrl+C to exit back to the Command Prompt, as shown by the following example:

```
C:\Users\Gil>nslookup
Default Server: UnKnown
Address: 192.168.1.1
> harvard.edu
Server: UnKnown
Address: 192.168.1.1
Non-authoritative answer:
Name: harvard.edu
Address: 72.3.199.7
> exit
C:\Users\Gil>
```

One key advantage of the nslookup command operation in interactive mode is its ability to support the use of the Help command. The use of Help from the Command Prompt results in the display of data concerning the use of a variety of nslookup options. Table 6.4 lists the items displayed from the use of Help in the nslookup interactive mode of operation.

One of the things that you can do with nslookup if security allows is to look up a specific type of DNS record. An example of this is an MX record, which points to an organization's mail server. For example, suppose that someone wanted to send you an email message.

Table 6.4   Using Help in the nslookup Interactive Mode of Operation

> help	
Commands: (identifiers are shown in uppercase, [] means optional)	
NAME	- print info about the host/domain NAME using default server
NAME1 NAME2	- as above, but use NAME2 as server
help or ?	- print info on common commands
set OPTION	- set an option
all	- print options, current server and host
[no]debug	- print debugging information
[no]d2	- print exhaustive debugging information
[no]defname	- append domain name to each query
[no]recurse	- ask for recursive answer to query
[no]search	- use domain search list
[no]vc	- always use a virtual circuit
domain = NAME	- set default domain name to NAME
srchlist = N1[/N2/.../N6]	- set domain to N1 and search list to N1,N2, etc.
root = NAME	- set root server to NAME
retry = X	- set number of retries to X
timeout = X	- set initial time-out interval to X seconds
type = X	- set query type (ex.A,AAAA,A+AAAA,ANY,CNAME,MX,NS,PTR,SOA, SRV)
querytype = X	- same as type
class = X	- set query class (ex. IN (Internet), ANY)
[no]msxfr	- use MS fast zone transfer
ixfrver = X	- current version to use in IXFR transfer request
server NAME	- set default server to NAME, using current default server
lserver NAME	- set default server to NAME, using initial server
root	- set current default server to the root
ls [opt] DOMAIN [> FILE]	- list addresses in DOMAIN (optional: output to FILE)
-a	- list canonical names and aliases
-d	- list all records
-t TYPE	- list records of the given RFC record type (ex. A,CNAME,MX,NS,PTR etc.)
view FILE	- sort an 'ls' output file and view it with pg
exit	- exit the program

One of the first things his or her mail server would do is resolve your domain's IP address. Thus if someone wanted to send me an email message his or her email client would have to resolve the IP address of my domain's mail server. This is where the MX record comes into play. The MX record is a record on a domain's DNS server that specifies the IP address of the domain's mail server. Suppose that your domain was having trouble receiving email and you suspected that a DNS server issue was to blame. You could use nslookup to confirm that the domain does indeed have an MX record and that the MX record is pointed to the correct IP address.

Sometimes the use of security will preclude issuing certain nslookup commands; however, there are other ways to determine the address of a mail server, as illustrated by the following example. In this example we cannot list MX records, but by using the Set Type = MX command followed by the ls command we can list information about the responsible mail address and the primary name server. Thus by examining the entries in Table 6.4 you may be able to locate alternative entries that can produce the data you need.

```
C:\Users\Gil>nslookup
Default Server: UnKnown
Address: 192.168.1.1
> ls mx
*** Can't list domain mx: No response from server
The DNS server refused to transfer the zone mx to your
computer. If this
is incorrect, check the zone transfer security
settings for mx on the DNS
server at IP address 192.168.1.1.
> set type = mx
> ls
Server: UnKnown
Address: 192.168.1.1
ls
  primary name server = mowgli.ru.ac.za
  responsible mail addr = postmaster.thaba.nul.ls
  serial = 2010121300
  refresh = 86400 (1 day)
  retry = 7200 (2 hours)
  expire = 2592000 (30 days)
  default TTL = 345600 (4 days)
```

6.10 The Getmac Command

If you're like this author you probably have no idea of the MAC address of your computer. While upon occasion you can turn a tablet or laptop upside down and perhaps read the Ethernet MAC address

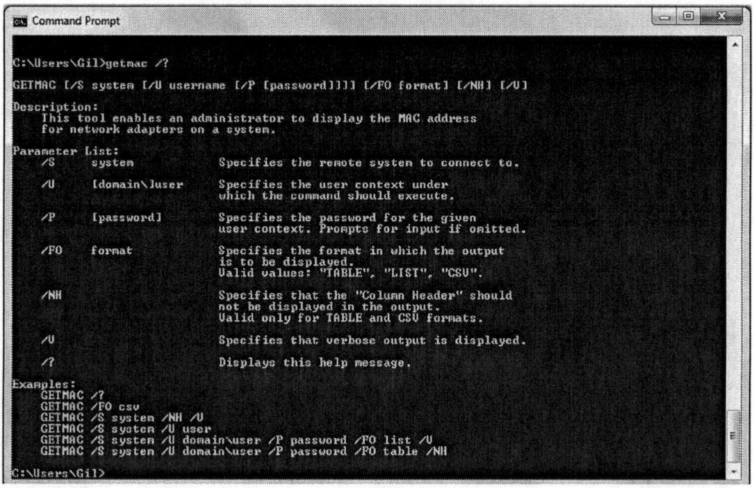

Figure 6.14   Viewing the getmac command options.

from a label, more often than not the address is not easily found. Thus the use of the getmac command can come in handy to determine the layer 2 address associated with a device.

Figure 6.14 illustrates the Help screen associated with the use of the getmac command. By itself, without any option, the getmac command will return the layer 2 address associated with your device. While you can use this command to obtain the MAC address of other devices, you need to have access rights to the other systems. Otherwise you will receive the error message "the RPC server is unavailable."

From Figure 6.14 note that the getmac command supports seven parameters or switches. The lower portion of that illustration includes six examples of the use of the command, to include its switches or parameters.

6.11 The Net Command

The Net command is used to update, fix, or view the network or selected network settings. The format or syntax of this command has minor variations based upon the version of Windows being used. For Windows 7 users the format or syntax of this command is shown below.

```
NET [ACCOUNTS | COMPUTER | CONFIG | CONTINUE | FILE |
GROUP | HELP | HELPMSG | LOCALGROUP | PAUSE | SESSION
| SHARE | START | STATISTICS | STOP | TIME | USE |
USER | VIEW]
```

6.11.1 *The Net Accounts Command*

The Net Accounts command is only used on a local computer and is employed to view and adjust policy settings, such as account policies and password policies. This command cannot be used on a domain controller. Through the use of the Net Accounts command you can display the user accounts database and modify password and logon requirements for all accounts.

When you type Net Accounts you will see the default settings in the local computer for the account lockout policy and password policy. The following illustrates the settings on this author's computer:

```
C:\Users\Gil>net accounts
Force user logoff how long after time expires?: Never
Minimum password age (days):0
Maximum password age (days):42
Minimum password length:0
Length of password history maintained:None
Lockout threshold:Never
Lockout duration (minutes):30
Lockout observation window (minutes):30
Computer role:WORKSTATION
The command completed successfully.
```

The above settings include a display concerning the successful execution of the command. If the computer upon which the command is executed is joined to a domain, the domain settings will take effect and only the settings from the domain are displayed.

6.11.1.1 Net Accounts Options There are several options associated with the use of the Net Accounts command. Those options:

FORCELOGOFF:{minutes | NO} The use of this command option sets the number of minutes a user has before being forced to log off when his or her account expires or valid logon hours expire. NO is the default and its use prevents forced logoff.

/MINPWLEN:length   This command option sets the minimum number of characters for a password. The range is 0–14 characters and the default is 6 characters.

/MAXPWAGE:{days | UNLIMITED}   This command option sets the maximum number of days that a password is valid. Note that /MAXPWAGE cannot be less than /MINPWAGE. The range is 1–999 with a default of 90 days.

/UNIQUEPW:number   This command option is used to requires a user's passwords to be unique through the specified number of password changes. The maximum value is 24.

/DOMAIN   This command option performs the operation on a domain controller of the current domain. Otherwise, the operation is performed on the local computer.

To illustrate the use of the Net Accounts command let's take a few examples. First, as we saw previously, to display the current settings, the password requirements, and the server role for a server, you would enter the command:

```
net accounts
```

As a second example, if you want to force users to log off after the logon time expires with a 10 min warning, you would enter the following command:

```
net accounts/forcelogoff:10
```

Note that if you are running various Net commands the error message "System error 5 has occurred. Access is denied" may appear. Reasons for this error message can include a time synchronization problem, missing permission to access a remote computer, firewalls or other products such as router access lists that may eliminate the ability to connect to the remote computer, or the account has an expired password. Fixing a system error 5 will depend on the cause. If Windows is not granting permission to local users, editing a key in the Windows registry can resolve the error. If time synchronization is the problem, updating the system time to match the network time should eliminate the error.

6.11.2 The Net Computer Option

This command option can be used to add or delete other networked computers on a Windows domain controller. The format of this command is as follows:

```
net computer \\computername {/ADD |/DEL}
```

6.11.3 The Net Config Option

The Net Config option is used to display the configurable workstation and server services that are running. The format or syntax of this option is:

```
net config [{server|workstation}]
```

To display the computer name, user name, software version of Windows, active NIC, logon domain, and data on communications you would enter the following command:

```
net config workstation
```

To display the server name, server active NIC, server hidden status, and maximum logged-on users you would enter the following command:

```
net config server
```

6.11.4 The Net Continue, Start, and Stop Options

The Net command includes four options to manage a service:

    net start [service]
    net stop [service]
    net pause [service]
    net continue [service]

where the service name represents an entry shown in the control panel under Services. Net start, when employed without parameters, is used to display a list of services that are currently operating. To stop a service you would enter net stop followed by the service. For example, to stop the tablet PC input service you would enter:

```
net stop tablet pc input service
```

Note that the other two options let you pause or continue a service. Thus Net Continue followed by a service continues the service while Net Pause allows a defined service to be paused.

6.11.5 *The Net File Option*

The Net File command is used to display the names of all open shared files on your server and the number of file locks. You can also use the Net File command to close individual files and release the locks. The format or syntax of the command is:

```
net file [id [/close]]
```

> id represents the identification number, returned by the Net File command. If you type "net file id," a formatted response will be displayed.
>
> /close closes an open file ID and releases locked records. Type this command from the server where the file is shared.

To display the names and IDs of open shared files, type Net File without any parameters. To close a file that has ID 5, type

```
net file 5/close
```

6.11.6 *The Net Group Option*

Through the use of the Net Group option you can add, delete, view, and manage network workgroups. The format or syntax of this command is:

```
NET GROUP [groupname [/COMMENT:"text"]] [/DOMAIN]
  groupname {/ADD [/COMMENT:"text"] |/DELETE} [/DOMAIN]
  groupname username [...] {/ADD |/DELETE} [/DOMAIN]
```

groupname specifies the name of the group to be added, deleted, or listed.

/comment adds the enclosed text as a comment for a new or existing group.

/domain indicates that the operation is to be performed on the domain controller. If not specified the operation is performed on the local computer.

/add results in the addition of a group or user name to a group. Note you must establish accounts that you add to a group with this command.

/delete results in the removal of a group or a user name from a group.

<username...> provides a list of one or more user names to add or remove from a group, with multiple user names separated with a space.

Let's turn our attention to a few examples of the use of the Net Group option. The following example adds a group called admin to the local user accounts database:

```
net group admin/add
```

In the next example we add a group called admin to the local user accounts database:

```
net group admin/add/domain
```

Next, let's add the existing user accounts alpha, beta, and gamma to the admin group on the local computer:

```
net group admin alpha, beta, gamma/add
```

If we want to add the three previously mentioned accounts to the admin group in the domain database we would enter:

```
net group admin alpha, beta, gamma/add/domain
```

To display the users in the admin group you would enter:

```
net group admin
```

Finally, to add a meaningful comment to the admin group record you could enter:

```
net group admin/comment:"The administration staff
members"
```

6.11.7 The Net Helpmsg

This Net command is used to determine why an error occurred and provides problem-solving information. The format or syntax of this command is the command followed by the message number, as shown below:

```
net helpmsg message-number
```

where message-number specifies the four-digit number of the message for which you want to obtain information.

6.11.8 The Net Send Command

The Net Send command is only applicable to Windows NT, Windows 2000, Windows XP, and Windows 2003, having been removed from later versions of Windows. The reason it will be briefly covered is due to its use in older versions of Windows, its versatility, and the fact that it is available as a third-party product from many companies.

Briefly, Net Send is used to transmit messages to other users, computers, or messaging names on a network. The format or syntax of this command is:

```
net send {name | * |/domain[:name] |/users} message
```

To send the message "this server will shut down in 30 minutes" to all users connected to the domain, you would enter the Net Send command as follows:

```
net send/domain:users This server will shut down in 30
minutes.
```

6.11.9 The Net Localgroup Option

The Net Localgroup command option is similar to the Net Group option, allowing you to add, display, or modify local groups. When used without parameters, Net Localgroup displays the name of the server and the names of local groups on the computer. For example, entering the command Net Localgroup on this author's computer resulted in the following display:

```
C:\Users\Gil>net localgroup
Aliases for \\GIL-PC
- - - - - - - - - - - - - - - - - - - - - - - - - - - -
*Administrators
*Backup Operators
*Cryptographic Operators
*Debugger Users
*Distributed COM Users
*Event Log Readers
*Guests
*HomeUsers
*IIS_IUSRS
*Network Configuration Operators
*Performance Log Users
*Performance Monitor Users
*Power Users
*Remote Desktop Users
*Replicator
*Users
The command completed successfully.
```

Note that since the command has the same format or syntax as the Net Group command readers are referred to the former command.

6.11.10 The Net Share Command Option

The use of the Net Share command option without parameters results in the display of information about all of the resources that are shared on the local computer. You can also use this command to create, delete, or modify shared resources. The format or syntax of this command is as follows:

```
net share [[sharename = drive:path [/grant:user,[read
| change | full]]
  [= drive:path]] [{/users:number |/unlimited}] [/
remark:"text"]
  [/cache: {manual | automatic |no}] [/delete]
```

sharename specifies the name of the shared resource.

drivepath denotes the absolute path of the directory to be shared.

number sets the maximum number of users who can simultaneously access the shared resource.

/unlimited is used to allow an unlimited number of simultaneous users to access the shared resource.

"text" adds a description enclosed in quotes about the resource.

/cache: manual enables offline client caching with manual
reintegration.

/cache: automatic enables offline client caching with automatic
reintegration.

/cache: no informs the client that offline caching is inappropriate.

/delete stops sharing of the shared resource.

You can use the net share command without parameters to quickly
view shared folders on your computer. In the wonderful world of
modern security shared resources are usually disabled on individual
computers by the network administrator and may be in limited use to
provide access to predefined directories on a local area network in large
organizations. The following illustrates the use of the net share command without any parameters. Note that any share name that ends in
a dollar sign ($) character will not appear when you browse the local
computer from a remote computer. However, if sharing is enabled and
you want to access a folder ending with a dollar sign you will need to
enter on the remote computer the exact path to the shared folder.

```
C:\Users\Gil>net share
Share name Resource  Remark

- - - - - - - - - - - - - - - - - - - - - - - - - - - -
C$  C:\  Default share
D$  D:\  Default share
print$ C:\Windows\system32\spool\drivers
  Printer Drivers
IPC$  Remote IPC
ADMIN$ C:\Windows    Remote Admin
```

```
Users  C:\Users
hp psc 1300 series
  USB001  Spooled hp psc 1300 series
The command completed successfully.
```

Suppose you have a directory named Familyphotos you wish to share with other users. You can create a new local file share by entering the following command:

```
c:\>net share allcanview = c:\familyphotos/remark:"see
my photos"
```

By executing this command you would make the folder labeled Familyphotos on the C drive available for other users on the network. Since this command would execute, assuming you have appropriate permissions, you would receive the message "allcanview was shared successfully" on your display. You could then use the command Net Share without parameters to view the share you just created. When you do so the name Allcanview will be listed under the Share name column, the path c:\familyphotos would be listed under the column labeled Resource, while the remark "see my photos" would be listed under the column heading of Remark.

If you wanted to limit the number of simultaneous users that can access the directory to 10 due to network bandwidth you could enter the following command:

```
net share allcanview/users:10
```

You can remove the previously set limit to the share by using the following net share command:

```
net share allcanview/unlimited
```

Now suppose you decided you goofed and do not wish to share family photos with other persons. You can delete the share by entering:

```
net share allcanview/delete
```

Note that if you wanted to delete all shares, you can specify the device name in the command. For example, to delete all shares on drive C you would enter:

```
net share c:\/delete
```

6.11.11 The Net Session Command

The Net Session command can be used to manage server computer connections. When used without parameters this command results in the display of information about all sessions with the local computer. You can also use the abbreviation Net Sess for this command. It should be noted that the use of Net Session results in a display limited to incoming connections. The format or syntax of this command is:

```
net {session|sess} [\\ComputerName] [/delete]
```

\\ *ComputerName* identifies the computer for which you want to list or disconnect sessions.

/delete is used to end the computer's session with the specified *ComputerName* and closes all open files on the computer for the session.

If you omit the *ComputerName*, all sessions on the local computer are canceled. Because the use of the Net Session command can result in a loss of data, you should consider warning users prior to disconnecting a session.

You can use the Net Session command to view the computer names and user names of users on a server. Thus you can see if users have files open as well as determine how long each user's session has been idle. The information displayed appears in a format similar to the following:

```
Computer  User name  Client type  Opens  Idle time
```

To illustrate the use of the Net Session command let's examine a few examples. To list all sessions connected to the computer you would enter the following:

```
net session
```

To list all sessions from a specified machine you would enter:

```
net session \\ComputerName
```

The resulting display will provide information about a single user, to include a list of shared resources to which the user has one or more connections. Note that a session is recorded whenever a user at a client successfully contacts a server and the two computers are on the same network. Obviously, the user will have a user name and password that are accepted by the server. In addition, a user at a client must have a session initiated with a server before he or she can use the resources of the server, requiring the user at a client to connect to a resource.

Suppose you want to terminate all sessions on your computer. You would enter the following command:

```
net session/delete
```

If you have permission to disconnect sessions on another computer, you would enter the following:

```
net session \\ComputerName/delete
```

Note that you can also set the length of time that a session can remain idle before being automatically disconnected. To do so you would use the Autodisconnect option in the Net Config command, as shown below:

```
net config server/autodisconnect
```

Also note that an automatic disconnection is transparent to the user. This results from the fact that the session is automatically reconnected when the user accesses the resource again.

6.11.12 *The Net Statistics Command*

This command, which can be abbreviated as Net Stats, displays the statistics log for the local workstation or server service, errors, logon time, and bytes transmitted and received. The format or syntax of this command is:

```
net {statistics|stats} [{workstation | server}]
```

Table 6.5 Statistics for a Workstation

Bytes received
SMBs received
Bytes transmitted
SMBs transmitted
Read operations
Write operations
Raw reads denied
Raw writes denied
Network errors
Connections made
Reconnections made
Server disconnects
Sessions started
Hung sessions
Failed sessions
Failed operations
Use count
Failed use count

As a result of the use of the Net Statistics command you will display a table of information that varies based upon the use of the workstation and server in the command. For a workstation's service you will display the number of bytes received, server message blocks received, bytes transmitted, server message blocks transmitted, number of read and write operations, reads and writes denied, network errors, connections made, and other data that are summarized in Table 6.5.

In examining the entries in Table 6.5, note that you can use this information to determine a variety of data concerning the connection between client and workstation. Here you can examine network errors, connections, and reconnections to check for abnormalities, as well as use bytes transmitted and received as a mechanism to determine if a station is hogging network bandwidth.

For the server service, Windows reports the computer's name, the date and time when the statistics were last updated, and the information concerning sessions, kilobytes sent and received, mean response time, system errors, permission and password violations, file and print job information, and data about buffers. Table 6.6 lists server statistics generated from the use of the Net Statistics Server command.

Table 6.6   Server Statistics Generated from the Net Statistics Server Command

Sessions accepted
Sessions timed out
Sessions errored out
Kilobytes sent
Kilobytes received
Mean response time (ms)
System errors
Permission violations
Password violations
Files accessed
Communication devices accessed
Print jobs spooled
Times buffers exhausted
Big buffers
Request buffers

Although not shown in Table 6.6, the use of the Net Statistics Server command can tell you the last time the server service started by displaying the day and time since statistics were accumulated. Since the server service is normally not restarted, this is a good method, but not a 100% certainty, to determine when the server last booted. The next block of information, which is shown at the top of Table 6.6, concerns server sessions. The session information can be a bit deceptive, partly because of the way the statistic is presented. This is because the "sessions timed-out" and "sessions errored-out" entries are cumulative; however, the "sessions accepted" entry represents the number of active sessions at the time the command was run.

The "sessions timed-out" entry represents sessions that have been disconnected because of how long they remained idle, while the "sessions errored-out" entry represents the number of sessions that were disconnected due to an error. However, when viewing the presented statistics it's important to note that the number of sessions that have timed out is included in the number of sessions that have errored out. Thus to determine actual errors, you need to subtract the time-outs from the errored-outs. This area of the report is useful for determining how many users are connected, whether the number of errors is disproportionately large, and whether the automatic time-out feature is working. Note that a time-out represents Windows' method for freeing up resources.

The information in the kilobytes section produced by the Net Statistics Server command is based on performance monitor data. Note that the numbers next to the "kilobytes sent" and "kilobytes received" entries represent the number of total kilobytes sent and received by the server service and not the system as a whole since the last boot. Also note that the mean response time in milliseconds is a metric that defines how quickly the server responded to a request, with the lower the number, the faster the response time.

The next section displayed consists of three types of errors. The "system errors" entry reports the number of system errors that have occurred since the last reboot. System errors typically represent a problem with the server, so this number should be zero. The next error indicates the number of permissions violations that have occurred since the last boot. Note that it is quite normal to have a few permissions violations if the server isn't configured correctly. However, if this number increases each time you run the Net Statistics Server command, it could mean that someone is trying to break into your computer. The third entry concerns password violations. This number represents the number of times users have entered passwords incorrectly. Here a large number could indicate a hack attempt, such as applying a dictionary against a password request.

The next section in Table 6.6 informs you about the manner by which your users are accessing the server. The "files accessed" entry denotes the total number of times files were accessed since the last boot. Note that this figure represents the total number of accesses and not the total number of individual files accessed. The next line entry, "communication devices accessed," shows how many times devices like modems were accessed. The "print jobs spooled" entry indicates how many print jobs have been spooled by the server since it was booted. The last section displayed by the use of the Net Statistics Server command provides data about buffers that have been exceeded.

6.11.13 The Net Time Command

The Net Time command is used to display and synchronize the computer's clock with that of another computer or domain. The format or syntax of this command is:

```
net time [{\\ComputerName |/domain[:DomainName] |/
rtsdomain[:DomainName]}] [/set]
```

To synchronize the computer's clock with the time on the specified computer or domain you would enter the following command, where computername is the name of the computer whose clock you wish to synchronize with:

```
net time \\computername/set
```

This action will result in the display of the current time at the entered computer name as well as a prompt asking you if you want to set the local computer's time to match the time at the entered computer name.

6.11.14 The Net Use Command

The Net Use command can be used for adding or modifying user accounts or for displaying user account information. In earlier versions of Windows you could control such parameters as when a user can connect to a computer or when an account expires, although this capability is not included in Windows 7. This command in Windows 7 controls persistent net connections, which means that such connections are reconnected at re-logon. The format or syntax of this command is:

```
net use [{devicename | *}] [\\computername\sharename[\
volume]] [{password | *}]] [/user:[domainname\]username]
  [/user:[dotteddomainname\]username]
  [/user: [username@dotteddomainname]
  [/smartcard]
  [{/delete |/persistent:{yes | no}}]
```

Devicename results in the assignment of a name to connect to the resource or specifies the device to be disconnected. There are two kinds of device names: disk drives (D: through Z:) and printers (LPT1: through LPT3:). Note that entering an asterisk (*) instead of a specific device name assigns the next available device name.

\\Computername\sharename is used to specify the name of the server and the shared resource. If the computername contains spaces, you need to use quotation marks around the entire computer name from the double backslash (\\) to the end of the computer name. The computer name can be from 1 to 15 characters in length.

> \volume is used to specify a NetWare volume on the server. You must have Client Service for NetWare installed and running to connect to NetWare servers.
>
> password is used to specify the password required to access shared resources. If you enter an asterisk (*) you will be prompted to enter a password.
>
> /user is employed to specify a different user name with which the connection is made.
>
> domainname is used to specify another domain. If you omit the domain name, the Net Use command will use the current logged-on domain.
>
> dotteddomainname is used to specify the fully qualified domain name for the domain where the user account exists.
>
> username is used to specify the name of the user account to add, delete, modify, or view. The name of the user account can be up to 20 characters in length.
>
> /smartcard is used to specify the network connection credentials on a smart card. If multiple smart cards are available, you are then prompted to specify the credential.
>
> /delete is used to cancel the specified network connection. If you specify the connection with an asterisk (*), all network connections will be canceled.
>
> /persistent:{yes | no} is used to control the use of persistent network connections. The default is the setting last used. Note that deviceless connections are not persistent. The entry of yes saves all connections as they are made, and restores them at next logon. The use of no does not save the connection being made or subsequent connections. Existing connections are restored at the next logon. Note that the use of /delete removes persistent connections.

To illustrate the use of this command let's first use the command to assign drive j to the share we previously created and named allcanview. Then, changing the drive to j and taking a directory listing would result in the following display:

```
C:\Users\Gil>net use j: \\gil-pc\allcanview
The command completed successfully.
C:\Users\Gil>j:
J:\>dir
Volume in drive J is HP
Volume Serial Number is D63D-3311
Directory of J:\
12/31/2010 09:01 PM <DIR> .
12/31/2010 09:01 PM <DIR> ..
11/02/2010 04:36 PM <DIR> AU Fall 1992-93
11/02/2010 04:36 PM <DIR> Beachway Drive Falls Church
- Macon 1977
11/02/2010 04:36 PM <DIR> Brooklyn NY
11/02/2010 04:36 PM <DIR> cherryblossom
12/23/2010 08:10 PM <DIR> HiltonHead2010
11/02/2010 04:36 PM <DIR> Jessica's Graduation Trip to
Israel 1992
11/02/2010 04:37 PM <DIR> Macon 1992
11/02/2010 04:37 PM <DIR> Macon the early years
11/02/2010 04:37 PM <DIR> maui-with Jon+Family
11/02/2010 04:37 PM <DIR> Reading PA
11/02/2010 04:37 PM <DIR> University of Pennsylvania
  0 File(s) 0 bytes
 13 Dir(s) 377,389,359,104 bytes free
J:\>
```

From the previous example we can note that you can control drive mappings through the Net Use command. The drive mapping capability is referred to as drive shares in a network environment. This command makes use of the server message block (SMB) and the NetBios protocol on port 139 or 445. Thus users can connect and disconnect from different shared resources, such as computers, printers, and drives. If you're a network administrator you might consider adding those ports in a routers access list if your organization permits this capability and you have a complex internal network interconnected by routers. Otherwise, routers deny anything not specifically permitted, and this could explain why mapping doesn't work between different areas within an organization.

Note that you can also use the Net Use command by itself to display a list of network connection information on shared resources. This is shown below.

```
C:\Users\Gil>net use
New connections will be remembered.
Status Local Remote Network

- - - - - - - - - - - - - - - - - - - - - - - - - - - -
OK J: \\gil-pc\allcanview Microsoft Windows Network
The command completed successfully.
```

Through the use of the Net Use command you can connect to the IPC$ (interprocess communication share). IPC$ represents the null session connection, which allows unauthenticated users. The basic syntax for connecting anonymously is shown below:

```
net use \\{computer name |IP address}\IPC$ ""/u:""
```

For example, typing at the Command Prompt

```
net use \\192.198.1.3\IPC$ ""/u:""
```

will result in an attempt to connect to the share IPC$ of the network 192.198.1.3 as an anonymous user with a blank password. If successfully connected to the target machine, a literal trove of information can be gathered, such as shares, users, groups, registry keys, and other information. This information will provide an unscrupulous person with a lot of information about a remote user and usually represents a security breach. Since you can enter either Net Use by itself to obtain a list of all of the computer's connections or Net Use device to obtain data about a specific connection, this represents a technique to look at possible network vulnerabilities. One last item is that you cannot disconnect from a shared directory if you use it as your current drive or an active process is using it.

6.12 The Net User Command

The Net User command should not be confused with the Net Use command, as it results in a completely different result. This command is used to display, create, modify, or delete users on the computer or domain. The format or syntax of this command is:

```
netuser [username [password | *] [options]] [/domain]
  username {password | *}/add [options] [/domain]
  username [/delete] [/domain]
  username [/times:{times | all}]
```

username represents the name of the user account you want to add, delete, modify, or view. The name of the user account can be up to 20 characters in length.

password represents a variable that assigns or changes a password for the user's account. A password must satisfy the minimum length set with the /minpwlen option of the Net Accounts command and can contain as many as 14 characters.

* results in a prompt for the password. The password is not displayed when you type it at a password prompt.

/domain results in the operation on the primary domain controller (PDC) of the current domain. This parameter applies only to computers running Windows Workstation that are members of a Windows server domain. By default, Windows server-based computers perform operations on the PDC.

/add adds a user account to the user accounts database.

/delete results in the removal of a user account from the user accounts database.

There are a variety of options supported by the Net User command. Those options are listed in alphabetical order in Table 6.7.

By itself, without parameters the Net User command displays information about your connections. For example, on this author's computer located at Hilton Head, entering Net User produces the following result:

```
C:\Users\Gil>net user
User accounts for \\GIL-PC
- - - - - - - - - - - - - - - - - - - - - - - - - - - - -
Administrator Bev  Gil
Guest
The command completed successfully.
```

As you can see, when the Net User command executes successfully you will receive a notice.

Table 6.7 Options for the Net User Command

/Active:{yes | no}	This option activates or deactivates the specified account. If the account is not active, the user cannot gain access to the server. The default is set to yes.
/Comment:"text"	This option provides a descriptive comment with a maximum of 48 characters about the user's account.
/Countrycode:nnn	This option uses the operating system country code in order to implement the specified language files for a user's help and error messages. A value of 0 signifies the default country code.
/Expires:{date | never}	This option causes the account to expire if a date is set. The **never** option sets no time limit on the account. The expiration date format is mm/dd/yy or dd/mm/yy, depending on the country code. Months can be a number, spelled out, or abbreviated with three letters. Years can be two or four numbers. Slashes (/) with no spaces are used to separate parts of the date.
/Fullname:"name"	This option represents a user's full name and not a user name. The name is enclosed in quotation marks.
/Homedir:pathname	This option sets the path for the user's home directory. The specified path obviously must exist.
Net help user | more	This option results in the display of the Help menu one screen at a time.
/Passwordchg:{yes | no}	This option is used to specify whether users can change their own password. The default is yes.
/Passwordreq:{yes | no}	This option specifies whether a user account must have a password. The default is yes.
/Profilepath[:path]	This option is used to set a path for the user's logon profile.
/Scriptpath:pathname	This option specifies the location of the user's logon script.
/Times:{times | all}	This option is used to specify the logon hours. The times option is expressed as day[-day][,day[-day]],time[-time][,time [-time]] and is limited to 1 h increments. Days can be spelled out or abbreviated and hours can entered in either 12 or 24 h notation. For 12 h notation, use am, pm, a.m., or p.m. The **all** option specifies that a user can always log on, while a blank value specifies that a user can never log on. Separate day and time entries with a comma, and separate multiple day and time entries with a semicolon.
/Usercomment:"text"	This option lets an administrator add or change the user comment for the account.
/Workstations:{computer name[,...] | *}	This option will list as many as eight computers from which a user can log on to the network. If the /workstations option has no list or if the list is an asterisk (*), the user can log on from any computer.

6.13 The Netsh Command

There is an old adage that you save the best for last. While this author recognizes that different commands are used by different persons with different types of problems, in concluding this chapter we turn our attention to the netsh command. Netsh or network shell is a command line utility included in Microsoft's Windows line of operating systems, beginning with Windows 2000. The use of this command allows local or remote configuration of network devices such as the interface, the display of the status of various network communications servers, assuming you have the required permissions, as well as the creation of a script in a text file that can be used for a variety of purposes. Concerning the latter, this enables the creation of batch files containing a series of commands that can be run as a script file. If you have previously worked with the Microsoft Management Console (MMC) you will note that the netsh command provides a similar capability and, in some cases, goes beyond by including commands for IPv6 and other functions that are presently not available in the user interface as an MMC snap-in. The general format or syntax of the netsh command is:

```
netsh [-a AliasFile] [-c Context] [-r RemoteMachine]
[-u [domain name\username]
[-p password] [Command | -f ScriptFile]
```

You can use the netsh command by entering the command *netsh* into a regular Command Prompt. The netsh shell has a hierarchical structure with some subshells that Microsoft refers to as context. From a user's point of view this means that commands can be entered as a sequence of terms. For example, you could first enter netsh and receive the prompt c:>netsh, after which you could enter a subcommand, such as wlan. This would result in the prompt becoming c:>netsh wlan, in effect allowing you to enter wireless LAN commands. Because many readers are new to the use of the Command Prompt, we will primarily reference the use of the netsh command at the first command line level; however, it is worthwhile for experienced users to "drill down" when using this command, similar to the manner that the nslookup command can be used.

Figure 6.15 Displaying the netsh command Help screen.

Figure 6.15 illustrates the netsh Help screen obtained by entering the command followed by the slash and question mark (/?) characters. Note that netsh commands are organized in a hierarchy with each netsh command having its own functionality and context. Both the format of the command and the commands in the context, which we can refer to as subcommands, are listed as a result of the Help screen entry. Note that similar to other commands, you can literally drill down help by entering, for example, netsh firewall/? to obtain a list of commands you can use with netsh firewall. In doing so you would obtain a display that informs you that you can use Add, Delete, Dump, Help, Set, and Show, after which the display informs you how to further drill down by entering the command followed by a space and a question mark. To illustrate this consider the following example :

```
C:\Users\Gil>netsh firewall dump ?
Usage: dump
Remarks:
Creates a script that contains the current
configuration. If saved to a
```

file, this script can be used to restore altered
configuration settings.
C:\Users\Gil>

One common use of the netsh command is to reset the TCP/IP
stack to its default setting, resulting in the use of known parameters that work but may not be optimized for a particular situation. To illustrate how far commands have come, this represents a
task that in Windows 98 required the reinstallation of the TCP/
IP adapter. To illustrate how you can drill down using the Help
display, let's consider the use of the netsh interface command. In
Figure 6.16 we are literally drilling down through the use of the
slash and question mark characters to display various levels of help.
First, in the top portion of Figure 6.16 we entered the netsh interface Help option, which results in a list of commands we can use
with the netsh interface command. Since we are concerned with
IPv4, we next drilled down a bit further by entering the Help command as follows:

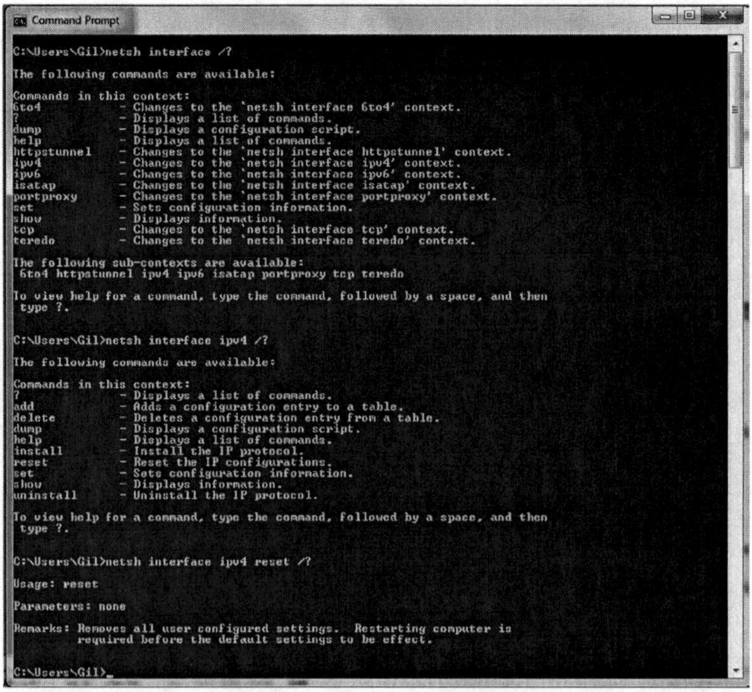

Figure 6.16 Drilling down the netsh interface set of commands.

```
netsh interface ipv4/?
```

This action resulted in the display of commands applicable to the netsh interface IPv4 command, to include the ability to reset the IP configuration through the use of the Reset subcommand. Drilling down further into the built-in help facility we entered the following command:

```
netsh interface ipv4 reset/?
```

Note that the resulting display informs us that Reset removes all user-configured settings and requires a computer reset for the default settings to take effect.

In addition to operating on workstations and tablets you can use the netsh command on servers. In a server environment you can configure the DHCP server roll by using the commands at the netsh dhcp context. Other communications roles include the Windows Internet Name Service (WINS), whose context for WINS is netsh wins; the Network Policy Server (NPS), which was previously known as Internet Authentication Service (IAS), whose context is netsh nps; the DHCP client, whose context is netsh dhcpclient; the Hypertext Transfer Protocol (HTTP), whose context is netsh http; the Routing and Remote Access, whose context is netsh rsa; and Internet Protocol version 4 and Internet Protocol version 6 (IPv6), whose context for IPv4 is netsh interface IP and for IPv6 is netsh interface IPv6. You can also specify an application proxy whose context is netsh interface port proxy.

Two areas that deserve special attention are the ability to use the netsh command to configure and display IEEE 802.11 wireless LAN connectivity and to create, administrator, and monitor Windows firewalls with advanced security. You can either do this for a single computer or configure multiple computers through the use of a logon script. In addition, you can use the netsh WLAN commands to view applied wireless group policy settings. Due to the importance of wireless LANs and security in networks we focus our attention upon these two areas in the remainder of this chapter. In doing so we examine the applicable commands supported by workstations.

6.13.1 The Netsh Wlan Command

The netsh wlan command set is restricted to being offered in Windows Vista and later versions of the Windows operating system. Through the use of this command you can configure wireless security settings, view wireless group policy settings, hide wireless networks from being viewed by end users, and even prevent users from connecting to certain wireless networks.

As we noted previously, the use of many Command Prompt commands includes the ability to drill down through a series of Help screens. The netsh wlan command is no exception, enabling you to drill down through a series of Help commands. Because these commands require elevation you will need to run the Command Prompt as an administrator. In the following example we can drill down to view the wireless commands supported by entering netsh wlan/? at the Command Prompt.

```
C:\Users\Gil>netsh wlan/?
```

The following commands are available:

?	Displays a list of commands
Add	Adds a configuration entry to a table
Connect	Connects to a wireless network
Delete	Deletes a configuration entry from a table
Disconnect	Disconnects from a wireless network
Dump	Displays a configuration script
Export	Saves WLAN profiles to XML files
Help	Displays a list of commands
Refresh	Refreshes hosted network settings
Reportissues	Generates WLAN smart trace report
Set	Sets configuration information
Show	Displays information
Start	Starts hosted network
Stop	Stops hosted network

To view help for a command, type the command, followed by a space, and then type ?.

To drill down further you can select a WLAN command such as Add and, no pun intended, add it to the prior netsh wlan command, entering netsh wlan add/?, as shown in the following example.

```
C:\Users\Gil>netsh wlan add/?
```

The following commands are available:

Add Filter   Add a wireless network into the wireless allowed or blocked list

Add Profile Add a WLAN profile to specified interface on the system

To obtain an appreciation for the use of WLAN-related commands we need to create a profile. However, prior to creating a profile you should first determine the name(s) of the wireless interfaces on targeted computers as well as the status of those interfaces. To do so you could use the netsh interface command, as shown below.

```
c:\>netsh interface show interface
Admin State State  Type  Interface Name
- - - - - - - - - - - - - - - - - - - - - - - - - - - - - - -
Enabled  Connected  Dedicated  Wireless Network
Connection
Enabled  Disconnected  Dedicated  Wireless Network
Connection 2
Enabled  Connected  Dedicated  Local Area Connection
```

Based upon the use of the netsh interface Show Interface command our computer has one connection and is disconnected from a second wireless network. To create a profile this author used the graphical user interface (GUI) interface instead of the Command Prompt. The reason for this is that after spending a few hours looking at Google and Bing searches for "netsh wlan create profile" this author could only find references to the use of GUI. In addition, this author noted that a number of persons were posting problems concerning not being able to create a profile in Command Prompt. Thus while it may be available, at the time of writing the author could not find a method other than the use of a GUI to create a WLAN profile.

Using the control panel's Network and Internet page this author created the profile netgear-densbc. Now that a profile was created on our Windows 7 computer that already has a working wireless network, you can execute the following command:

```
netsh wlan export profile name = "netgear-
densbc"folder = C:\Netgear\wlan interface = "Wireless
Network Connection"
```

This command would create a file named Wireless Network Connection-netgear-densbc.xml in the folder C:\netgear\wlan. You will note that the message "netgear-densbc" is saved in file C:\netgear\wlan\Wireless Network Connection-netgear-densbc.xml successfully. To view the file you just saved you can use the Command Prompt Type command to display the contents of the .xml file. You can also use the Command Prompt to verify the creation of a WLAN profile. To do so you could enter the netsh WLAN Show Profile command as follows:

```
C:\Windows\system32>netsh wlan show profile
Profiles on interface Wireless Network Connection:
Group policy profiles (read only)
- - - - - - - - - - - - - - - - -
<None>
User profiles
- - - - - - -
All User Profile :netgear-densbc
```

The file just created is shown below:

```
<?xml version = "1.0" ?>
- <WLANProfile xmlns =
"http://www.microsoft.com/networking/WLAN/profile/v1">
<name>netgear-densbc</name>
- <SSIDConfig>
- <SSID>
<hex>6E6574676561722D64656E736263</hex>
<name>netgear-densbc</name>
</SSID>
<nonBroadcast>false</nonBroadcast>
</SSIDConfig>
<connectionType>ESS</connectionType>
<connectionMode>manual</connectionMode>
- <MSM>
```

```
- <security>
- <authEncryption>
<authentication>open</authentication>
<encryption>none</encryption>
<useOneX>false</useOneX>
</authEncryption>
</security>
</MSM>
</WLANProfile>
```

Once a profile is created you can manipulate it in a variety of ways. For example, to create a profile to connect to the WLAN you would enter:

```
C:> netsh wlan add profile filename = "c:\netgear\
wlan\wireless network connection-netgear-densbc.xml"
```

As a result of this command you will receive the display "profile netgear-densbc is added on interface wireless network connection," assuming you entered the path and file name correctly. Note that you could choose to add this profile only for a certain wireless interface or for certain users. Since we just demonstrated the use of the Add subcommand, let's discuss it in a bit more detail.

6.13.1.1 The Add Subcommand   There are two commands available in this context: Add Filter and Add Profile. The Add Filter subcommand results in the addition of a wireless network, by its service set identifier (SSID), to the wireless allowed or blocked list. The format or syntax of this command is:

```
netsh add filter permission = {allow|block|denyall}
ssid = WirelessNetworkNamenetworktype =
{infrastructure|adhoc}
```

Permission specifies the permission type of the filter.
Ssid represents the SSID of the wireless network.
Networktype represents the wireless network type, infrastructure or ad hoc.

Note that the SSID parameter is required if permission is allowed or blocked. If permission is deny all, then you should not specify the SSID parameter. To illustrate an example of the use of the Add Filter subcommand, consider the following. Also note that when the filter is applied successfully you receive a message to that effect.

```
C:\Windows\system32>netsh wlan add filter permission =
block ssid = "1909 SBC" networktype = infrastructure
The filter is added on the system successfully.
C:\Windows\system32>
```

The next Add subcommand is Add Profile. This command adds a WLAN profile to the specified interface on the computer. The format or syntax of this command is:

```
add profile filename = pathandfilename[[interface =]
interfacename] [[user =]{all|current}]
```

Filename is required and is used to specify both the path to and name of the XML file containing the profile data.

Interface is optional and when used specifies the name of the wireless interface on which to add the profile. Note that interfacename represents the name of the wireless interface either listed in network connections or obtained by the use of the netsh wlan Show Interfaces command. If the interface parameter is specified the profile will be added to the specified interface. When specified the profile is added to the specified interface. You can also use the wildcard characters * and ? to replace one or more letters of the interface name.

User is optional and when used specifies whether the profile is applied only to the current user or to all users. If not specified, it applies the profile to all users.

To illustrate the use of the Add Profile subcommand let's assume you want to use the file profile1.xml located on the C drive in the directory wlandoc. To do so you would enter the following command:

```
add profile filename = C:\\wlandoc\profile1.xml inter-
face = "Wireless Network Connection"
```

6.13.1.2 The Connect Subcommand Once you have a profile you can use a variety of netsh wlan subcommands, such as Add, Connect, and Delete. As a result of the use of the Connect subcommand your computer will connect to a wireless network by using the specified parameter.

The format or syntax of this command is:

```
connect [[ssid =]wirelessnetworkname] name = profile-
nameinterface = interfacename
```

Ssid, which is optional, is used to specify the SSID of the wireless network.

Name, which is required, is used to specify the name of the wireless profile to use for the connection attempt. Note that the profilename is the name of the wireless profile that is listed in Manage Wireless Networks, or as shown by the netsh wlan Show Profile command.

Interface, which is required, specifies the wireless interface to use for the connection attempt. Note that the interfacename represents the name of the wireless interface that is listed in Network Connections, or displayed by the netsh wlan Show Interfaces command.

It's important to note that if only one SSID is specified in the profile, then the specified SSID is used to connect. Thus under this situation the SSID parameter is not required. If the profile specifies multiple SSIDs, the SSID parameter is then required. In addition, the interface parameter is required only if there is more than one wireless interface on the computer and wildcards are not supported to specify the interface name.

The use of the Connect subcommand will result initially in a disconnect if the specified interface is already connected to a wireless network. Then the command will attempt to connect to the new network. Note that if the command attempts to connect to a network to which the interface is already connected, this command returns a message that the connection was successful, and does not change the state of the wireless adapter.

To illustrate the use of the Connect subcommand consider the following two examples.

```
netsh wlan connect name = Profile1 ssid = SSID1
netsh wlan connect name = Profile2 ssid = SSID2 inter-
face = "Wireless Network Connection"
```

Here the format or syntax of the Connect subcommand is:

```
netsh wlan connect [name =]<string> [[ssid =]<string>]
[[interface =]<string>]
```

Ssid represents the SSID of the wireless network.

Name represents the name of the profile to be used in the connection attempt.

Interface represents the name of the interface from which connection is attempted.

Once you connect to the network the use of the Show Interfaces command should result in a display similar to the following:

```
C:\>netsh wlan show interfaces
There is 1 interface on the system:
Name : Wireless Network Connection
Description : 802.11n Wireless LAN Card
GUID : 51ba5c3e-0fcc-4efb-8dd6-6c07614865b3
Physical address : 00:16:44:d7:4a:be
State : connected
SSID : NETGEAR-DENSBC
BSSID : 00:22:3f:09:75:db
Network type : Infrastructure
Radio type : 802.11g
Authentication : Open
Cipher : None
Connection mode : Discovery (unsecured)
Channel : 1
Receive rate (Mbps) : 150
Transmit rate (Mbps) : 150
Signal : 90%
Hosted network status : Not started
```

6.13.1.3 The Delete Subcommand   There are two Delete subcommands supported by the netsh wlan command: Delete Filter, which is used to remove a wireless network from an allowed or blocked wireless list, and Delete Profile, which is used to remove a WLAN profile from one or more interfaces. The format or syntax of each command is:

```
delete filter permission = {allow|block|denyall} ssid
= WirelessNetworkNamenetworktype =
{infrastructure|adhoc}]
```

Permission is required and specifies the permission type of the filter.

SSID is required and specifies the SSID of the wireless network.

Networktype is required and specifies whether the wireless network type is ad hoc or infrastructure.

Note that the SSID parameter is required, unless the value of the permission parameter is set to deny all, which avoids the setting of the SSID. A few examples of the use of the Deny Filter subcommand follow:

```
netsh wlan delete filter permission = allow ssid =
"netgear-densbc" networktype = infrastructure
netsh wlan delete filter permission = block ssid =
"netgear-densbc" networktype = adhoc
netsh wlan delete filter permission = denyall network-
type = infrastructure
```

Now let's discuss the second version of the Delete subcommand. As previously noted, the Delete Profile subcommand is used to remove a WLAN profile from one or multiple interfaces. The format or syntax of this command is:

```
delete profile name = profilename [[interface
=]interfacename]
```

Name is required and specifies the name of the wireless profile to delete.

Profilename is the name of the wireless profile.

Interface is optional and specifies the name of the interface.

InterfaceName is the name of the wireless interface on which to delete a profile and is optional.

Note that when you delete a profile the result will be the display of a message informing you of the profile that was deleted. For example, entering

```
netsh wlan delete profile name = "netgear-densbc"
```

would delete the profile of netgear-denpc. You can verify that the profile was removed by entering the command netsh wlan Show Profile. Similar to other subcommands, you can use wildcards such as the asterisk (*) and question mark (?) in the name parameter. Thus you could delete multiple profiles through their use.

6.13.1.4 The Export Profile Subcommand The Export Profile subcommand represents a powerful tool, as it allows you to save WLAN profiles as XML files at a specified location. The format or syntax of this subcommand is:

```
export profile folder = pathandfilename [[name =]
profilename] [[interface =] interfacename]
```

Folder is optional and when included specifies the path and file where the profile XML file is to be saved, and the name to use for the saved file.

Name is optional and when included specifies the name of the wireless profile to export where *profilename* is the name of the wireless profile.

Interface is optional and when included specifies the name of the wireless interface on which the profile is configured, with *interfacename* being the name of the wireless interface.

Note that the folder parameter must specify an existing folder that is accessible from the local computer via either an absolute path or relative path to the current working directory. If the name parameter is specified but the interface parameter is not, then only that profile is saved. Otherwise, all profiles on the computer with the specified name are saved. If both the interface parameter and name parameter are specified, only the specified profile for that interface is saved.

To illustrate the use of the Export Profile subcommand let's first view the profiles on our computer. To do so we would enter the netsh wlan Show Profile command as shown below.

```
C:\Users\Gil>netsh wlan show profile
Profiles on interface Wireless Network Connection:
Group policy profiles (read only)
_ _ _ _ _ _ _ _ _ _ _ _ _ _ _ _ -

<None>
User profiles
_ _ _ _ _ _ -

All User Profile : netgear-densbc
```

Note that we have one user profile named netgear-densbc. To export this profile we would enter:

```
C:\Users\Gil>netsh wlan export profile name = "net-
gear-densbc" folder = c:\netgear\wlan interface =
"Wireless Network Connection"
```

And receive the following message:

```
Interface profile "netgear-densbc" is saved in file
"c:\netgear\wlan\Wireless Network Connection-netgear-
densbc.xml" successfully.
```

Note that in addition to executing the command you will receive a display that informs you the file was saved and the location of the file. Now suppose you wanted to manipulate the profile by first deleting it. The following example shows how you would delete the profile and then use Show Profile to verify it is gone, or is it?

```
C:\Users\Gil>netsh wlan delete profile name = "net-
gear-densbc"
Profile "netgear-densbc" is deleted from interface
"Wireless Network Connection".
C:\Users\Gil>netsh wlan show profile
Profiles on interface Wireless Network Connection:
Group policy profiles (read only)
_ _ _ _ _ _ _ _ _ _ _ _ _ _ _ _ -

<None>
User profiles
_ _ _ _ _ _ -

<None>
```

While the profile is gone, it is literally not forgotten, as we exported it just a few minutes ago. Thus if we errored in deleting the profile we can add it back. Before deleting a profile it makes sense to save it through the use of the Export Profile subcommand.

6.13.1.5 Other Netsh Wlan Functions   In concluding our examination of netsh and the wlan subcommand we discuss some of the uses of the command netsh wlan besides just adding or deleting profiles and connecting or disconnecting to wireless networks. Those uses include dumping wireless settings, displaying and blocking networks, displaying and setting the autoconfiguration status, setting the order in which profiles are used on an interface, automatically connecting to a wireless network, and as a marketing person would say, much more. Thus let's turn our attention to a few of these techniques.

6.13.1.5.1 Dumping Wireless Settings   One of the reasons to use the netsh wlan Dump command is to create a script file that can be used to reconfigure your wireless network adapter. To do so you should direct the dump to a text file, as shown in the following example:

```
C:\>netsh wlan dump>mywlan.txt
```

To view the previously dumped file you could enter the command:

```
C:\>type mylan.txt
```

Through the use of the WLAN Dump subcommand you can in effect export your adapter settings, examine those settings, and decide if you wish to use those settings as a script.

6.13.1.5.2 Displaying and Blocking Networks   Wireless networks can be hidden or blocked. Suppose you want blocked networks to be shown in the list of available networks but listed as blocked. To hide blocked networks from the list of available networks you would enter the following command:

```
netsh wlan set blockednetworks display = hide
```

Now, if you follow that command with "netsh wlan show blocked-networks," this action would result in a display of blocked networks. This author might add that it is worthwhile for readers to experiment with the use of the netsh wlan Show All command, to include displaying the names of profiles as well as data about networks currently visible.

6.13.1.5.3 Display and Set Autoconfiguration The enabling of auto-configuration on a wireless interface means that the interface will automatically connect with its wireless profile. By default its setting should be enabled. You can check your settings with the command netsh wlan show autoconfig. You can change your autoconfiguration settings with the command netsh wlan set autoconfig enabled = {yes|no} interface = "Wireless Network Adaptor," where you would enter yes to set autoconfiguration and no to disable its use. Note that when set to no this action will result in the computer not connecting to any wireless network.

6.13.1.5.4 Show and Set the Profile Order If there are multiple profiles previously developed then the profile order is used. With the show and set profile commands you can view or change this profile order from the command line. For example, entering netsh wlan show profile will result in the display of profiles previously developed. Then you could enter netsh wlan set profileorder to set the profile order you desire.

6.13.1.5.5 Automatically Connecting to a WLAN The use of the Autoconfiguration subcommand on a wireless interface means that the interface will automatically connect with its wireless profile. You can check your settings with the command netsh wlan show autoconfig. If necessary, you can change your autoconfiguration settings with the command netsh wlan set autoconfig enabled = {yes|no} interface = "Wireless Network Adaptor".

6.13.1.5.6 Execute the Netsh Command with a Script Netsh can run either interactively or through the execution of a script file. To execute netsh with a script file you would use the following netsh command:

```
netsh -f <scriptfile>
```

Scriptfile indicates the path to and name of the scriptfile.

Note that at the beginning of Figure 6.15, when we listed the initial netsh Help screen, there were a series of parameters that could be used with the command, such as -a, -c, -f, and -r. Although each parameter can be important depending upon user requirements, we will conclude our examination of the netsh command by noting how, if you know the remote machine name, IP address, and applicable permission by knowing the administrator password, you can perform various netsh commands against a remote device.

6.13.1.5.7 Enabling Remote Machine Access   As shown at the top portion of Figure 6.15, when you enter netsh/? note that you can enter the name, IP address, and password for a remote machine. Once the password is correctly entered you can then execute netsh commands against the remote machine. The parameters used include -r for the machine, -u for the username, and -p for the password. For example,

```
netsh -r Sales -u robert-s\administrator -p MyPassword
interface ip show config
```

In the preceding example we supplied the remote machine name (Sales), the remote user name (robert-s), and password (MyPassword), which allows us to perform this command (interface ip show config) over the network. Note that you can perform any of the netsh commands over the network as long as the remote machine supports that command since different versions of the Windows operating systems may support different variations of commands.

7

NETWORK MONITORING WITH WIRESHARK AND WINDUMP

In this chapter we focus on the use of two network monitoring programs. Each program provides users with a comprehensive tool to obtain insight into what is occurring on a network. The first tool we examine is the program Wireshark. We then turn our attention to the program WinDump.

7.1 Wireshark

Wireshark can be downloaded for Windows-based computers at the uniform resource locater (URL) address of www.wireshark.org/download. This program includes a significant amount of valuable features, to include the ability to inspect hundreds of protocols, capture data on the fly as well as perform an offline analysis, use a variety of filters to reduce data to your field of interest, perform an analysis of Voice over IP (VoIP), and read and write a variety of file formats, ranging from Microsoft's Network Monitor to Cisco IDS to Network General's Sniffer and Sniffer Pro to Network Instruments Observer. Through the use of this program you can even capture compressed files, and it also supports Novell's LANalyzer. You can output data to extensive markup language (XML), PostScript, CSV, or as a standard text file. If you go to the home page of Wireshark, move your cursor over the term *Wireshark* and select About from the drop-down menu. This action will result in a display of program features followed by the name of the original author and his email address, and a comprehensive list of contributors and their email addresses.

7.1.1 Program Evolution

The origin of Wireshark dates to the 1990s. This is when Gerald Combs was working for a small ISP. At that time commercial protocol analysis products were priced between $1500 and $2000 and did not operate on Solaris or Linux operating systems, which were then the ISPs' primary computer platforms. Due to this Mr. Combs commenced writing code for a protocol analyzer that became known as Ethereal. During 2006 Mr. Combs accepted a job with CACE Technologies. Since he held the copyright on a majority of Ethereal's source code, while the rest was redistributable under the GNU general public license (GPL), he used the contents of the Ethereal Subversion repository as the basis for the Wireshark repository. Because he did not own the Ethereal trademark, he changed the name of the product to Wireshark. In 2010 Riverbed Technology purchased CACE and became the primary sponsor of Wireshark. Today all Ethereal development has ceased and Wireshark now has over 500 contributors listed on its website.

7.1.2 Obtaining the Program

Figure 7.1 shows the home screen of Wireshark.org in late February 2012. Note that you need to go to www.wireshark.org (not .com) to access the correct location. Also note that the top portion of the screen is subdivided into three key areas: a download section, a learning section, and an area to obtain an enhanced version of the program. Under the top portion of the screen is a series of areas where you can

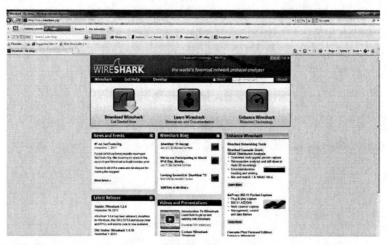

Figure 7.1   The Wireshark home screen at www.wireshark.org.

view news and events, Wireshark blog data, and obtain information about other products.

The use of this program requires one to first download it. If you click on the Download Wireshark icon a screen is displayed that indicates a series of stable releases of the program for Windows 32-bit and 64-bit machines as well as a version for Windows mobile and versions for various Apple operating systems, with the correct installer for your computer highlighted. For most of you this will reduce your effort to simply clicking on an entry. You can also select an older release or decide to download documentation that you can read online or save as Windows HTML or in a PDF or even in a PDF A4 format. Assuming you are downloading the selected file a dialog box with options to run or save the file or cancel the operation will be displayed. This author selected the Run option, which resulted in the downloading of a 21.7 Mbyte file to a temporary folder, after which a setup wizard walked this author through a licensing agreement, and the selection of such components as Wireshark, TShark, Plugins/Extensions, Tools, and a User's Guide occurred. After this selection process the wizard displayed such options as selecting a Start Menu and desktop icon that were accepted by this author, resulting in the wizard displaying the space requirements for a destination folder and the space available on the drive. Continuing, the wizard extracted the files necessary to run the program, to include WinPcap version 4.1.2.

WinPcap represents the Windows version of the libpcap library and includes a driver that supports capturing packets. Since Wireshark uses this library to capture network data on Windows, it is critical that it is installed and operating correctly. While this author did not encounter any problem with WinPcap, according to the Wireshark documentation you can encounter problems with different versions of Windows and the documentation suggests various workarounds. In addition, you will require administrator privileges to capture live data using the WinPcap driver, which is called NPF and loaded automatically by the Wireshark program.

Assuming you downloaded the applicable Windows version of Wireshark, you may not be able to use the program to capture packets until you start Wireshark with applicable privileges. As mentioned in the comprehensive documentation that accompanies the program, there are three ways to start Wireshark with the privilege to capture.

For each method the documentation describes one or more advantages and disadvantages associated with the method. This author ran the command line as administrator as follows:

```
sc config npf start = auto
```

This resulted in the display of the following message, which indicated that the command was executed:

```
[SC] ChangeServiceConfig SUCCESS
```

Note that the equal sign must follow "start" and you must leave a space between the equal sign and "auto."

7.1.3 Program Overview

Figure 7.2 illustrates the Wireshark Network Analyzer initial screen, which is subdivided into four sections: Capture, Files, Online, and Capture Help. In the Capture section the interfaces on your computer are listed. You can use the pull-down Capture menu to select a capture option from Interfaces, Options, Start, Stop, Restart, and Capture Filters. Since you first need to select an interface, some options, such as the Options and Start options, cannot be selected and appear grayed out on your screen. In addition to selecting an applicable interface for

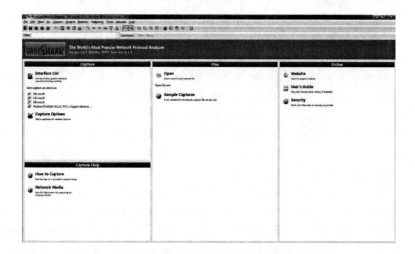

Figure 7.2   The initial Wireshark screen is divided into five main sections.

the capture, another important option is Capture Filters. This results from the fact that by incorporating certain filters, you can narrow the captured packets to your area of interest, such as packets flowing to a particular IP or Ethernet address, eliminating broadcast and multicast addresses, selecting IP, TCP, or UDP traffic or another filter, as we note below.

A second reason for incorporating filtering results from the fact that this author is using a high-speed Gigabit Ethernet network interface card (NIC), which in turn is connected to a high-speed cable modem. Thus the sheer volume of packets flowing between his computer and the Internet would require the use of a very large buffer area that would soon overflow. In fact, even if data are recorded to a file you could conceivably run out of available disk storage space. Thus filtering not only allows you to focus your attention upon a problem area, but in addition provides you with a mechanism to minimize the quantity of data that you need to possibly store as well as investigate.

The second main area in the Wireshark screen, Files, shown in Figure 7.2, allows you to open a previously saved file or select sample captured files. In fact, after you save two or more files they will be listed, so that a simple click will allow you to view a previously captured series of packets. As an alternative you could go to the Files menu and select the Open option.

The third section in the main area of the Wireshark screen, shown in Figure 7.2, is labeled Online. Selecting this option provides you with a link to view Wireshark's website, examine the user guide to the program, or work with the program as securely as possible.

The fourth area of the main display, Capture Help, provides you with the ability to learn how to set up the Capture facility, which we will perform below and obtain information about capturing data on different types of media, such as a wireless local area network (LAN) and Ethernet.

Of the five sections shown in Figure 7.2, the most important obviously is Capture. From this section you could select an interface that would then immediately initiate packet capturing on that interface. If you want you could select Stop from the Capture drop-down menu and then select an applicable filter to employ. As an alternative you could select Capture Options to run a capture with a series of options you select, such as the interface that will be used for packet capturing, to include specifying a local or remote interface, with the latter requiring you to enter the host name and port as well as authentication information, buffer size in Mbytes, capture filters, and other data. Because Capture Options is probably best used after you have an appreciation of the general operation of the program, we will examine its use below.

7.1.4 The Capture Screen

Figure 7.3 illustrates the Capture screen after 96 packets were captured. As we examine the two dialog boxes shown superimposed on the Capture screen we will learn a little about the capabilities of Wireshark.

7.1.4.1 Packet Colors   In examining Figure 7.3 note that the interface selected is shown at the upper left portion of the display. Also note that the packets are color coded, which in this book will be shown in shades of gray. If you are working with Wireshark note that there are four colors used with the display of packets: blue, red, green, and light blue. A packet colored blue represents the frame you are currently viewing and which the program decodes. In Figure 7.3 we examine the first frame, Frame 1, which is colored blue. If you move the cursor down to Frame 2, it would then be colored in blue and be decoded.

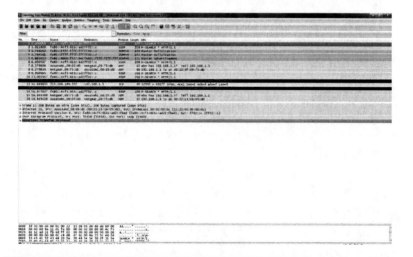

Figure 7.3   Examining a previously captured sequence of packets.

The next color used is green, which indicates packets flowing to your computer. The third color used is red, which indicates packets originated by the source. The fourth color, light blue, is used to denote the capture of wireless packets.

Returning to Figure 7.3, note that the file name saved from a previous capture is displayed in the upper left corner of the screen. This author used the program's Save As capability from the File menu so that he could take a capture and use different computers with the same capture file when authoring this book.

7.1.4.2 Examining a Packet To illustrate how you can use Wireshark to probe deeper into activity occurring, let's examine the second packet that was captured. If you double-click on Frame 2 this action (double-clicking on packet 2) will result in the display of a pop-up box, as illustrated in Figure 7.4. At the same time the pop-up box is displayed the second frame shown in Figure 7.3 will be highlighted in a white background, which informs you of the frame you are working with. In examining Figure 7.4 note the frame number is placed in the upper left corner. This is followed by the time of occurrence (2.691024) in seconds since capturing commenced; the source address (192.168.1.3); the destination address (75.126.14.205); the fact that the packet transported TCP data that were 66 bytes in length and data about the source port (52535); the destination port shown as HTTP, which is port 80; the window size (8192 bytes); the maximum segment size (MSS), the value of which is shown as 1460; the window scale (WS), the value of which is shown as 4; and if TCP slack is permitted. To determine if TCP slack is permitted requires you to either double-click on the top bar or select the restore icon, with either

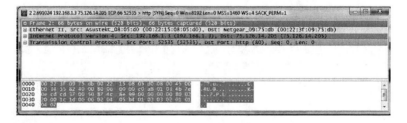

Figure 7.4 Selecting a frame results in a pop-up display that provides detailed information about what data are being transported.

action resulting in the display of the frame in a full screen, which then allows you to note that TCP slack is permitted or enabled.

Although we are working at the frame level and are examining a captured Ethernet frame, we need to remember that the frame flows at the data link layer, which is layer 2 in the protocol stack. The Ethernet frame is transporting IP, which in turn, in this case, is transporting TCP. Thus we can begin our examination at the frame level and work our way up the protocol stack as the Ethernet frame we captured transported an IP packet, which in turn was transporting a TCP datagram.

Since we previously mentioned how you can open the view of a frame for further examination, let's do so. In Figure 7.4 we were working with Frame 2, so let's either double-click on the top bar of the pop-up or select the restore icon in the upper right corner of the display. Either action will result in a display similar to the one shown in Figure 7.5.

The reason this author said similar is due to the fact that he clicked on a series of icons to expand the display. Thus the small box on the left of Figure 7.5 that has a minus sign was clicked on to display its contents in place of viewing a summary line. If you examine the display shown in Figure 7.5 for Frame 2 you will note that Wireshark displays the contents of the frame in what can be considered a step-up ISO Reference Model, with information about the frame at layer 2

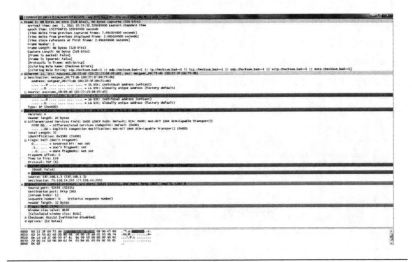

Figure 7.5 Expanding the decoding capability of Wireshark.

first displayed, followed by IP information at layer 3, which in turn is followed by TCP information transported at layer 4 in the Reference Model. At the top of Figure 7.5 you will find information concerning when the frame was captured, the capture length, and other information, such as how coloring rules are used to indicate certain situations. Under the Ethernet II heading, which identifies the type of frame that was captured, we can note that the frame being examined was sent from an Asustekc adapter with a defined layer 2 address to a Netgear wireless router, which was connected to the computer used by this author. Thus the Ethernet II section in the display provides you with information about the source (scr) and destination (dst) devices, to include their layer 2 addresses.

Moving up the protocol stack to layer 3, we can examine the IP header transported by the Ethernet II frame. In doing so we note that IPv4 was being transported, the source IPv4 address was 192.168.1.3, and the destination IPv4 address was 75.126.14.205. From the IPv4 information we note that the IP header was 20 bytes in length, which represents a standard length, the Differentiated Services field was not used, only the Don't Fragment field bit was set in the Flags field, and IP transported protocol 6, which is TCP.

Once again we can move up the protocol stack by looking lower into Figure 7.5. When we do so we arrive at TCP information. In examining the initial TCP data we see the source and destination ports used. In this example the source port was 52325 while the destination port was 80. From our knowledge of TCP ports we know that the source port is either set to zero or obtained randomly, so we focus our attention on the destination port. That port number is 80, which represents HTTP or web service, so TCP is flowing to the Netgear wireless router at the IP address we previously mentioned. We can also note that none of the flags in the header are set, the sequence number is zero, and the window size is 8192 bytes. Thus we can obtain a significant amount of information concerning the flow of data via packet capturing from the automatic decoding of captured frames through the use of Wireshark.

Now that we have a basic appreciation for the manner by which we can capture, save, and open previously saved files, let's examine some of the additional capabilities of this program.

7.1.4.3 File Menu Options We can save a capture as a file by clicking on the Open Recent file name in the Files section in the main menu or by selecting an interface in the Capture section in the main menu or when you're in the program mode of operation by selecting Open from the File menu. In addition to using Open from the File menu, that menu includes several additional options, including Open Recent, which points to recently used files; Merge, which allows you to merge a previous capture file with the capture you are working with; and Import, which supports input from a text file. In addition to those options you can select a Save or Save As option to save a capture file as well as File Set, Export, Close, and Quit. While Close closes the current capture and Quit exits the program, the File Set and Export options deserve a bit of explanation.

While capturing data the capturing engine used by the program acquires packets from the network card and keeps the data in a small buffer. Such data are then read by Wireshark and can be saved to one or more user-specified capture files. Since working with large files can be quite slow, especially if your computer has a single core and slow disk drives, you might consider using one of the programs Multiple Files options to spread captured packets over a series of smaller files that can be easier to work with. When doing so the series of captured files is referred to as a file set. Thus selecting File Set from the File menu allows you to view through the List option files in the file set as well as work with the next or previous file by selecting one of those options. Concerning the Export option, its selection allows you to save the capture in a variety of formats as well as to select packet bytes, SSL session keys, or objects, with the latter including the ability to export certain types of packets captured, such as HTTP.

7.1.5 Working with Filters

Let's return our attention to Figure 7.3 Note that when you select the Capture menu the last entry in that drop-down menu is Capture Filters. The reason filters can be important results from the fact when attempting to resolve a problem you will want to narrow your focus to one or more specific areas that enable your efforts to be more focused than attempting to wade through literally hundreds to thousands of packets. Through the use of Wireshark you can define filters and then assign them labels for later use. This action can make you more productive, as it will save you time in remembering and retyping some of the more complex filters you may desire to develop and use.

Selecting Capture Filters or Display Filters from the Analyze menu results in the display of a dialog box similar to the one shown in Figure 7.6. In examining the Wireshark Capture Filter dialog box shown in Figure 7.6, note that under the Edit column located in the left portion of the box are buttons labeled New and Delete. Selecting New results in the addition of a new filter to the list of filters. The currently entered values from Filter Name and Filter String will be used. If any of these fields are empty, they will be set to "new." Selecting Delete results in clearing of the filter. It will be grayed out if no filter is selected.

Under the Capture Filter column are the filters we can use. Once you select a filter it will be displayed in the Filter Name bar at the bottom of the dialog box. You can change the name of the filter once it is selected. The filter name is only used in this dialog to identify the filter for convenience and is not be used elsewhere by the program. Thus you can add multiple filters with the same name; however, this is not very useful. The last entry at the bottom of Figure 7.6 is labeled Filter String. You can change the filter string of the currently selected filter in this bar. To the right of the Filter String bar is a button labeled

Figure 7.6   The Wireshark Capture Filters dialog box is similar to the Define Filters box accessed from the Analyze menu.

Expression…. Clicking on this button results in the display of a new dialog box, which enables you to add relationships and values to filters, a situation we examine below.

At the bottom of Figure 7.6 are a series of buttons that will vary based on the manner by which the Display Filters box was invoked—via the Capture menu or from the Display Filters entry in the Analyze menu. If you selected Capture Filter you would see three buttons labeled Help, Ok, and Cancel, while selecting Display Filters from the Analyze menu would result in a dialog box with that name that would have four buttons at the bottom of the box labeled Help, Ok, Apply, and Cancel, respectively. Clicking on the Help button results in the display of an online help facility in the form of a user's guide, which allows you to view specific content or search for a specific topic. Clicking on Ok results in the selected filter being applied to the current display and closes the dialog. Moving to the right, the button labeled Apply, as its name implies, applies the selected filter to the current display and keeps the dialog open. Although the version of Wireshark used by this author did not permit the use of a button labeled Save to save filters, other versions of the program refer to the use of a Save button to permanently save your filters. Thus if your version of Wireshark does not contain a Save button your filters will be lost when Wireshark closes.

Figure 7.7 illustrates the result of clicking on the button labeled Expression… when you first select the Display Filter option from the Analyze menu. The left portion of Figure 7.7 illustrates the resulting display obtained by selecting Display Filters, while the right

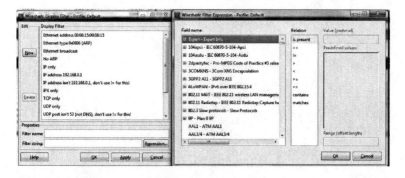

Figure 7.7   Viewing the Filter Expression dialog box after selecting the button labeled Expression on the Display Filter dialog box.

dialog box, labeled Filter Expression, resulted from clicking on the Expression… button in the left box.

When you select Expression… the resulting display of the Filter Expression dialog box will show a tree list of field names that are organized alphabetically by protocol, a field for selecting relationships, and text blocks for entering a value, accepting or modifying a predefined value associated with some protocols, or entering a range via an offset. Let's examine each of the columns shown in the dialog box labeled Filter Expression.

7.1.5.1 Filter Expressions   The first column in the Filter Expressions dialog box, labeled Field Name, provides you with the ability to select a protocol field from the protocol field tree. Every protocol with filterable fields is listed at the top level. Note that you can also search for a particular protocol entry by entering the first few letters of the protocol name. By clicking on the + symbol next to a protocol name you can get a list of the field names available for filtering for that particular protocol. The second column in the dialog box, Relation, is used to select a relation from a list of available relations. At the top of the column are the words "is present," which represents a unary relation that is true if the selected field is present in a packet. All of the other relations in the column represent binary relations, which require a value to be entered in the box with that name, which is in a column to the right of the Relation column. Depending upon the protocol selected, some protocol fields will have predefined values, which are then displayed in the box on the right of Figure 7.7 with that label. If one or more predefined values are defined you can select one of them in the box labeled Predefined Values. The third box in the right column in Figure 7.7 is Range. You can add a range for the filter by entering an offset length into this box. At the bottom of the Filter Expression dialog box are buttons labeled Ok and Cancel. You would click on the first button once you have built a satisfactory expression and a filter string will be created. Clicking on the button labeled Cancel results in closing of the dialog box without any effect occurring from previous entries.

In working with filters this author discovered what may appear as an initial quirk to some new users of this packets capture tool. For example, let's assume you wished to filter your packets to view

TCP on port 80, which is HTTP traffic. If you selected TCP from the Display Filter dialog box and then clicked on the button labeled Expression and opened the TCP entry in the Filter Expression dialog box, selecting the equal relation and entering a value of 80, you would receive an error message when you clicked on the button labeled Ok. This is because you were attempting to set a filter of TCP equal to port 80, a bit redundant and not acceptable when using Wireshark. Instead, you would use the Filter Expression dialog box, scroll down until you view TCP in the Field Name column, open the protocol by expanding the + sign, selecting the destination port entry, and entering a value of 80 in the value box for the port value. Next, clicking on the button labeled Ok would result in the newly created filter being displayed in the box labeled Filter in the packet capture display previously illustrated in Figure 7.3 prior to the creation of a filter.

Since Ethernet represented the layer 2 type of data flowing to this author's computer, those entries are placed as possible filters we can employ. If you are using a different computer and different layer 2 protocol, the layer 2 address and protocol would then be listed at the beginning of the Capture Filters column. Continuing our examination of the filters listed in Figure 7.6, the next possibility is to select No Broadcast and No Multicast. Thus it's possible to filter out broadcast and multicast frames if that is not a problem area. Continuing down the list, the No ARP entry allows you to filter Address Resolution Protocol packets. The next filter allows you to filter on IP only, while the next entry allows you to filter on the IP address indicated, which in this situation represents the gateway used by this author's computer. Note that to the right of the box labeled Filter are three buttons: Expression, Clear, and Apply. Clicking on the Expression button results in the display of the Filter Expression dialog box previously illustrated in the right portion of Figure 7.7. Clicking on the Clear button cancels and clears the application of the filter, resulting in the display of the original packet capture. Perhaps the most important button is the one labeled Apply because once you create a filter you need to apply it to the packet capture. Thus let's apply the filter we previously discussed to our packet capture.

7.1.5.2 Applying a Filter   In Figure 7.8 this author is illustrating both the creation of a filter and its application after the filter was applied.

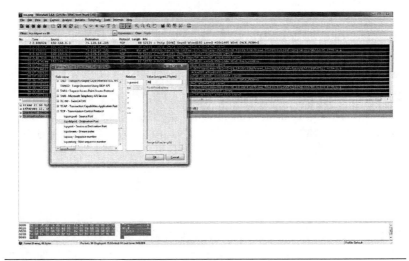

Figure 7.8 Creating a filter based upon TCP destination port 80.

Thus from a reality point of view the dialog box in the foreground, labeled Filter Expression, was actually created prior to clicking on the button labeled Apply. Concerning the dialog box, we scrolled down through its Field Name entries until we reached TCP. To the left of the TCP entry was a plus sign, indicating that that entry could be exploded to show additional items. Thus we clicked on the plus sign, which resulted in the plus sign turning into a minus sign and the entries under TCP being displayed. Those entries included the TCP source port and the TCP destination port, as well as several other fields from which we could select. In this simple situation we decided that we wanted to select the TCP destination port whose value equaled 80. Thus we first selected TCP Destination Port and then selected the Relation field value of double equal sign (= =), and entered a value of 80 into the value box. If you carefully examine Figure 7.8 you can note that in the Filter Expression dialog box both one Field Name and one Relation are colored in very light gray to indicate that they were selected.

Once you are satisfied with your filter you would click on the button labeled Ok, which would result in the filter being listed in the box labeled Filter. Since we previously created the TCP filter it is already listed in the box as tcp.dstport = =80. In addition, we clicked on the button labeled Apply, which explains why the button is grayed out and cannot be clicked upon. If you examine the packets now shown in the Capture screen, shown in the background of Figure 7.8, you will note that in the protocol field they are all TCP or HTTP, with the latter representing TCP on destination port 80. If you turn your attention to the bottom of Figure 7.8 you will note that we reduced the 96 packets previously captured to 25 packets, which are marked per our recently created filter. Thus out of the 96 packets captured a total of 25 packets, or a drop below 25%, represented TCP datagrams sent to destination port 80.

7.1.6 Statistics

Another valuable feature of Wireshark is its statistics capability. In fact, Statistics has its own drop-down menu in the program that can be easily accessed and provides you with over 20 methods by which data can be analyzed. That menu entry is the seventh from the left, following the Capture and Analyze drop-down menus. Through the use of the Statistics drop-down menu you can perform a variety of functions, ranging from examining the response time to determining if such functions as VoIP are not performing correctly due to excessive delays at your end of a connection to investigating data flow on wireless networks. In addition, you can use the Statistics menu to obtain numerous types of information about a previously captured file, ranging from packet counts to a breakdown about the protocols captured.

Figure 7.9 illustrates the contents of the drop-down Statistics menu, to include selecting one of several entries that will result in the display of a second list of items to select from. In Figure 7.9 the Conversation List entry is shown selected, which results in the display of a list of conversations for which statistics will be displayed, ranging from Ethernet to IPv4 and IPv6 and even wireless LAN (WLAN) conversations.

7.1.6.1 Summary Data

The first entry in the Statistics menu, labeled Summary, provides a summary of information about the captured file: the file name, its length, format, and time of capture for the first and last packet in the file, and information concerning the number of packets in the file. In addition, the time between the first and last packet and statistics concerning the packet flow in packets per second,

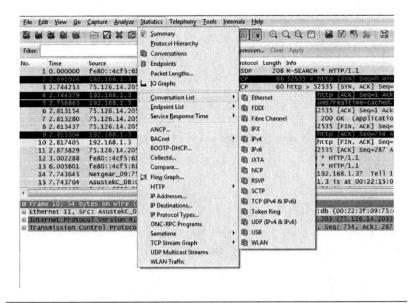

Figure 7.9 Viewing the Statistics menu to include an expansion of the conversation list.

average packet size in bytes, total bytes, average bytes per second, and average million bits per second (Mbits/s) are computed and displayed.

7.1.6.2 Protocol Hierarchy The second entry in the Statistics menu is labeled Protocol Hierarchy. Selecting this entry results in the display of data in a hierarchical manner, from the frame level up the protocol stack to actual data transported in terms of a percent of packets, total packets, percent of bytes, total bytes, Mbits/s, end packets, end bytes, and end Mbps. Thus for each row entry for a protocol there are eight columns of information.

7.1.6.3 Conversations The third entry in the Statistics menu is labeled Conversations. Selection of this entry results in the display of statistics of the captured conversations where a network conversation represents the traffic between two specific endpoints. For example, an IP conversation is all the traffic between two IP addresses. Other common conversations may include information about broadcast and multicast traffic. The resulting display consists of a series of tabs across the top of the dialog box display, with each tab indicating a supported protocol. If a specific protocol is not supported, the data in the capture tab label will be grayed out. If your traffic was being monitored on an Ethernet network that would be indicated on a separate row, after which, by default, a pair of addresses are in the first two columns in a following row, labeled Address A and Address B. This would be followed by columns for traffic in bytes, the time in seconds between the start of the capture and the start of the conversation, the duration of the conversation in seconds, and the average bits per second in each direction. By clicking on a tab you can display the statistics for a protocol supported by the captured data, such as IPv4, IPv6, TCP, or UDP.

Figure 7.10 illustrates an example of the Conversations window displayed when this author selected that entry from the Statistics menu. In this example the IPv4 tab was selected and the resulting display indicated four conversations. Note that each tab that corresponds to a protocol that occurred will include a numeric count. Thus the IPv4 tab was followed by a colon (:) and a numeric value of 4 for this example. If we selected the Ethernet tab we would then see six conversations. If you are working with a live capture or a large previously captured file you can expect a delay to occur that will be related to the capability of the processor in your computer. That is, the lower the performance of the processor in your computer (assuming other activity is constant) the longer it will take to display conversation information.

One of the more interesting aspects of working with Wireshark is its well-thought-out features, some of which are literally not a big

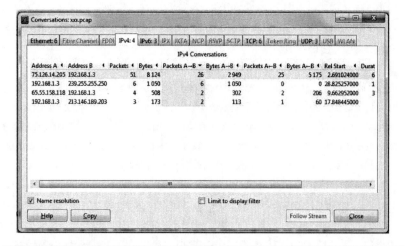

Figure 7.10 Displaying IPv4 conversations.

deal individually, but their inclusion can cumulatively result in a significant level of assistance to users. For example, clicking on an arrow can result in the reorder of rows based upon the value of a selected column. Thus if you wanted to rearrange conversations by packets you would click on the arrow that would toggle between being upward and downward to provide you with options concerning the conversations based upon packet flow. Thus if you had a large number of conversations and were interested in a certain level of activity, the ability to sort conversations by many column entries provides a good facility that may reduce the time otherwise required to obtain such data.

7.1.6.4 Endpoints Returning to the Statistics menu, the fourth entry for selection is labeled Endpoints. A network endpoint represents the logical endpoint of separate protocol traffic for a specific protocol layer, such as an Ethernet's Media Access Control (MAC) address, an IP address, or for TCP and UDP. However, when we discuss TCP and UDP an endpoint actually represents a combination of the IP address and the TCP or UDP port used, so different ports on the same IP address represent different TCP and UDP endpoints. Note that both broadcast and multicast traffic will be shown separately as additional endpoints. Both endpoints are virtual and the actual traffic is received by all (broadcast, and some when multicast) of listed unicast endpoints.

7.1.6.5 Packet Lengths The fifth entry in the Statistics menu, Packet Lengths, when selected, first displays a rectangular dialog box that enables you to specify a filter. You can either click on the Filter button and select a filter or ignore the addition of a filter. Clicking on a button labeled Create Stat will result in the display of packet lengths either as captured or based upon a filter.

7.1.6.6 IO Graphs The sixth entry in the Statistics menu provides you with the ability to view packet flow by time. That entry, IO Graphs, allows you to define up to five differently colored graphs. You can even apply a filter to a graph so that only packets associated with the filter are taken into account for the resulting graph. Similar to other graphing programs, you can specify the style of the graph, several *X*-axis and *Y*-axis intervals, as well as a scale for the *Y*-axis.

7.1.6.7 Conversation List The seventh entry in the Statistics menu is the Conversation List, whose entries were previously shown in Figure 7.9. In the version of Wireshark used by this author there were 15 possible conversations you could select. Selecting Ethernet results in the display being similar to the one shown in Figure 7.10, while selecting another entry in the Conversation List would result in the display of conversations associated with the selected protocol.

7.1.6.8 Endpoint List and Other Entries The Endpoint List, which is the eighth entry in the Statistics menu, produces the same options to select as the Conversation List shown in Figure 7.9. While many of the remaining selections available in the Statistics menu are self-explanatory, a few deserve mention as their use can be valuable in certain situations. For example, consider the Service Response Time entry. Selecting this entry results in a display of 16 protocols for which you can determine the time between a request and the corresponding response. You can even set a display filter to determine the service response time for packets meeting a predefined criterion. Another entry in the Statistics menu that deserves mention is the HTTP entry. The HTTP selection results in the ability to display HTTP in three ways. You can display a load distribution, which shows statistics based upon HTTP requests and responses from servers, by selecting Load Distribution; packets transmitted to and from servers by selecting a Packet Counter entry; or HTTP requests by HTTP hosts by clicking on a Request entry. This capability can be very important if you suspect that your server is slowing down due to either a growing workload or a denial of service attack. For either situation, this program provides you with the tool to examine packet flow that can be a valuable addition to making a rational decision concerning your organization's server operations.

Another interesting Statistics menu entry is the one labeled UDP Multicast Streams. Selecting this entry will display multicast by IP address and UDP port as well as the average and maximum bandwidth used. This information can be most useful in determining if multicast data streams are using too much of available bandwidth, either as the rationale for upgrading a network or the possible filtering of the ability of users to watch online videos of the Victoria's Secret yearly shindig. In addition, the resulting UDP Multicast Streams display will indicate the maximum buffer utilization in kilobytes, which may allow you to adjust buffer size to smooth out audio or video streams.

7.1.7 Telephony

To the right of the Statistics drop-down menu shown in Figure 7.9 is the menu labeled Telephony. Selecting this menu results in the ability to select from a series of 14 protocols, several of which enable a further selection to be made. For example, selecting ANSI, an acronym for American National Standards Institute, from the drop-down Telephony menu results in a display of an additional menu from which you can select one of three entries: A-Interface BSMAP, A-Interface DTAP, and MAP Operation. Selecting each entry will result in the display of a dialog box illustrating the messages by message name and count for each entry. The first entry, A-Interface BSMAP, where A-Interface references the interface between the mobile switching center (MSC) and the base station system (BSS) or radio subsystem, while BSMAP is an acronym for Base Station Management Protocol, is a cellular series of messages passed from a base station supporting Radio Resource Management and Facility Management procedures between the MSC and the base station (BS), or calls within the base station. BSMAP messages use 8 bits to define the message type, enabling up to 256 messages to be defined. This field uniquely defines both the function and format of the message. The second option, A-Interface DTAP, references Direct Transfer Application Part Radio Resources Management messages for the interface located between the MSC and the BS or radio subsystem. The third option, MAP Operation, represents a mobile application standard that provides a means to perform intersystem handoff, delivery of short messages, and roaming. Other capabilities of the Telephony drop-down menu include the ability to analyze Real-Time Transport Protocol (RTP), VoIP calls, and generate statistics for a number of different protocols that either transport or enhance traffic for VoIP operations.

7.1.7.1 RTP   The RTP represents a standardized packet format for transportation of audio and video over IP-based networks. RTP is used for telephony, video conferencing, and even the delivery of television over IP networks. This protocol is used in conjunction with other protocols, such as H.323 and RTSP. The RTP standard actually defines a pair of protocols, RTP and Real-Time Control Protocol (RTCP), with the former used for the transfer of multimedia and the latter for transfer control information as well as quality of service (QoS) data. RTP is originated and received on even port numbers, while the associated RTCP communication uses the next higher odd port number.

RTP permits end-to-end real-time transfer of a stream of data, to include jitter compensation as well as the detection of packets that arrive out of sequence, which can commonly occur on an IP network. Regarded as the primary standard for the transport of audio and video in an IP network, RTP is often used with a signaling protocol for setting up and tearing down a connection. Although TCP can be used with RTP, since TCP is a reliable connection that supports retransmission of packets, this would not be conducive for real-time streaming applications. Thus the vast majority of RTP implementations are constructed using the UDP protcol.

RTP was developed to support a range of multimedia formats, from H.264 to MPEG-4, MJPEG, and MPEG. In addition, the design of RTP allows new formats to be added without revising the standard. The design of this standard results in a specific application's requirements provided through RTP profiles and payload formats instead of the protocol header. Thus a complete RTP specification includes both a profile and a payload format. The profile defines the codec used to encode payload data as well as their mapping to payload format codes in the Payload Type field in the RTP header. Each RTP profile can include several payload format specifications that describe the transport of a defined type of encoded data. Examples of audio payload formats include DTMF, G.711, G.723, G.726, G.729, GSM, QCELP, and MP3, while examples of video payload formats include H.261, H.263, H.264, and MPEG-4. Note that although RTP's header includes a 16-bit sequence number that can allow packets to be reassambled in order, if a packet is lost it is left to the application to take appropriate action. In fact, most digital voice application packets contain a very short duration of a voice conversation, typically 20 ms. Thus if a packet is lost, which is a common occurrence on the Internet, as when a router cannot handle traffic, it is programmed to drop packets; dropping a packet containing a 20 ms segment of a voice conversation is normally not noticeable to the parties of the conversation. Only when traffic through one or more routers on the path between endpoints becomes saturated and a large number of packets are dropped do the conversations begin to sound awkward.

7.1.7.2 Stream Analysis Returning our attention to Wireshark's Telephony menu, the RTP option provides two additional options. You should first select RTP and then Select All Streams, which is at the top of an additional menu. Once you select Select All Streams and select a packet, you can then choose the second option, which is labeled RTP Stream Analysis, which will operate on a previously selected packet.

Figure 7.11 illustrates the resulting dialog box once you select the RTP option from the Telephony menu and then select the Select All Streams option. In addition to showing the source and destination IP addresses and ports you can view the synchronization source (SSRC) as well as data concerning the payload, packets, and packets lost, and when you scroll the window information, you can view data about delay time and jitter. Note that SSRC represents the source of a stream of RTP packets, identified by a 32-bit numeric SSRC identifier in the RTP header so that it is not dependent upon the network address. All packets from a synchronization source form part of the same timing and sequence number space, so a receiver will group packets by synchronization source for playback.

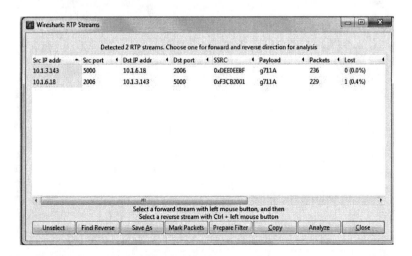

Figure 7.11 Viewing the RTP Streams dialog box.

In examining the RTP Streams display shown in Figure 7.11 note that there are eight buttons at the bottom of the window, from Unselecting (a previously selected stream) to Close, which closes the window. Those eight buttons remain displayed as you scroll through the window. This display was based upon the use of an RTP example file, which is mentioned in Section 7.1.7.3.

One of the key buttons you may wish to use in Figure 7.11 is the one labeled Analysis. Through the use of this button you can determine a wealth of information concerning a selected RTP data stream. For example, assume you selected the first data stream shown in Figure 7.11 and then clicked on the button labeled Analysis at the bottom of the window. This action would result in the analysis of the selected RTP data stream in both forward and reverse directions.

An example of the RTP stream analysis is shown in Figure 7.12. Note that a summary of computations for the maximum and mean jitter and skew are provided at the bottom of the window as well as a packet analysis for individual packets. Although in the example shown there were no lost packet or sequence errors, information about lost packet and sequence errors is provided, which can be quite helpful when attempting to analyze the quality of a connection used to transport voice. In addition to providing both individual and key summary data for the selected stream, you can click

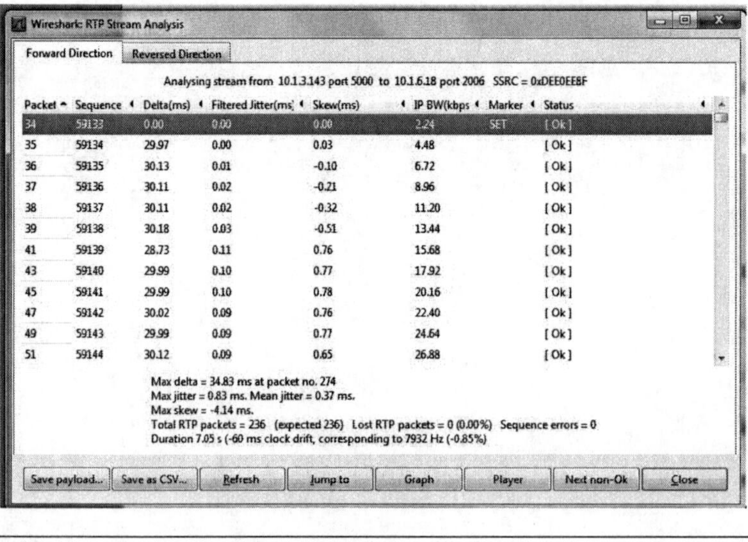

Figure 7.12 Viewing an RTP Stream Analysis display.

on any column arrow to adjust the relationship of the display. For example, clicking on the arrowhead associated with the column labeled Filtered Jitter(ms) will result in the display changing so that maximum jitter packets are displayed in a decreasing jitter amount along each row instead of the increasing jitter amount shown in Figure 7.12.

If you select the button labeled Player you can view a graph of the voice stream captured. From the resulting dialog box labeled VoIP - RTP Player you can then select the Play button to hear the conversation. According to documentation that accompanied the program this feature works only for G711 A-Law and G711 u-Law RTP streams; other codecs had not been implemented when this program was examined.

7.1.7.3 VoIP Calls One of the more interesting Telephony menu options is the VoIP Calls entry in the drop-down menu. This entry has a telephone handset to its left and you can use it to display a list of all VoIP detected calls in captured data. Although the VoIP facility detects calls by their signaling, this author found one common omission in its inability to capture calls from a well-known VoIP provider. Since this author primarily used the facilities of a VoIP provider that Wireshark could not capture in its VoIP facility, he used a capture file containing a VoIP call found at samplecaptures/rtp_example.raw. gz, which contains an example of an H323 call, including H225, H245, RTP, and RTCP packets. Note that this is an archive file that will need to be uncompressed to operate with Wireshark.

Figure 7.13 illustrates a sequence of several operations against the previously mentioned capture file containing a VoIP call. The captured sequence of packets is shown in the background of Figure 7.13. Note that the file name rtp_example.raw is shown in the upper left corner of the background window. This represents the file extracted from the archive previously mentioned. Next, the second window, titled rtp_example.raw VoIP Calls, was displayed by selecting the VoIP option from the Telephony menu. In this example one call has been detected by the previously mentioned Telephony option being invoked. For each VoIP call listed in this window, data concerning the start and stop time of the call will be displayed. In addition, the Initial Speaker represents the IP source of the packet that initiated

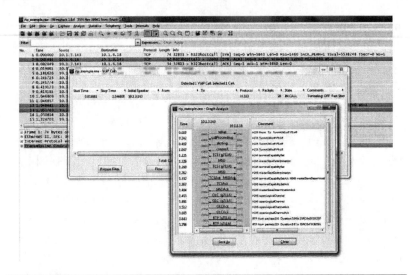

Figure 7.13 Examining a sequence of operations on a VoIP call.

the call while the From and To fields vary based upon the protocols employed. For H.323 and ISUP calls the From field will show the calling number. For SIP calls, this field will be from the From field of the INVITE. For Media Gateway Control Protocol (MGCP) calls, the EndpointID or calling number will be used, while for Unified Networks IP Stimulus Terminal ID (UNISTIM), the TerminalID will be displayed. Currently for other protocols the field will be blank. Concerning the To field, for H323 and ISUP calls, this field will show the called number. For SIP calls, this field will show the To field of the INVITE. For MGCP calls, the EndpointID or dialed number will be displayed, while for UNISTIM, the field will display the dialed number. Again, for other protocols the field at this time will be blank. Continuing our examination of the fields in the middle window shown in Figure 7.13, the field labeled Protocol informs us that the H.323 protocol is in use, while the field labeled Packets shows the number of packets involved in the call, which in our example is 28. Next, the field labeled State represents the current call state, whose value can be CALL SETUP, where the call can be in a Setup, Proceeding, Progress, or Alerting state; RINGING (currently only supported for MGCP calls); IN CALL, where the call is still connected; CANCELLED, where the call was released from the originating caller; COMPLETED if the call was connected and then released; REJECTED if the call was released prior to a connection by the destination side; or UNKNOWN if the call is in an unknown state. In the middle window in Figure 7.13 the state is shown as IN CALL, which informs us that the call is still connected at the time of the display. The last field shown in the middle window of Figure 7.13, labeled Comment, provides an additional comment and is dependent upon the protocol. For example, for the H.323 protocol this field will denote if the call uses H.245 Tunneling or Fast Start.

Once you select a call the first three buttons at the bottom of the window will become selectable. Those buttons are labeled Prepare Filter, Flow, and Player. Two additional buttons, Select All and Close, which are obscured from view in Figure 7.13, can be used at anytime. After you select a call you can examine the sequence of events or flow by time. This is shown in the third or foreground window in Figure 7.13, which occurred when the button labeled Flow was selected from the middle window.

When you focus on the foreground window shown in Figure 7.13, labeled Graph Analysis, you can view the entire call setup process. For example, at a time of 0.019 the call setup began with the use of the H.225 protocol. Next, at 0.242 H.225 responded with a call proceeding, and so on. Thus you can view what is occurring on a voice call by both time and protocol, a very important capability for diagnosing problems.

7.1.7.3.1 Filtering a Call You can prepare to filter a particular call by selecting the desired call and then pressing the button labeled Prepare Filter. This action will create a filter in the Wireshark main windows to filter the packets related to the selected call.

7.1.7.3.2 Playing VoIP Calls One most interesting capability of the VoIP capture provided by Wireshark is the ability to play captured VoIP calls. Although this feature was only available for G.711 A-Law and G.711 u-Law RTP streams at the time this book was prepared, this capability supports two of the most prevalent codecs. This may also explain why those that need security require the ability to encrypt voice calls, due to the calls' ability to be captured and easily decoded if sent in the clear.

To play an audio stream you would first select one or more calls from the VoIP list of calls displayed in the middle window shown in Figure 7.13. You would then select a button labeled Player that is obscured in the middle window, resulting in the display of a dialog box labeled RTP Player, which allows you to adjust the jitter buffer if you desire, or select a button labeled Decode. The jitter buffer, whose default is 50 ms, is emulated by Wireshark and can be used to reproduce what persons can effectively hear during the VoIP call. The selection of the Decode button will result in the display of a screen similar to the one shown in Figure 7.14, in which the available RTP streams are displayed. Selecting a stream will then allow the Play button to be selected, as shown in Figure 7.14. Then you can click on that button to hear the captured call.

In Figure 7.14 the stream from IP address 10.1.6.18.2006 to 10.1.3.145 at port 5000 is shown selected. Pressing the button labeled Play plays the RTP stream from within Wireshark. As the stream is played a progress bar in the display indicates the position in the stream. The progress bar is also synchronized among all RTP streams that are played. Note that one packet is shown as dropped by the jitter buffer, while a second packet is shown as being out of sequence.

Although the ability to listen to a conversation can be an effective tool in diagnosing problems, it can also represent a potential security problem. That is, since you can capture conversations, to include data about the originating and destination IP addresses, it doesn't require

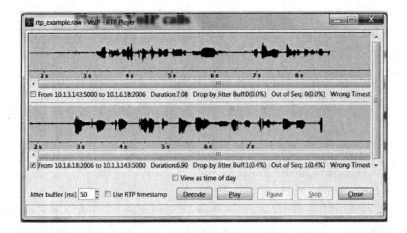

Figure 7.14   Preparing to play a captured VoIP conversation.

much effort to determine the IP address of the CEO or company trea-surer and selectively search a list of captured calls to determine whom they talked with and what they said. Thus this feature of Wireshark needs to be carefully used.

7.1.8 *The Tools Menu*

To the right of the Telephony menu is the Tools menu. At the time this book was developed there were two entries available for selection from this drop-down menu, Firewall ACL Rules and Lua. Selecting Firewall ACL Rules allows you to develop and save an access control list that can be applied to an outside interface. The use of this entry in the Tools menu allows you to create command line ACL rules for many different firewall products, such as Cisco IOS, Linux Netfilter (iptables), OpenBSD, and Windows Firewall, via netsh. Rules for MAC addresses, IPv4 addresses, TCP and UDP ports, and IPv4 + port combinations are supported. The second entry, Lua, represents an interpreter built into Wireshark. Selecting this option from the Tools menu results in the ability to select Console, Evaluate, Manual, or Wiki from another displayed menu. Lua was designed and implemented by a team at the Pontifical Catholic University of Rio de Janeiro.

7.2 WinDump

WinDump can be used to observe, analyze, and save network traffic. In addition, as we note later in this section, you can use the program to enhance network security, as with an appropriate configuration it can alert you to a variety of network probes that could signify your organization's network is under attack or simply being probed prior to an attack.

WinDump requires you to install the WinPcap library and drivers. Thus if you previously installed WinPcap, you probably do not need to reinstall this program. The reason this author says "probably" is because this author does not know what version of WinPcap you are using, with version 4.1.2 being the latest available for download at the time this book was prepared. By going to the following URL you can check for the lat-est version of the program: http://www.winpcap.org/install/default.htm.

7.2.1 Overview

WinDump is from Riverbed Technologies, which is also the developer of Wireshark. Figure 7.15 illustrates the home screen for WinDump, located at the URL of http://www.winpcap.org/windump/.

You can download WinDump by first pointing your browser to http://www.winpcap.org/windump/. Note that although you might assume you could go to www.windump.com, doing so will show that the domain was for sale during mid-2012. If you go to www.windump.org, however, you will be redirected to the WinPcap home page, which also provides you with the ability to download WinDump. At the time this author downloaded WinDump the latest version available was version 3.9.5. Downloading WinDump occurs with an uncompressed executable file, so you might wish to first create a directory named WinDump and install the executable in the directory. As previously mentioned, this program requires the installation of WinPcap. WinPcap represents an industry standard tool for link-layer network access in Windows environments and is also required to operate Wireshark. This program allows applications to capture and transmit network packets bypassing the protocol stack and includes kernel-level packet filtering, a network statistics engine, and support for remote packet capture. To download WinPcap, you can either

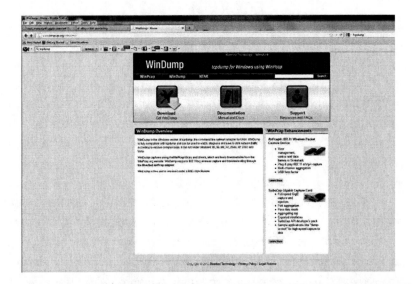

Figure 7.15   Viewing the WinDump screen through a Firefox browser.

click on the WinPcap entry under the Required Software area on the WinPcap website or go directly to winpcap.org, where you can download the program. Downloading WinPcap is relatively simple, with an executable file generating instructions and even including an applet that automatically detects your operating system and installs the correct drivers. If for some reason you decide to remove this program at a later date, you can do so by going to the control panel on the computer and clicking on Add/Remove Programs after selecting WinPcap as the program to remove. Assuming you downloaded both programs, you would then use the Command Prompt window to execute the WinDump program.

7.2.1.1 Initial Operation If you enter the Command Prompt window, and assuming you placed the executable WinDump in the directory of the same name, your display might appear as follows in response to issuing the WinDump command, with Ctrl+C required to display packet information.

```
C:\>cd\windump
C:\WinDump>windump
windump: listening on \Device\NPF_{9D740838-0199-40C7-
A3E6-99E6DCA8AF8A}
0 packets captured
0 packets received by filter
0 packets dropped by kernel
C:\WinDump>
```

7.2.1.2 Selecting an Interface If you're a bit puzzled as to why, after a long period of time, no packets were captured, do not fear, as this author was literally in the same boat. In this author's situation WinDump displayed the fact that it was listening on a device that was a tunnel adapter for which the media was disconnected. You can ascertain if you have this or a similar problem by entering the command ipconfig/ all in the Command Prompt window. Since WinDump was listening on a bad interface, one of the first commands we need to review is the one associated with selecting an interface.

One key switch associated with WinDump is the -i switch or parameter. This switch defines the interface that WinDump will use for displaying the contents on a specified network interface. Thus let's use the -i switch to make the program listen on system interface 3. As a side item, according to documentation associated with the program, if you do not specify an interface the program searches the system interface list for the lowest configured interface, excluding loopback. In the following example WinDump was entered into the Command Prompt window using the -i 3 option. Then a few seconds later a Ctrl+C multikey combination was entered to break the capturing of data. Note that 38 packets were received by the program, of which 10 were captured.

```
C:\WinDump>windump -i 3
windump: listening on \Device\NPF_{AC59CE79-70D8-4E78-
BCE2-0A943F848EDF}
17:55:32.328072 IP Kitchen-Home.Belkin.57614 >
239.255.255.250.1900: UDP, length 133
17:55:32.329232 IP Kitchen-Home.Belkin.57613 >
239.255.255.250.1900: UDP, length 133
17:55:32.627022 IP Kitchen-Home.Belkin.51796 >
94.245.121.253.3544: UDP, length 61
17:55:32.926219 IP Kitchen-Home.Belkin.137 >
239.255.255.250.137: UDP, length 50
17:55:32.926824 IP Kitchen-Home.Belkin.137 >
239.255.255.250.137: UDP, length 50
17:55:34.425982 IP Kitchen-Home.Belkin.137 >
239.255.255.250.137: UDP, length 50
17:55:34.426818 IP Kitchen-Home.Belkin.137 >
239.255.255.250.137: UDP, length 50
17:55:35.365257 IP Kitchen-Home.Belkin.57614 >
239.255.255.250.1900: UDP, length 133
17:55:35.365959 IP Kitchen-Home.Belkin.57613 >
239.255.255.250.1900: UDP, length 133
17:55:35.405153 IP
10 packets captured
38 packets received by filter
0 packets dropped by kernel
C:\WinDump>
```

Although you can use ipconfig/all as a mechanism to check system interfaces, WinDump has an uppercase -D switch that can be used to display the interfaces available for selection. Although we will discuss the use of this switch below, you may wish to use it if, when you execute the program, you do not receive any results after monitoring for a period of time and then entering Ctrl+C as a break. You might be monitoring on an interface that receives no traffic, which is why the -D switch can be an important tool in determining the interface that the program should use.

7.2.1.3 Program Format The general format of WinDump is as follows, where items in brackets {[]} are optional. Note that the first group of switches from A to X are not as commonly used as the switches followed by a word that defines an option required, such as -c count, where you would specify the number of packets to be counted prior to the program exiting. In actuality the format shown excludes the Help facility, which results in the display of the general format or structure of the program. You can display the general structure of WinDump by entering windump -/?. Doing so will display the versions of WinDump and WinPcap as well as the usage of WinDump, similar to that shown below. As indicated by the two examples that follow, you can use windump -? or windump -/ to generate the following Help display. Just remember that you need to place a dash before either character.

```
C:\WinDump>windump -?
windump version 3.9.5, based on tcpdump version 3.9.5
WinPcap version 4.1.2 (packet.dll version 4.1.0.2001),
based on libpcap version 1.0 branch 1_0_rel0b (20091008)
Usage: windump [-aAdDeflLnNOpqRStuUvxX] [-B size] [-c
count] [-C file_size]
  [-E algo:secret] [-F file] [-i interface] [-M secret]
  [-r file] [-s snaplen] [-T type] [-w file]
  [-W filecount] [-y datalinktype] [-Z user]
  [expression]
C:\WinDump>windump -/
windump version 3.9.5, based on tcpdump version 3.9.5
WinPcap version 4.1.2 (packet.dll version 4.1.0.2001),
based on libpcap version 1.0 branch 1_0_rel0b (20091008)
Usage: windump [-aAdDeflLnNOpqRStuUvxX] [-B size] [-c
count] [-C file_size]
  [-E algo:secret] [-F file] [-i interface] [-M secret]
  [-r file] [-s snaplen] [-T type] [-w file]
  [-W filecount] [-y datalinktype] [-Z user]
  [expression]
C:\WinDump>
```

7.2.1.4 Using Multiple Switches   When executing the WinDump program it will either display or log to a file (depending upon the use of switches) a description of the contents of packets on a network interface that match the entered Boolean expression. In this section we will primarily use the term *display* to reference the output from the use of this program; however, it should be noted that this program can also create files. Since we previously discussed the use of the -i switch, let's add information about the use of another switch. In the next example let's incorporate the use of the -c switch and assume we want the program to terminate after five packets are received. The following example illustrates the use of the -i and -c switches, where the -c switch results in the graceful exit of the program once the indicated packet count is reached.

```
C:\WinDump>windump -i 3 -c 5
windump: listening on \Device\NPF_{AC59CE79-70D8-4E78-
BCE2-0A943F848EDF}
19:54:30.593476 IP Kitchen-Home.Belkin.137 >
192.168.2.255.137: UDP, length 50
19:54:31.091008 IP Kitchen-Home.Belkin.63852 >
192.168.2.1.53: 40249+ PTR? 255.2.168.192.in-addr.
arpa. (44)
19:54:31.137818 IP 192.168.2.1.53 > Kitchen-Home.
Belkin.63852: 40249 NXDomain 0/1/0 (121)
19:54:31.138788 IP6 Kitchen-Home.Belkin.63989 >
ff02::1:3.5355: UDP, length 44
19:54:31.138802 IP6 Kitchen-Home.Belkin.63989 >
ff02::1:3.5355: UDP, length 44
5 packets captured
65 packets received by filter
0 packets dropped by kernel
C:\WinDump>
```

A few words are in order concerning program switches. First, under WinDump they are prefixed with a negative sign (–), and while some can be grouped together, others cannot and fail to provide an error message. For example, entering

```
windump -i3 -c5
```

does not work the same as

```
windump -i3c5
```

In fact, if you enter the latter the program will ignore the count and continuously display packets on your screen. Another item that warrants a brief discussion and will be repeated in this section is the fact that switches are case sensitive. This means that −c and −C are different switches and their uses have different effects and may require different parameters to be specified after the switch.

Although the output of WinDump is protocol dependent and can be affected by the switches used in the command, we can use the preceding output as an example. If we focus our attention upon the WinDump output we note that the first 12 numerics on a line indicate the time the packet was received in military format, where 19:54:31 indicates the time was 7:54 p.m. and 31 seconds in the evening. Note that the next six digits following the second number provide a mechanism to differentiating timing on even 10 Gbit networks. Next, we see the protocol, which in the five packets previously captured is either IP or IPv6 (IP6), followed by the packet flow, the type of packet carried by IP or IPv6, for which in this example the last two packets displayed were UDP, and their length, which was 44 bytes. If we added the -e option we could add the link-level header, resulting in the source and destination addresses, protocol, and packet length being displayed. To do so you would enter the command as follows:

```
windump -i 3 -e -c 5
```

While the previous WinDump entry was written for clarity, note that we could also enter the command as follows:

```
windump -i3 -e -c5
```

However, if you entered the command with everything grouped together as follows,

```
windump -i3ec5
```

the program would not stop at five packets and would continue to display packet data on interface 3 as well as ignore your request for the display of Ethernet headers. Thus when in doubt you should consider both clarity when entering switches and a test of what you wish to accomplish. Now that we have a general appreciation for the use of WinDump, let's turn our attention to its comprehensive series of switches by going through them in alphabetical order, with particular emphasis placed on those switches this author believes will be used by many readers. Thus certain switches will not be covered in detail and readers are referred to the WinDump manual at the previously mentioned URL for additional information.

7.2.1.5 Program Switches   WinDump supports a large number of switches that encompass the alphabet from A to Z.

7.2.1.5.1 The -A Switch   The uppercase -A switch causes each packet less its link-level header to be displayed in American Standard Code for Information Interchange (ASCII). The use of this switch can facilitate capturing information that appears in ASCII code, such as web pages. The following example illustrates the use of the -A switch, which in this situation is not particularly helpful.

```
C:\WinDump>windump -i 3 -A -c 4
windump: listening on \Device\NPF_{AC59CE79-70D8-4E78-
BCE2-0A943F848EDF}
20:41:55.508641 IP Kitchen-Home.Belkin.137 >
192.168.2.255.137: UDP, length 50
E..NN.....e................:...5..........
FHEPFCELEHFCEPFFFACACACACACACABL....
20:41:56.100913 IP Kitchen-Home.Belkin.45225 >
192.168.2.4.36824: UDP, length 3
E...N.....................s..-
20:41:57.260569 IP Kitchen-Home.Belkin.138 >
192.168.2.255.138: UDP, length 174
E...N.....e..................9..........
ELEJFEEDEIEFEOCNEIEPENEFCACACAAA. FHEPF
20:41:57.260710 IP Kitchen-Home.Belkin.137 >
192.168.2.255.137: UDP, length 50
E..NN.....e................:...;..........
FHEPFCELEHFCEPFFFACACACACACACABL....
4 packets captured
50 packets received by filter
0 packets dropped by kernel
```

7.2.1.5.2 The -c Switch The use of the lowercase -c switch causes the program to exit after receiving the number of packets specified. In the format of WinDump note that the option -c was followed by *count*, which indicates the number of packets that must be received prior to the program exiting. Of course, at any time you can issue Ctrl+C as a program break.

7.2.1.5.3 The -C Switch The uppercase -C switch serves as a file check mechanism and is followed by a file_size entry that you would specify in bytes. That is, the -C switch checks prior to writing a raw packet to a file if the file is larger than a specified file_size. If so, WinDump will close the current file and open a new file. Files saved by the program after the first file will have their name specified through the use of the -w switch with a number appended, commencing at 1 and progressing higher. Note that file_size units are millions of bytes (1,000,000) and not 1,048,576 bytes.

7.2.1.5.4 The -d Switch The purpose of the -d switch is to dump the compiled packet-matching code in a human readable form to standard output and then terminate. Note that standard output is normally your display but can be altered via the Command Prompt.

7.2.1.5.5 The -dd and -ddd Switches The purpose of the lowercase -dd switch is to dump packet-matching code as a C program fragment. When the lowercase -ddd switch is used this results in the dump of packet-matching code as decimal numbers that are preceded by a count.

7.2.1.5.6 The -D Switch The use of the uppercase -D switch results in the display of a list of network interfaces for which WinDump can capture packets. An example of the use of this switch is shown below.

```
C:\WinDump>windump -D
1.\Device\NPF_{4EE46A76-4F1D-4603-922D-80C1986680E1}
(Microsoft)
2.\Device\NPF_{9D740838-0199-40C7-A3E6-99E6DCA8AF8A}
(Microsoft)
3.\Device\NPF_{AC59CE79-70D8-4E78-BCE2-0A943F848EDF}
(Realtek RTL8168C/8111C PCI-E Gigabit Ethernet NIC)
```

```
4.\Device\NPF_{124CC1EE-2C1B-43D3-880D-A7927B7E5DA4}
(Microsoft)
C:\WinDump>
```

Note that the resulting display of interfaces is of the form of an interface number followed by the interface. By using the -i switch with the interface number provided by the use of the -D switch you can define where the program will capture packets.

7.2.1.5.7 The -e Switch   The purpose of the lowercase -e switch is to display the link-level header on each packet display line. In the following example we used the -e, -i, and -c switches. Remember that the -c switch causes the program to exit after receiving a defined number of packets, which is two in this example, while the -i switch sets the packet capture to interface 3. Also note that although you can combine switches, such as specifying windump -ei 3 -c 2, this author does not recommend doing so, as your intentions are more clear when entering windump -e -i 3 -c 2.

```
C:\WinDump>windump -e -i 3 -c 2
windump: listening on \Device\NPF_{AC59CE79-70D8-4E78-
BCE2-0A943F848EDF}
20:05:03.855854 90:e6:ba:04:ac:8c (oui Unknown) >
00:11:50:23:32:a6 (oui Unknown), ethertype IPv4
(0x0800), length 158: K
itchen-Home.Belkin.57351 > webcs202p2.msg.sp1.yahoo.
com.5050: P 1400012877:1400012981(104) ack 311432368
win 252
20:05:03.950472 00:11:50:23:32:a6 (oui Unknown) >
90:e6:ba:04:ac:8c (oui Unknown), ethertype IPv4
(0x0800), length 166: w
ebcs202p2.msg.sp1.yahoo.com.5050 > Kitchen-Home.
Belkin.57351: P 1:113(112) ack 104 win 8212
2 packets captured
6 packets received by filter
0 packets dropped by kernel
C:\WinDump>
```

7.2.1.5.8 The -E Switch   Once again we go to uppercase, this time with the -E switch. The actual use of the -E switch is as follows:

```
-E spi@ipaddr algo:secret,…
```

The use of the -E switch is for decrypting previously encrypted IPSec Encapsulating Security Payload (ESP) packets. Here ipaddr represents the IP address of IPSec ESP packets that contain a security parameter index value of spi. Note that this combination of spi@ ipaddr can be repeated via the use of a comma or a new line.

7.2.1.5.9 The -f Switch Reverting back to lowercase, the -f switch is used to display IPv4 addresses numerically rather than symbolically. The following example illustrates the use of the -f switch. Note that IPv4 addresses include the port number; thus 173.194.53.212.80 actually represents port 80 from the IPv4 address of 173.194.53.212.

```
C:\WinDump>windump -i 3 -f
windump: listening on \Device\NPF_{AC59CE79-70D8-4E78-
BCE2-0A943F848EDF}
19:55:52.590863 IP 173.194.53.212.80 > Kitchen-Home.
Belkin.52928:. 3100584710:3100586170(1460) ack
796470366 win 137
19:55:52.591027 IP 173.194.53.212.80 > Kitchen-Home.
Belkin.52928:. 1460:2920(1460) ack 1 win 137
19:55:52.591108 IP Kitchen-Home.Belkin.52928 >
173.194.53.212.80:. ack 2920 win 16425
19:55:52.612322 IP 173.194.53.212.80 > Kitchen-Home.
Belkin.52928:. 2920:4380(1460) ack 1 win 137
19:55:52.612645 IP 173.194.53.212.80 > Kitchen-Home.
Belkin.52928:. 4380:5840(1460) ack 1 win 137
19:55:52.612722 IP Kitchen-Home.Belkin.52928 >
173.194.53.212.80:. ack 5840 win 16425
```

7.2.1.5.10 The -F Switch Proceeding up the alphabet, the uppercase -F switch permits a file to be specified as an input for filter expressions. Thus it represents a powerful tool that can be used to create filters on a file that can be run at a later date. Since the -F switch requires a file name to be specified the actual format of this switch is -F file, where file represents the location and name of the file.

7.2.1.5.11 The -i Switch The lowercase -i switch is used to specify the system interface where WinDump will listen for packets. Since spaces are not considered by the WinDump command line windump -i 3 is treated the same as windump -i3; however, for clarity this author's personal preference is to use the former.

7.2.1.5.12 The -l Switch   The use of the lowercase -l switch causes standard output, which by default is the display to be buffered. That is, you can view data as they are being captured and piped to a file through the use of the greater than (>) sign. If you simply use the lowercase -l switch each display line occurs twice, which, as the following example illustrates, may result in you thinking you have a slight case of double vision.

```
C:\WinDump>windump -i 3 -l
windump: listening on \Device\NPF_{AC59CE79-70D8-4E78-
BCE2-0A943F848EDF}
20:21:15.674855 IP Kitchen-Home.Belkin.6646 >
192.168.2.255.6646: UDP, length 170
20:21:15.676411 IP Kitchen-Home.Belkin.6646 >
192.168.2.255.6646: UDP, length 170
20:21:15.803573 arp who-has 192.168.2.1 tell Kitchen-
Home.Belkin
20:21:15.803647 arp who-has 192.168.2.1 tell Kitchen-
Home.Belkin
```

7.2.1.5.13 The -L Switch   The purpose of the uppercase -L switch is to list the known data link types for the interface and then exit. The following example shows the use of the uppercase -L switch on this author's computer.

```
C:\WinDump>windump -L
windump: listening on \Device\NPF_{9D740838-0199-40C7-
A3E6-99E6DCA8AF8A}
Data link types (use option -y to set):
EN10MB (Ethernet)
C:\WinDump>
```

Note from the preceding that you can also use the -y switch followed by a datalinktype to set the interface for the capture of a defined type of data link.

7.2.1.5.14 The -m Switch The lowercase -m switch enables one or more Simple Network Management Protocol (SNMP) management information base (MIB) modules to be loaded. Since the module is on a file the switch is followed by the location of the file and its file name.

7.2.1.5.15 The -M Switch The uppercase -M switch provides a shared secret for validating the digest found in TCP segments, assuming that the TCPMD5 option is present. Since you need to specify a shared secret when using this switch, its format is -M secret.

7.2.1.5.16 The -n Switch Through the use of the lowercase -n option you inform WinDump that addresses should not be converted to names. The following example illustrates the use of the -n switch. Note that IP addresses are shown.

```
C:\WinDump>windump -i 3 -n
windump: listening on \Device\NPF_{AC59CE79-70D8-4E78-
BCE2-0A943F848EDF}
17:27:18.765016 IP 192.168.2.3.53075 >
98.137.80.32.80: P 1817248954:1817249340(386) ack
3739024666 win 16425
17:27:18.851115 IP 98.137.80.32.80 >
192.168.2.3.53075:. 1:1461(1460) ack 386 win 44
```

Since we need a frame of reference let's use WinDump without the -n switch. As shown by the following example, we note host names such as Yahoo as well as a wireless router named Kitchen-Home-Belkin. Both with or without the use of the -n option we can view the port number associated with packets.

```
C:\WinDump>windump -i 3
windump: listening on \Device\NPF_{AC59CE79-70D8-4E78-
BCE2-0A943F848EDF}
17:28:12.813916 IP l3.ycs.vip.a4e.yahoo.com.80 >
Kitchen-Home.Belkin.53081: F 4003815248:4003815248(0)
ack 3570894289 win 32
17:28:12.814045 IP Kitchen-Home.Belkin.53081 > l3.ycs.
vip.a4e.yahoo.com.80:. ack 1 win 16425
17:28:12.814112 IP Kitchen-Home.Belkin.53081 > l3.ycs.
vip.a4e.yahoo.com.80: F 1:1(0) ack 1 win 16425
```

```
17:28:12.878950 IP 13.ycs.vip.a4e.yahoo.com.80 >
Kitchen-Home.Belkin.53081:. ack 2 win 32
```

7.2.1.5.17 The -N switch The uppercase -N switch is used to inhibit the display of the domain name qualification of host names. For example, using the -N flag abc will be displayed instead of abc.fbi.gov, where fbi.gov represents the domain name qualifier. The use of this switch reduces the amount of packet data displayed and represents a method to better focus upon troubleshooting a localized event.

7.2.1.5.18 The -O Switch The uppercase -O switch inhibits the running of packet-matching code optimizer. The use of this switch is recommended if you suspect a bug is in the optimizer.

7.2.1.5.19 The -p Switch The lowercase -p switch inhibits placing the interface into a promiscuous mode of operation where it reads every packet passing the interface.

7.2.1.5.20 The -q Switch The use of the lowercase -q switch places output in what is referred to as a quiet mode of operation. In this mode of operation less protocol information is displayed resulting in shorter output lines. The following example illustrates the use of the lowercase -q switch on interface 3 in which five packets are captured through the use of the -c switch.

```
C:\WinDump>windump -i3 -c5 -q
windump: listening on \Device\NPF_{AC59CE79-70D8-4E78-
BCE2-0A943F848EDF}
12:27:32.521865 IP 192.168.2.4.5353 >
224.0.0.251.5353: UDP, length 251
12:27:32.525844 IP6 fe80::e2b9:baff:fe08:ccf7.5353 >
ff02::fb.5353: UDP, length 251
12:27:33.151975 IP Kitchen-Home.Belkin.56094 >
192.168.2.1.53: UDP, length 42
12:27:33.211137 IP 192.168.2.1.53 > Kitchen-Home.
Belkin.56094: UDP, length 99
12:27:33.212328 IP6 Kitchen-Home.Belkin.63026 >
ff02::1:3.5355: UDP, length 42
5 packets captured
92 packets received by filter
0 packets dropped by kernel
```

7.2.1.5.21 The -R Switch   Because there is no protocol version field in the ESP/AH (authentication header) specification WinDump cannot determine the version of the ESP/AH protocol. Thus the uppercase -R switch is used to inform WinDump to assume ESP/AH packets are based upon the old specifications defined in RFC 1825 to RFC 1829. When specified WinDump will not display the Replay Prevention field.

7.2.1.5.22 The -r Switch   The lowercase -r switch is used to read packets previously created through the use of the -w switch, which is used to create a file. Since the location and file name must be specified the actual use of this option is -r file, where file defines the location and file name to be read by the program.

7.2.1.5.23 The -S Switch   The uppercase -S switch causes absolute rather than relative TCP sequence numbers to be displayed.

7.2.1.5.24 The -s Switch   The lowercase -s switch is used to define the number of bytes of data obtained or snarfed from each packet rather than the default of 68. While 68 bytes is typically sufficient for IP, ICMP, TCP, and UDP, it can result in the truncation of protocol data from name server and Non Stop Forwarding (NSF) packets. When packets are truncated they are indicated in the output by [proto], where proto represents the name of the protocol level at which truncation occurred. There is a relationship between the time required to process packets and snapshot length, with longer snapshots requiring an increase in processing time.

7.2.1.5.25 The -T Switch   The uppercase -T switch is used to force packets selected by an expression to be interpreted by the specified *type* following the switch. Thus its full format is -T type. WinDump currently supports the -T type values listed in Table 7.1.

7.2.1.5.26 The -t Switch   The lowercase -t switch is used to inhibit the display of a timestamp on each packet line. The following example illustrates the removal of the timestamp based upon the use of the -t switch. Although the timestamp can be a valuable tool, as the following example illustrates, there can be situations where its removal adds

Table 7.1   -T Type Values

VALUE	MEANING
aodv	Ad Hoc On-Demand Distance Vector Protocol
cnfp	Cisco NetFlow Protocol
rpc	Remote Procedure Call
rtp	Real-Time Applications Protocol
rtcp	Real-Time Applications Control Protocol
snmp	Simple Network Management Protocol
tftp	Trivial File Transfer Protocol
vat	Visual Audio Tool
wb	White Board

clarity to the display. Because packets are listed or displayed in time order, its removal can facilitate examining a sequence of packets as well as maintain its time sequence.

```
C:\WinDump>windump -i 3 -t
windump: listening on \Device\NPF_{AC59CE79-70D8-4E78-
BCE2-0A943F848EDF}
IP Kitchen-Home.Belkin.52312 > 65.55.158.118.3544:
UDP, length 61
IP Kitchen-Home.Belkin.137 > 65.55.158.118.137: UDP,
length 50
```

7.2.1.5.27 The -tt Switch   The double t (-tt) switch is used to display an unformatted timestamp on each packet line. The following example illustrates its use on interface 3.

```
C:\WinDump>windump -i 3 -tt
windump: listening on \Device\NPF_{AC59CE79-70D8-4E78-
BCE2-0A943F848EDF}
1331257009.492843 arp who-has 192.168.2.4 tell
Kitchen-Home.Belkin
1331257009.650370 IP Kitchen-Home.Belkin.63186 >
192.168.2.1.53: 49480+ PTR? 4.2.168.192.in-addr.
arpa. (42)
1331257009.698004 IP 192.168.2.1.53 > Kitchen-Home.
Belkin.63186: 49480 NXDomain 0/1/0 (119)
1331257009.698855 IP6 Kitchen-Home.Belkin.58030 >
ff02::1:3.5355: UDP, length 42
```

7.2.1.5.28 The -ttt Switch The lowercase triple t (-ttt) switch is used to display in microseconds (10^{-3}) the time or delta between the current and previous packet. In the following example note that the first packet by default has a delta time of six zeros.

```
C:\WinDump>windump -i 3 -ttt
windump: listening on \Device\NPF_{AC59CE79-70D8-4E78-
BCE2-0A943F848EDF}
000000 IP Kitchen-Home.Belkin.49701 >
213.146.189.206.12350: P 796224157:796224162(5) ack
65474505 win 253
115180 IP 213.146.189.206.12350 > Kitchen-Home.
Belkin.49701: P 1:6(5) ack 5 win 7
199668 IP Kitchen-Home.Belkin.49701 >
213.146.189.206.12350:. ack 6 win 253
```

7.2.1.5.29 The -tttt Switch The lowercase quad t (-tttt) switch is used to have WinDump display timestamps in their default format preceded by the date for each packet. Note that the date is displayed as a four-digit year followed by a two-digit month and two-digit date, with dashes connecting each in the format of yyyy-mm-dd. In the following example we first used the triple -ttt switch to display two packets followed by the use of the quad -tttt switch. As you can visually note from the use of the quad -tttt option, adding date information can significantly increase the amount of characters displayed, and while there are good reasons to use this option, its use should be carefully considered.

```
C:\WinDump>windump -i 3 -c 3 -ttt
windump: listening on \Device\NPF_{AC59CE79-70D8-4E78-
BCE2-0A943F848EDF}
000000 IP6 Kitchen-Home.Belkin.546 > ff02::1:2.547:
dhcp6 solicit
000557 IP6 Kitchen-Home.Belkin.546 > ff02::1:2.547:
dhcp6 solicit
990628 IP Kitchen-Home.Belkin.54468 > 192.168.2.1.53:
24775+[|domain]
3 packets captured
31 packets received by filter
0 packets dropped by kernel
C:\WinDump>windump -i 3 -c 3 -tttt
```

```
windump: listening on \Device\NPF_{AC59CE79-70D8-4E78-
BCE2-0A943F848EDF}
2012-03-14 12:57:28.982156 IP 157.55.130.142.40002 >
Kitchen-Home.Belkin.50525: P 3084560502:3084560505(3)
ack 2562842087
win 60
2012-03-14 12:57:29.182407 IP Kitchen-Home.
Belkin.50525 > 157.55.130.142.40002:. ack 3 win 256
2012-03-14 12:57:29.235481 IP 157.55.130.142.40002 >
Kitchen-Home.Belkin.50525: P 3:13(10) ack 1 win 60
3 packets captured
8 packets received by filter
0 packets dropped by kernel
```

7.2.1.5.30 The -u Switch   The lowercase -u switch is used to display undecoded NFS handles.

7.2.1.5.31 The -U Switch   The uppercase -U switch causes output saved through the use of the -w switch to be directly written to the output file instead of being written only when the output buffer fills.

7.2.1.5.32 The -v Switch   Through the use of the lowercase -v switch the program will generate verbose output. In the following example of the use of the -v switch note that the type of service (TOS), time to live (TTL), offset, flags, and protocol are displayed for the IP packet. In addition, the -v switch also enables additional packet integrity checks, to include verifying IP and ICMP checksums.

```
C:\WinDump>windump -i 3 -v
windump: listening on \Device\NPF_{AC59CE79-70D8-4E78-
BCE2-0A943F848EDF}
20:57:33.378468 arp who-has Kitchen-Home.Belkin tell
192.168.2.1
20:57:33.378529 arp reply Kitchen-Home.Belkin is-at
90:e6:ba:04:ac:8c (oui Unknown)
20:57:33.633607 IP (tos 0x0, ttl 56, id 39061, offset
0, flags [DF], proto: TCP (6), length: 43)
64.4.23.147.40011 > Kit
chen-Home.Belkin.51562: P, cksum 0xf310 (correct),
537736013:537736016(3) ack 355993396 win 57
```

7.2.1.5.33 The –vv and –vvv Switches The double -vv switch results in an extended verbose output, while the triple -vvv switch provides the most verbose output. You should experiment between using the -v, -vv, and -vvv switches to match your requirements for output to the capability of WinDump.

7.2.1.5.34 The –w Switch The lowercase -w switch is used to write raw packets to a specified file. Thus the location and file name follow this switch. You can display the packets at a later date using the -r switch. Since a file name must follow the -w switch its actual format is -w file.

7.2.1.5.35 The –W Switch The uppercase -W switch is used with the uppercase -C switch to limit the number of files created to the file-count following the -W switch, which represents a specified number. The file_size following the -C switch limits the size of the file, which when reached results in overwriting of the file similar to a rotating buffer.

7.2.1.5.36 The –x and –xx Switches The use of the lowercase -x switch results in the headers of each packet as well as any data in the packet (less its link-layer header) being displayed in hex. In comparison, the double lowercase -xx switch causes headers of each packet, to include its link layer, to be displayed in hex.

7.2.1.5.37 The –X and –XX Switches The use of the uppercase -X switch displays the headers and data in each packet less its link-layer header in both hex and ASCII. In comparison, the double uppercase -XX switch results in the headers of each packet, to include its link layer, to be displayed in both hex and ASCII.

7.2.1.5.38 The –y Switch The lowercase -y switch is used to define the type of packets to be captured on the data link. Thus this switch is followed by the variable *datalinktype*.

7.2.1.5.39 The –Z Switch The last switch in WinDump is the uppercase -Z switch. The use of this switch will drop privileges and change the user ID to *user* and the group ID to the primary group of *user.*

7.2.2 WinDump Expressions

When you use WinDump without an expression every packet encountered will be displayed or dumped unless you use one or more switches that affect packets, such as the -c or -w switch. Since the use of most switches has a limited effect upon packet display, by themselves the use of switches can result in an excessive number of packets, many of which will not be of interest to you. Thus you will more than likely want to consider the use of an expression to control or narrow the display of packets that satisfy your requirements.

In WinDump an expression consists of one or more primitives, with a primitive normally consisting of an identification or ID (name or number) proceeded by one or more qualifiers.

7.2.2.1 Qualifiers   Concerning qualifiers, under WinDump there are three different kinds we need to know. Those qualifiers are type, dir, and proto, each of which we discuss below.

7.2.2.1.1 The Type Qualifier   The type qualifier defines the entry that the identification name or number references. Possible types include host, net, port, and portrange. Examples of the use of the type qualifier include host fbi, net 192.37, port 80, and portrange 257-3000. Note that if no type qualifier is specified a host qualifier is assumed.

7.2.2.1.2 The Dir Qualifier   The dir qualifier references a transfer direction either to or from the identification or ID. Possible directions are source specified as src, destination specified as dst, src or dst, and src and dst. Examples of the use of the dir qualifier include scr fbi, dst net 192.37, and scr or dst port 80. Note that if no dir qualifier is present src or dst is assumed. Also note that for some device types *inbound* and *outbound* qualifiers can be used to denote a desired direction.

7.2.2.1.3 The Proto Qualifier   The use of this qualifier restricts packet matching to a specified protocol. Those protocols are listed in Table 7.2.

Table 7.2 Protocol Qualifiers Supported by WinDump

QUALIFIER	PROTOCOL
ether	Ethernet
fddi	Fiber Data Distribution Interface
tr	Token-Ring
wlan	Wireless LAN (802.11)
ip	Internet Protocol version 4
ip6	Internet Protocol version 6
arp	Address Resolution Protocol
rarp	Reverse Address Resolution Protocol
decent	Digital C
tcp	Transmission Control Protocol
udp	User Datagram Protocol

The following example illustrates the use of the proto qualifier as this author entered UDP in the WinDump command line and pointed his browser to eBay.com.

```
C:\WinDump>windump -i 3 udp
windump: listening on \Device\NPF_{AC59CE79-70D8-4E78-
BCE2-0A943F848EDF}
19:36:21.758731 IP Kitchen-Home.Belkin.6646 >
192.168.2.255.6646: UDP, length 170
19:36:21.759130 IP Kitchen-Home.Belkin.6646 >
192.168.2.255.6646: UDP, length 170
19:36:25.020515 IP Kitchen-Home.Belkin.138 >
192.168.2.255.138: UDP, length 174
19:36:25.020658 IP Kitchen-Home.Belkin.137 >
192.168.2.255.137: UDP, length 50
19:36:25.267413 IP Kitchen-Home.Belkin.65207 >
192.168.2.1.53: 1602+ A? ebay.com. (26)
19:36:25.312539 IP 192.168.2.1.53 > Kitchen-Home.
Belkin.65207: 1602 4/4/4 A pages.ebay.com, A[|domain]
19:36:25.725559 IP Kitchen-Home.Belkin.58957 >
192.168.2.1.53: 12042+ A? www.ebay.com. (30)
19:36:25.760675 IP Kitchen-Home.Belkin.59500 >
192.168.2.1.53: 45641+ A? www.ebay.com. (30)
```

If you do not specify a protocol qualifier all protocols consistent with the type are assumed. For example, port 53 means both TCP and UDP port 53, while scr fbi means IP or ARP or RARP src fbi.

7.2.2.2 Expression Primitives Through the use of WinDump primitives you can construct a variety of expressions to satisfy just about any filtering capability you need to perform. WinDump includes a large number of primitives, of which a majority of the more popular ones are listed in Table 7.3. For a full list of WinDump primitives, to include Asynchronous Transfer Mode (ATM)-related ones, readers are referred to the WinDump user manual, which can be obtained at www.winpcap. org/windump/docs/manual.htm.

7.2.2.3 Relationship Operators Within a WinDump expression you can use a variety of relationship operators using the format expr relop expr. Here the relation is true where relop is one of the relations greater than (>), less than (<), less than or equal (< =), greater than or equal (> =), equal (=), or not equal (! =), and expr is an arithmetic expression composed of integer constants that are expressed in standard C syntax, the normal binary operators [+, −, *, /, &, |, <<, >>], a length operator, and special packet data accessors. If you need to access data within a packet you would use the following format:

```
proto [expr: size]
```

where proto represents the protocol layer, expr references the byte offset, and size indicates the number of bytes of interest. Note that only certain ICMP Type field values can be used, as well as certain TCP Flags field values. Readers are referred to the WinDump manual for a listing of currently available field values.

7.2.2.4 Utilization Examples While we examine the use of WinDump in this section, as a refresher we need to review its operation. Using the old adage that a picture is worth a thousand words, let's use an illustration to discuss the basic WinDump syntax or format (Figure 7.16).

In examining Figure 7.16 note that the protocol field can have a value such as ether, fddi, ip, arp, rarp, tcp, udp, and so on, with a full list in the previously referenced manual. If no protocol is specified then all the protocols are used.

The second field shown in Figure 7.16 is Directions. The values in this field can be source (src), destination (dst), source and destination (src and dst), and source or destination (src or dst). If no source or

Table 7.3 Popular WinDump Primitives

PRIMITIVE	DESCRIPTION
dst host host	True if the IPv4/6 destination field of the packet matches the host either as an IP address or hostname
drc host host	True if the IPv4/6 source field of the packet is host
host host	True if either the IPv4/6 source or destination of the packet is host
Note: You can prefix any of the above host expressions with the keywords *ip, arp, rarp, or ip6.*	
ether dst ehost	True if the Ethernet destination is ehost, which can be a name or number
ether src ehost	True if the Ethernet source address is ehost
ether host ehost	True if either the Ethernet source or destination address is ehost
ether broadcast	True if the packet is an Ethernet broadcast packet; note that ether is optional
ether multicast	True if the packet is an Ethernet multicast packet; note that ether is optional
ether proto protocol	True if the packet is of an ether type protocol, such as ip, ip6, arp, rarp, atalk, aarp, decent, sca, lat, mopdl, moprc, iso, stp, ipx or netbeui; note that these identifiers are also keywords and must be escaped via the use of a backslash (\) character
dst net net	True if the IPv4/6 destination address of the packet has a network address of net
src net net	True if the IPv4/v6 source address of the packet has a network address of net
net net	True if either the IPv4/v6 source or destination has a network address of net
net net mask netmask	True if the IPv4 address matches net with the specified netmask; can qualify with scr or dst but is not valid for IPv6
dst port port	True if an ip/tcp or ip/udp packet (IPv4/v6) has a destination port value of port
src port port	True if the port has a source value of port
port port	True if either the source or destination port of the packet is port
dst portrange port1-port2	True for packets that have a destination port value between port1 and port2 for ip/tcp and ip/udp where ip is ipv4/v6
src portrange	True if the packet has a source port value between port1 and port2
Note: You can prefix the keyword *tcp or udp* to any port or portrange primitive, such as tcp dst port 80. The above matches only TCP packets whose destination is port 80.	
ip proto protocol	True if the packet is an IPv4 packet of protocol type protocol; protocol names can be icmp, icmp6, igmp, pim, ah, esp, vrrp, udp, or tcp; since tcp, udp, and icmp are also keywords, they must be escaped via the back slash (\) character
ip6 proto protocol	True if the packet is an IPv6 packet of protocol type protocol
ip broadcast	True if the packet is an Ipv4 broadcast packet
ip multicast	True if the packet is an IPv4 multicast packet
ip6 multicast	True if the packet is an IPv6 multicast packet

(continued)

Table 7.3   Popular WinDump Primitives (continued)

PRIMITIVE	DESCRIPTION
mpls [label_num]	True if the packet is an MPLS one; if label_num is specified, it's only true if the packet has the specified label_num
pppoed	True if the packet is a PPP-over-Ethernet Discovery packet
pppoes	True if the packet is a PPP-over-Ethernet Session packet
vlan [vlan_id]	True if the packet is an IEEE 802.1Q virtual LAN packet; if the vlan_id is specified, then only true for packets with that vlan_id

Protocol	Direction	Host(s)	Port	Logical Operands	Other Expressions

Figure 7.16   The basic WinDump format.

destination is specified, then the source or destination (src or dst) will be used for packet matching.

The third field, labeled Host(s) in Figure 7.16, can have a value of host, net, port, or portrange. If this field is omitted, the keyword *host* is then used by default.

The fourth field, Logical Operations, can have the values *and, or,* or *not*. In order of program precedence, *not* has the highest precedence, while *or* and *and* have equal precedence. Operations are then performed left to right.

The fifth field, Other Expression, can include a combination of one or more of the preceding fields, such as udp dst 198.78.46.8. Now that we have a basic understanding of how WinDump can be used, let's examine a few examples in what we can consider increasing levels of complexity.

To display the standard WinDump output you would enter:

```
windump
```

To display network interfaces available for packet capturing you would enter:

```
windump -D
```

To use the standard packet capturing on interface 3 you would enter:

```
windump -i 3
```

To capture all Ethernet broadcast traffic on interface 3 you would enter:

```
windump -i 3 ether broadcast
```

To capture the TCP port 80 (HTTP) traffic on interface 3 you would enter:

```
windump -i 3 tcp port 80
```

or you could enter:

```
windump -i 3 tcp port http
```

To capture the first 20 TCP packets on interface 3 on port 80 (HTTP) you would enter:

```
windump -i 3 -c 20 tcp port 80
```

or you could enter:

```
windump -i 3 -c 20 tcp port http
```

Now suppose you want to capture packets of interest onto a file named packet.cpt. To do so we would use the -w switch followed by the location and name of the file we wish to save. Assuming we want to capture the first 100 packets on interface 3 and the saved file will be located on Drive C under the directory \windump, we would then enter the following command:

```
windump -i 3 -c 100 -w packet.cpt
```

Now that we saved a file containing a hundred packets on interface 3, let's assume we want to display the results of our effort. To do so we would use the -r switch as follows:

```
windump -r packet.cpt
```

Note that in the preceding example the -r switch is followed by the location and file name, which in our example was assumed to be in the same location as the program. In the next example we note how we can combine two or more switches with a single negative sign (–).

In this example we will continue monitoring packets on interface 3 as well as display Ethernet headers and data in a very verbose mode. Note that we use the -e switch to display Ethernet headers and the -nn switch to display information in a very verbose mode. Thus our command line entry now becomes:

```
windump -i 3 -enn
```

We could also combine the -i and -enn operators; however, you need to be a bit careful in doing so. This is because while windump -enni 3 as well as windump -i3enn would work, if you entered windump -3ienn this would result in the display of the format or syntax of the program and it would then halt operations. The reason the last entry is no good lies in the fact that it violates the basic structure of the -i switch, which requires the interface number to follow and not the reverse, where it was the prefix to the -i switch.

Suppose we only wanted to capture 125 packets of data. We could then use the -c switch. If we also wanted to display Ethernet headers of captured packets in a very verbose mode again using interface 3, our command line would be as follows:

```
windump -i3ennc125
```

In actuality WinDump would continuously display packets, similar to the song about riding the train in Boston forever. The reason for this is that you need to separate the count from the -c switch. Thus entering the following would work:

```
windump -i3enn -c 125
```

7.2.2.4.1 Working with Expressions Although we have examined a number of examples of the use of WinDump, until now we have ignored the full capability of this program, which enables us to create complex filters. Thus in this section we will gradually increase our use of WinDump by creating command line entries that enable us to display certain types of network traffic that can significantly enhance our ability to solve network problems. First, let's commence our series of examples by looking for traffic based upon a specific IP address. For our series of examples that address will be 192.168.2.2. Thus to display packets with source and destination IP addresses matching our IP address on interface 3 we would enter:

```
windump -i 3 host 198.168.2.2
```

Now let's assume we need to focus on destination packets. To slightly change our command line entry we need to add the keyword *dst* as follows:

```
windump -i 3 dst 198.168.2.2
```

Note that in the preceding example we need to remove the *host* keyword while adding the *dst* keyword. Now suppose you want to focus upon source packets instead of destination packets. To do so you would enter:

```
windump -i 3 src 198.168.2.2
```

7.2.2.4.2 Watching Specific Protocols Now suppose our interest resides in examining one or more specific protocols. If we remember that proto works for a range of protocols from ether and Fiber Data Distribution Interface (FDDI) to TCP and UDP, we can focus on some specific protocols. Assuming we wanted to display TCP packets we could enter the following into the Command Prompt window, again assuming we are examining interface 3:

```
windump -i 3 tcp
```

Now let's expand our analysis and assume we want to examine TCP packets with a destination of port 80. Again, assuming monitoring on interface 3, we would enter:

```
windump -i 3 tcp dst port 80
```

7.2.2.4.3 Working with Operators WinDump supports three operators: *and*, *or*, and *not*. You can enter *and* into the command line as either *and* or &&. *Or* can be used as *or* or ||, while the *not* operator can be entered as *not* or |.

Now let's get a bit creative and use the power of WinDump. To do so let's expand our monitoring so that we display TCP packets

destined to the World Wide Web on port 80 and UDP packets that
flow to port 53, the well-known Domain Name Service (DNS). Since
we want both, we would use the *or* capability of the program as follows:

```
windump -i 3 tcp dst port 80 or udp dst port 53
```

In the preceding example we used the *or* operator. Note that *or* can
also be entered as ||. Thus we could also enter the preceding command
line entry as:

```
windump -i 3 tcp dst port 80 || udp dst port 53
```

One of the nicer aspects of WinDump is that when you do something foolish it may give you a hint that what you just did will not
work. For example, if you for some reason entered an *and* operator
instead of the *or* operator and wanted to display packets with both
TCP and UDP, a physical impossibility, you would receive the message "expression rejects all packets," which is a nice method of informing you that what you entered will not work.

Since we just worked with the *or* operation and briefly discussed
a way the *and* operator can get us into an area of unintended conse-
quences, let's continue by using a few operators in our examples.

To illustrate the use of the *and* operator let's assume we want to
monitor traffic originating from the 198.72.0.0/16 network flowing
to either the 192.168.0.0/16 network or the 98.174.0.0/16 network.
This example will result in the use of both an *and* operator and an *or*
operator as follows:

```
windump -i 3 src net 198.72.0.0/16 and dst net
192.168.0.0/16 or 98.174.0.0/16
```

Now suppose we only wanted to display ICMP traffic from the
198.72.0.0 network flowing to the two previously mentioned networks. In this example we would need to add "and icmp" to the prior
example. Now suppose we still wanted the same network data flow
but did not want to view ICMP traffic. This means that we would
need to use both another *and* operator and the *not* operator, as follows:

```
windump -i 3 src net 198.72.0.0/16 and dst net
192.168.0.0/16 or 98.174.0.0/16 and not icmp
```

Based upon the previous examples we can easily note how we can use WinDump to construct queries to satisfy our operational requirements. To use this program effectively, however, requires you put on your thinking cap, as many of its capabilities only become apparent when you use the program. For example, most persons rightly are concerned about security but may be a bit puzzled when thinking about how WinDump could be used to assist us in this area. Thus let's discuss its potential use in this area.

7.2.2.4.4 Use as a Security Monitor If you were wearing a black hacker hat one of the things you would probably perform is a port scan of a targeted network. If we put on our good guy or girl white hat, we want to note when it appears our network is under attack. Thus by the use of either the port or the portrange primitive you can display activity that can indicate your network is under attack. For example,

```
windump -i 3 tcp portrange 64-6400
```

would display TCP packets with either source or destination port numbers between 64 and 6400. If you wanted to restrict packet display to those packets whose destination is in that portrange, you would then enter:

```
windump -i 3 tcp dst portrange 64-6400
```

While the preceding might be useful, it doesn't let us know if a UDP attack is underway. Thus we might consider entering the following in the Command Prompt:

```
windump -i 3 tcp dst portrange 64-6400 or udp dst
portrange 64-6400
```

Of course, you would set the portrange values to satisfy your organization. For example, if your organization has a router access list that blocks most but not all ports, you could consider placing a computer on a demilitarized zone (DMZ) where the router is connected to the Internet to examine packets filtered by the router before they are sent to the great bit bucket in the sky. In addition, you could operate the program on the other side of the router to display packets that are allowed into your network. By selectively using either the port or por-trange command you can operate WinDump as an intrusion detection system that can be added to your bag of tricks to determine the state of your organization's network.

8

NETWORK INTRUSION
AND SECURITY

In this chapter we turn our attention to topics that are security related. First we examine a program referred to as Snort®. Snort represents an open-source network intrusion prevention and detection system (IPS/IDS) that was developed by a firm named Sourcefire. This program combines the benefits of signature examination, protocol, and anomaly-based inspection. According to Sourcefire, Snort is the most widely deployed IPS/IDS program on a worldwide basis, with millions of downloads and approximately 400,000 registered users, and has become a *de facto* standard for intrusion detection and prevention. After we examine Snort we continue with an examination of several additional security-related programs. Next is a discussion of the use of SpywareBlaster, a program that can be used to prevent the installation of spyware and other potentially unwanted software. This is a Windows-based program that while simple to install and operate has some key operational capabilities. Following our discussion of SpywareBlaster we then turn our attention to a program that monitors our computer for keyboard loggers, referred to as keyloggers, as well as other suspicious software. Referred to as Online Armor, this program has some very interesting capabilities.

8.1 Snort

You can download Snort by first pointing your browser to www.snort.org. Once you arrive at the Snort home page you should first click on the Requirements button located under the label New to Snort to verify that you have the required software on your computer prior to clicking on the Download button, which is prominently displayed in the upper right corner of the display. Figure 8.1 illustrates the Snort home screen viewed through this author's Firefox browser in early 2012.

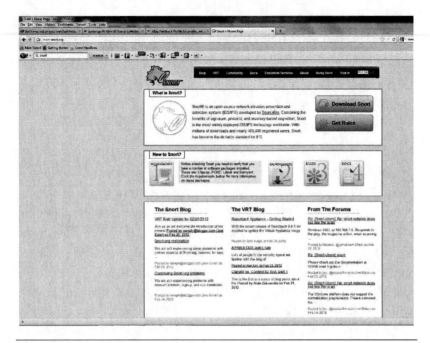

Figure 8.1   Viewing the Snort home page through a Firefox browser.

8.1.1 Requirements

Prior to downloading Snort you should examine its software requirements. While the Linux version requires five software products,
Windows only has a requirement for two of the products when you
download the binary version of this program. Those products required
to support Snort in a Windows environment are WinPcap and
Barnyard. WinPcap represents an industry standard tool for link-layer
network access in Windows environments and was also required to
operate Wireshark, which was described in Chapter 7. This program
allows applications to capture and transmit network packets bypassing
the protocol stack and includes kernel-level packet filtering, a network
statistics engine, and support for remote packet capture. At the time
this book was written the latest stable version of WinPcap was version
4.1.2. You can either click on the WinPcap entry under the Required
Software area on the Snort website or go directly to winpcap.org,
where you can download the program. Downloading WinPcap is
relatively simple, with an executable file generating instructions and
even including an applet that automatically detects your operating
system and installs the correct drivers. If for some reason you decide

to remove this program at a later date you can do so by going to the Control Panel and clicking on Add/Remove Programs after selecting WinPcap as the program to remove.

The second program required to operate Snort in a Windows environment is referred to as Barnyard2. Barnyard2 represents an output system for Snort. Barnyard2 reads a Snort binary output format referred to as unified and resends the data to a back-end database as well as stores data temporarily when the database cannot accept connections. Barnyard2 is available from Securixlive at http://www. securixlive.com/barnyard2/download.php. Because the program is in a tar-compressed form you will need a decompression performing utility program once you download it. This author used the free Stuffit Expander located on the web at http://www.stuffit.com/win-expander-download.html to decompress the series of files. Once both of the previously mentioned programs were installed it was then time to install Snort.

Figure 8.2 illustrates several items that warrant a bit of explanation when downloading Snort and using the Firefox browser. First, regardless of the browser used, you want to direct your browser to the web address http://www.snort.org/snort-downloads#latest to determine the latest information about Snort releases as well as the ability to download information. That URL is shown in the

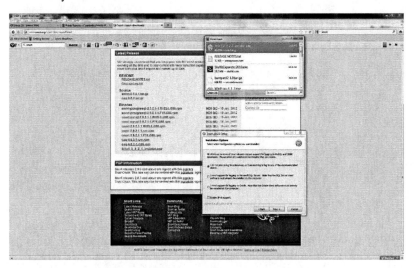

Figure 8.2 Downloading Snort.

background of Figure 8.2, which has two Readme files ending in .txt, two compressed tar files containing source data, and ten binary files. Concerning the latter, this author selected the Snort installer file, which is the tenth binary file. Once this file was selected this author simply double-clicked on the downloaded file, which appears in the dialog box labeled Download, which was positioned toward the top right position on Figure 8.2. Once that file executed the dialog box labeled Snort 2.9.2.1 Setup was displayed. Through the use of this dialog box you can select the configuration options you wish to be installed, to include support for Microsoft's SQL Server, Oracle, and IPv6. Once you select the configuration options for installation the setup program will prompt you to select the components of the program to be installed. By default all four components displayed are checked, Snort, Dynamic Modules, Documentation, and Schemas, with the amount of storage required for the selected modules listed. As you click or unselect each component you can determine its storage requirements as well as obtain an explanation of what the component does as a brief description will be displayed to the right of the entry as you move the cursor over each component. Figure 8.3 illustrates the Choose Components dialog box.

8.1.2 Installation

This author had a professor who was fond of the saying "the proof of the pudding is in its taste." While we cannot exactly taste the program,

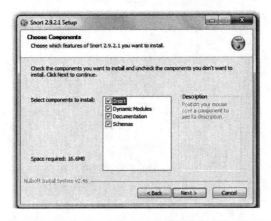

Figure 8.3   Selecting Snort program components to install.

we can obtain a taste of what it does by installing and operating it. Let's do so.

Once you select or deselect applicable components the setup program will provide you with the ability to define the location where the program will be installed. By default the program will be installed in a directory named Snort on the C drive; however, you can select a different directory, drive, or combination of directory and drive if you so desire. Once you either accept the default or enter a different location the program will extract a number of files, delete a file not needed, and then display "Completed" both at the top of the box and within the box, after which you can close the Snort Setup dialog box. Although most installation programs will terminate when you click on a Close button, that it not the case with Snort. Instead of terminating the Snort installation program will inform you that the program was sucessfully installed and requires WinPcap 4.1.1 to be installed on your computer as well as the web location where it can be obtained. In addition, you will be informed that you need to manually modify the snort.conf file to specify proper paths that will enable the program to find the rules and classification files. This information is shown in Figure 8.4.

Assuming that you installed Snort in its default location on your C drive the configuration file will be located at c:snort\etc\snort.conf. Although you might be a bit perplexed when you first attempt to open it and obtain the typical Windows message asking if it should either search the web or use an existing program to open the file of unknown

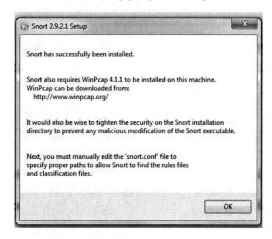

Snort 2.9.2.1 Setup

Snort has successfully been installed.

Snort also requires WinPcap 4.1.1 to be installed on this machine.
WinPcap can be downloaded from:
http://www.winpcap.org/

It would also be wise to tighten the security on the Snort installation directory to prevent any malicious modification of the Snort executable.

Next, you must manually edit the 'snort.conf' file to specify proper paths to allow Snort to find the rules files and classification files.

OK

Figure 8.4 Once Snort is successfully installed you need to carefully read its requirements.

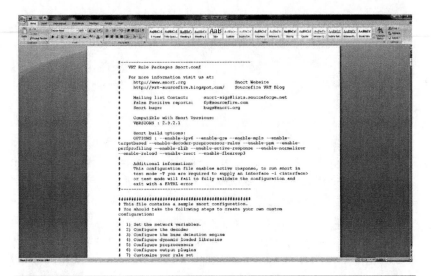

Figure 8.5   Viewing the first of 11 pages in the snort.conf file.

type, the file can be opened using Word. In fact, Figure 8.5 illustrates the first of 11 pages of the snort.conf file. While we will defer discussing this file until later in this chapter, remember its location.

8.1.3 Commencing Snort

Snort can operate in three modes, referred to as sniffer mode, packet logger mode, and Network Intrusion Detection System (NIDS) mode. In the sniffer mode of operation snort continuously reads packets on the network and displays them in a continuous stream. In the packet logger mode packets are logged to disk, while in the NIDS mode Snort will analyze packets against user-defined rules. As you might expect, NIDS is the most complex of the three modes. Prior to turning our attention to Snort's NIDS mode let's begin with the basics by using its sniffer mode of operation. In doing so we will use a few parameters or switches to gain an appreciation of their use.

8.1.3.1 Sniffer Mode   To use Snort we need to first locate its presence in the directory structure we just established. Since we are working with Windows, which requires downloading binary data, a good and logical place to commence our examination is in the snort\bin directory, where you will see the application named Snort.

Like several Command Prompt types of programs, you can use Snort with the -? switch to display a Help screen. In doing so you will note that the -v switch is used to place the program into a verbose mode of operation. Thus by using the -v switch with Snort we can simply display TCP/IP packet headers.

Since Snort runs in the Command Prompt you can open that window and change your location to c:\snort\bin, after which you would enter the following command:

```
c: \snort\bin -v
```

Entering the command with the -v parameter or switch will display the message "Running in packet dump mode" followed by initializing information, the display of the version of the program being executed, and some copyright data, followed by the display that packet processing has commenced and the actual packet processing. When this author commenced using Snort in its sniffer mode of operation with the -v switch the first three lines of display were as follows:

```
Commencing packet processing (pid = 6552)
02/28-17:59:04.394853 ARP who-has 192.168.2.2 tell
192.168.2.4
02/28-17:59:04.625760 ARP who-has 192.168.2.2 tell
192.168.2.3
```

In addition to displaying ARP information the sniffer mode resulted in the display of TCP/IP packet headers. For example, at 17:59 and 30.023 s on February 28 a UDP packet was displayed as follows:

```
= + = + = + = + = + = + = + = + = + = + = + = + = + =
+ = + = + = + = + = + = + = + = + = + = + = + = + = +
= + = + = + = +          02/28-17:59:30.023113
192.168.2.3:57113 -> 239.255.255.250:1900
UDP TTL:1 TOS:0x0 ID:27509 IpLen:20 DgmLen:161
Len: 133
= + = + = + = + = + = + = + = + = + = + = + = + = + =
+ = + = + = + = + = + = + = + = + = + = + = + = + = +
= + = + = + = +
```

While the sniffer mode will continuously display packets, once the buffer area in the Command Prompt window is filled the program will in effect write over previously displayed data. Thus if you wish to analyze a portion of the display you can consider issuing a Ctrl+C pair of keystrokes to in effect break the program's execution. When you do so the program will catch the interrupt and display summary statistics prior to terminating. In fact, sometimes you may just consider running Snort in its sniffer mode for a prolonged period of time and then come back to your computer and issue Ctrl+C to obtain a summary of activity on a network, in effect using a free counter of activity. The following illustrates a small portion of data generated by Snort when you enter Ctrl+C when in its sniffer mode. Note that the program will actually list a large number of protocols; however, because this author only used the program for a short period of time, the breakdown by protocol was limited.

```
Packet I/O Totals:
Received:    60
Analyzed:    26 (43.333%)
Dropped:     0 ( 0.000%)
Filtered:    0 ( 0.000%)
Outstanding: 34 (56.667%)
Injected:    0
= = = = = = = = = = = = = = = = = = = = = = = = = = = =
= = = = = = = = = = = = = = = = = = = = = = = = = = = =
Breakdown by protocol (includes rebuilt packets):
Eth:   26 (100.000%)
VLAN:  0 ( 0.000%)
IP4:   14 (53.846%)
Frag:  0 ( 0.000%)
ICMP:  0 ( 0.000%)
UDP:   14 (53.846%)
```

If you wanted to display application data you would then enter the switch -vd, where d represents application data. Thus the dual switch -vd, which can also be entered as -v -d, results in the display of both TCP/IP headers and application data. Now suppose you want to go one layer lower and display local area network headers. To do so you would add the switch -e, either entering

```
snort -vde
```

or

```
snort -v -d -e
```

8.1.3.2 Packet Logger Mode   In the packet logger mode of operation Snort will record packets to disk. To commence logging you would use the -l switch or parameter, followed by the directory where you want the log file to reside. When you install the Windows version of Snort it automatically will create a directory named Log under the Snort directory. Thus you would enter the following command to record packet data to a log file:

```
c:\snort\bin\snort -l \snort\log
```

As a result of the entry of the above command the program will create the file named snort.log in the directory c:\snort\log. Since the program will continuously log packet data to the file, at some point in time you will probably issue a Ctrl+C resulting in the file being saved and a summary of packet processing time, the number of packets processed, packet I/O totals, and a breakdown by protocols of the packets captured.

When working in a network environment you need to consider the frequency of packet flow. This is because the size of the recorded file can considerably grow over time. If you refer to the Snort user manual they suggest recording data in binary to reduce storage requirements. To do so you would add the -b switch to the logging command. That is, you would enter the following command:

```
c:\snort\bin\snort -l c:\snort\log -b
```

Note that in this example you need to enter the -b switch after the directory and file name.

One additional switch that deserves mention prior to moving on is the -r switch, which I like to think of as a rewind. This switch allows you to display previously recorded packets. In using the -r switch you need to be sure of the name of the previously logged file. On this author's computer the file name was snort.log.1330478336 and the file was located in the directory c:\snort\log. Thus to use this command switch correctly this author entered the following command in the Command Prompt window:

```
c:\Snort\log>c:\snort\bin\snort -r snort.
log.1330478336
```

After displaying the message "Running in packet dump mode" Snort will display initialization information followed by copyright data. After a quick display of the preceding Snort will display the previously captured packets followed by how long the program requires to process the packets, packet I/O totals, and a breakdown of protocols encountered, in essence everything that was previously logged to disk.

8.1.3.3 Network Intrusion Detection System Mode   The third and for many persons the most important mode of operation is the program's NIDS. However, prior to discussing NIDS we need to discuss the use of a special switch that can be of considerable assistance. That is the -? switch, which will result in the display of a Help screen concerning the usage of Snort and its various options. However, unlike the Help facility in the Command Prompt, to use Snort's facility you must prefix the question mark with a dash (-). Thus to access the Snort Help facility you would enter the following command in the Command Prompt, again assuming Snort was installed on the C drive in the directory snort\bin:

```
c:\Snort\bin>snort -?
```

The general format of the Snort program is:

```
snort [-options] <filter options>
```

Through the use of this program you can also install various services, display services, as well as uninstall the program. To install services and display services you would use the following two commands, with the second command used to display services previously installed.

```
snort \service\install [-options] <filter options>
snort \service\show
```

To uninstall services as you might expect you would enter the following command:

```
snort \service\uninstall
```

Table 8.1 lists the various options available. Note that the options are case sensitive. Also note that you can use options individually with

Table 8.1   Snort Command Line Switch Options

OPTION	DESCRIPTION OF USE
-A	Set the alert mode: fast, full, console, test, or none (alert file alertsonly)
-b	Log packets in tcpdump format
-B <mask>	Obfuscated IP addresses in alerts and packet dumps using CIDR mask
-c <rules>	Configure program by the use of Rules file <rules>
-C	Print out payloads with character data only (no hex)
-d	Dump the application layer
-e	Display the second layer header information
-E	Log alert messages to NT Eventlog (Win32 only)
-f	Turn off fflush() calls after binary log writes
-F <bpf>	Read BPF filters from file <bpf>
-G <0xid>	Log identifier (to uniquely ID events for multiple snorts)
-h <hn>	Set home network = <hn>
	(for use with -l or -B, does *not change* $HOME_NET in IDS mode)
-H	Make hash tables deterministic
-i <if>	Listen on interface <if>
-I	Add interface name to alert output
-k <mode>	Checksum mode (all, noip, notcp, noudp, noicmp, none)
-K <mode>	Logging mode (pcap [default], ascii, none)
-l <ld>	Log to directory <ld>
-L <file>	Log to this tcpdump file
-n <cnt>	Exit after receiving <cnt> packets
-N	Turn off logging (alerts still work)
-O	Obfuscate the logged IP addresses
-p	Disable promiscuous mode sniffing
-P <snap>	Set explicit snaplen of packet (default: 1514)
-q	Quiet; doesn't show banner and status report
-r <tf>	Read and process tcpdump file <tf>
-R <id>	Include "id" in snort_intf<id>.pid file name
-s	Log alert messages to syslog
-S <n = v>	Set Rules file variable n equal to value v
-T	Test and report on the current Snort configuration
-U	Use UTC for timestamps
-v	Be verbose
-V	Show version number
-W	Lists available interfaces (Win32 only)
-X	Dump the raw packet data starting at the link layer
-x	Exit if Snort configuration problems occur
-y	Include year in timestamp in the alert and log files
-Z <file>	Set the performonitor preprocessor file path and name
-?	Show this information

a minus sign prefix for each option or you can group options together with a single minus sign prefix. Thus snort -vde produces the same result as snort -v -d -e.

Concerning <Filter Options>, in Snort they are standard Berkeley Packet Filter (BPF) options that provide an interface to data link layers. Returning to the command line options, in addition to the use of letter and puncuation mark characters Snort also supports what is referred to as longname options. For example, you can enter either snort –help or snort– ? to display information about the various Snort options. While many longnames have a corresponding single-character version there are also dual and triple hyphenated longnames. Table 8.2 lists the Snort longnames available in the version of the program downloaded by this author. Note that you can obtain an up-to-date list of longnames by entering snort -? at any time after you download the program.

As an example of the use of Snort in its NIDS mode of operation let's dump the application layer (using the -d switch) and the network layer (using the -e switch) and specify the home network as 192.168.2.3 through the use of the -h switch. To do so we could enter the following command into the Command Prompt window.

```
\snort\bin\snort -d -e -l \snort\log -h 192.168.2.3/24
\snort\etc\snort.conf
```

where snort.conf represents the name of the Snort configuration file.

8.1.4 Command Switches

In the following paragraphs we review the use of several switches, and periodically include an example of the use of a switch. Note that because Snort distinguishes between upper- and lowercase switches it is important to verify the composition of switches to preclude an error or inadvertent operation from taking effect.

8.1.4.1 The -A Switch   The uppercase -A switch is used to set the alert mode: fast, full, console, test, or none. Thus the use of snort -A console would send alerts to the console.

Table 8.2 Snort Longname Options

LONGNAME OPTIONS	CORRESPONDING SINGLE-CHARACTER VERSION
— logid <0xid>	Same as -G
— perfmon-file <file>	Same as -Z
— pid-path <dir>	Specifies the directory for the Snort PID file
— snaplen <snap>	Same as -P
— help	Same as -?
— version	Same as -V

OTHER LONGNAME OPTIONS

— alert-before-pass	Processes alert, drop, sdrop, or reject before pass, default is pass before alert,drop …
— treat-drop-as-alert	Converts drop, sdrop, and reject rules into alert rules during start-up
— treat-drop-as-ignore	Uses drop, sdrop, and reject rules to ignore session traffic when not inline
— process-all-events	Processes all queued events (drop, alert, …); default stops after first action group
— enable-inline-test	Enables inline test mode operation
— dynamic-engine-lib <file>	Loads a dynamic detection engine
— dynamic-engine-lib-dir <path>	Loads all dynamic engines from directory
— dynamic-detection-lib <file>	Loads a dynamic rules library
— dynamic-detection-lib-dir <path>	Loads all dynamic rules libraries from directory
— dump-dynamic-rules <path>	Creates stub Rule files of all loaded rules libraries
— dynamic-preprocessor-lib <file>	Loads a dynamic preprocessor library
— dynamic-preprocessor-lib-dir <path>	Loads all dynamic preprocessor libraries from directory
— pcap-single <tf>	Same as -r
— pcap-file <file>	Contains a list of pcaps to read—read mode is implied
— pcap-list "<list>"	Contains a space-separated list of pcaps to read—read mode is implied
— pcap-loop <count>	Contains Reads the pcaps specified on command line continuously
— for <count> times	A value of 0 will read until Snort is terminated
— pcap-reset	If reading multiple pcaps, resets Snort to post-configuration state before reading next pcap
— pcap-show	Prints a line saying what pcap is currently being read
— exit-check <count>	Signals termination after <count> callbacks from DAQ_Acquire(), showing the time it takes from signaling until DAQ_Stop() is called
— conf-error-out	Same as -x
— enable-mpls-multicast	Allows multicast MPLS
— enable-mpls-overlapping-ip	Handles overlapping IPs within MPLS clouds
— max-mpls-labelchain-len	Specifies the max MPLS label chain

(continued)

Table 8.2   Snort Longname Options (continued)

LONGNAME OPTIONS	CORRESPONDING SINGLE-CHARACTER VERSION
— mpls-payload-type	Specifies the protocol (IPv4, IPv6, Ethernet) that is encapsulated by MPLS
— require-rule-sid	Requires that all Snort rules have SID specified
— daq <type>	Selects packet acquisition module (default is pcap)
— daq-mode <mode>	Selects the DAQ operating mode
— daq-var <name = value>	Specifies extra DAQ configuration variable
— daq-dir <dir>	Tells Snort where to find desired DAQ
— daq-list [<dir>]	Lists packet acquisition modules available in dir

8.1.4.2 The -b Switch   The lowercase -b switch is used to log packets in a format that can be read by the tcpdump program, which in a Windows environment is WinDump. Through the use of this switch data are logged in binary, which is faster and very useful when you are monitoring a high-speed network.

8.1.4.3 The -B Switch   The uppercase -B switch is used to obfuscate IP addresses in alerts and packet dumps using a Classless Interdomain Routing (CIDR) mask. Thus this switch needs to be followed by an IP address and CDIR mask. An example of its use follows:

```
snort -B 192.168.1.1/16
```

An example of the use of this switch is illustrated below, with two packets displayed. Note that while the packet display continued as shown below, any alert with the given IP address and CDIR mask would be obfuscated.

```
Commencing packet processing (pid = 2992)
03/14-20:47:47.938291 192.168.2.4:5353 ->
192.168.0.251:5353
UDP TTL:255 TOS:0x0 ID:56096 IpLen:20 DgmLen:279
Len: 251
= + = + = + = + = + = + = + = + = + = + = + = + = + =
+ = + = + = + = + = + = + = + = + = + = + = + = + = +
= + = + = + = +
03/14-20:47:51.704988 192.168.2.3:6646 ->
192.168.2.255:6646
UDP TTL:128 TOS:0x0 ID:14426 IpLen:20 DgmLen:897
Len: 869
```

```
= + = + = + = + = + = + = + = + = + = + = + = + = + = + =
+ = + = + = + = + = + = + = + = + = + = + = + = + = + = +
= + = + = + = +
The -c, l and h switches
```

The lowercase -c switch is probably the most important switch, as it directs Snort to apply the rules in its configuration file. There are three "gotcha" issues you need to consider. The first is running as the administrator in the command mode, which will then let you relocate the configuration file if you so desire. A second issue is you need to enter the location of the configuration file. For example, in its default setting the file snort.conf is located at c:\snort\etc. Thus you might enter:

```
snort -v -c c:\snort\etc\snort.conf
```

where snort.conf is the name of your configuration file. This action will apply the rules configured in the snort.conf file to each packet, and based upon the rule type in the file, one or more actions may be taken. Note that if you do not specify an output directory the program will use the \snort\log directory, placing output in a file named snort.log, followed by a nine-digit generated number. A third gotcha was the last paragraph in the Setup menu shown in Figure 8.4 and which is very easy to miss when you are installing this program. As a refresher, the last paragraph in the Setup menu informs you to "manually edit the snort.conf file to specify proper paths to allow snort to find rules and classification files." Thus when you specify the snort.conf file you should make sure it was previously altered to allow path information to reflect where the applicable files are located on your computer.

Another item that is worth mentioning is the fact that when using the -l switch you may notice that Snort sometimes uses the address of the remote computer as the directory in which it places packets. Other times it uses the local host address. Thus to log relative to the home network, you need to tell Snort which network is the home network. To do so you would use the -h switch as follows, remembering that by default the binary version of Snort is located in the directory \snort\bin, while logging occurs into the directory snort\log:

```
c:\Snort>cd\snort\bin
c:\Snort\bin>snort -l \snort\log -h 192.168.2.0/16
```

```
Running in packet logging mode
- = = Initializing Snort = =-
```

In the preceding example we will log packets relative to the 192.168.2.0 network, with all incoming packets recorded into the log subdirectory.

8.1.4.4 The -C Switch   The uppercase -C switch is used to print out payloads with character data only, which eliminates hexadecimal characters. You can append the -C switch to the prior example as follows:

```
c:\Snort\bin>snort -l \snort\log -h 192.168.2.0/16 -C
```

8.1.4.5 The -d Switch   The lowercase -d switch is used to dump the application layer. Similar to the preceding example, you can simply add the -d switch to a command line entry.

8.1.4.6 The -E Switch   The uppercase -E switch is only applicable to Win32. This switch results in log alert messages being sent to the Windows NT Eventlog.

8.1.4.7 The -f Switch   The lowercase -f switch is employed to turn off fflush() calls after binary log writes.

8.1.4.8 The -F Switch   The uppercase -F switch is used to read BPF filters from a file. Thus the switch must be followed by the location and file name containing <bpf>. Note that BPF provides some Unix-like systems with a raw interface to data link layers, permitting raw link-layer packets to be sent and received

8.1.4.9 The -G Switch   The purpose of the uppercase -G switch is to enable multiple snorts to be identified by unique ID events. Thus the -G switch must be followed by an identifier of the form 0xid.

8.1.4.10 The -H Switch   The uppercase -H switch is used to make hash tables deterministic. Note that a hash table represents a data structure that uses a hash function to map identifying values, referred to as keys to their associated values, such as a person's name to a telephone number or address.

8.1.4.11 The –i Switch The lowercase -i switch is used to inform Snort of the interface it should listen on for packets. When used the -i switch is followed by the interface number; thus its format or syntax is:

```
-i <if>
```

where <if> is the interface number.

When used with the uppercase G switch you can run multiple instances of Snort on the same computer to monitor different interfaces. Each instance will use the value specified to generate unique event IDs. Note that you can specify either a decimal value or a hex value preceded by 0x for the -G option. For example,

```
c:\snort\bin\snort -i3 -G2
```

will result in Snort monitoring interface 3 as instance 2.

8.1.4.12 The –I Switch The uppercase -I switch is used to add an interface name to alert output. Through its use the specified interface name is appended to alert.

8.1.4.13 The –k and –K Switches The lowercase -k switch is employed to place the program in its checksum mode, while the uppercase -K switch is used for its logging mode. Both letters are followed by the applicable mode indicator, such as all, noip, notcp, noudp, noicmp, and none for the -k switch, and pcap [default], ascii, or none for the -K switch. Thus the format for either switch is a negative sign followed by the lower- or uppercase letter followed by the mode.

8.1.4.14 The –l and –L Switches The lowercase -l switch is used to log packets to a directory, while the uppercase -L switch causes packets to be logged to a tcpdump (WinDump) file. Thus the lowercase -l switch is followed by the log directory, while the uppercase -L switch is followed by the location and file name of the tcpdump file.

8.1.4.15 The –n Switch The lowercase -n switch causes the program to terminate after receiving a defined number of packets. Thus the -n switch is followed by a count value. An example of its use to exit after 10 packets are displayed follows:

```
C:\snort\bin>snort -n 10
```

8.1.4.16 The -O Switch   The uppercase -O switch is employed to hide or obfuscate the logged IP addresses. The following example illustrates its use to hide IP addresses as well as have the program exit after five packets. To facilitate the use of space, the copyright, runtime, and packet I/O statistics are not shown in the output.

```
C:\Snort\bin>snort -n 5 -O
Running in packet dump mode
Commencing packet processing (pid = 3600)
03/31-16:34:22.263077 xxx.xxx.xxx.xxx:6646 -> xxx.xxx.
xxx.xxx:6646
UDP TTL:128 TOS:0x0 ID:12192 IpLen:20 DgmLen:1036
Len: 1008
= + = + = + = + = + = + = + = + = + = + = + = + = + =
+ = + = + = + = + = + = + = + = + = + = + = + = + = +
= + = + = + = + = + = + = + = + = + = +
03/31-16:34:22.396596 xxx.xxx.xxx.xxx:6646 -> xxx.xxx.
xxx.xxx:6646
UDP TTL:128 TOS:0x0 ID:32465 IpLen:20 DgmLen:1036
Len: 1008
= + = + = + = + = + = + = + = + = + = + = + = + = + =
+ = + = + = + = + = + = + = + = + = + = + = + = + = +
= + = + = + = + = + = + = + = + = + = +
03/31-16:34:25.163871 xxx.xxx.xxx.xxx:6646 -> xxx.xxx.
xxx.xxx:6646
UDP TTL:128 TOS:0x0 ID:12193 IpLen:20 DgmLen:198
Len: 170
= + = + = + = + = + = + = + = + = + = + = + = + = + =
+ = + = + = + = + = + = + = + = + = + = + = + = + = +
= + = + = + = + = + = + = + = + = + = +
03/31-16:34:25.257706 xxx.xxx.xxx.xxx:6646 -> xxx.xxx.
xxx.xxx:6646
UDP TTL:128 TOS:0x0 ID:32476 IpLen:20 DgmLen:198
Len: 170
= + = + = + = + = + = + = + = + = + = + = + = + = + =
+ = + = + = + = + = + = + = + = + = + = + = + = + = +
= + = + = + = + = + = + = + = + = +
```

```
03/31-16:34:25.358748 ARP who-has 192.168.2.1 tell
192.168.2.2
```

8.1.4.17 The -p and -P Switches The lowercase -p switch is used to disable promiscuous mode sniffing. In comparison, the uppercase -P switch is used to set the snaplen (snap length, which is the amount of data in each packet actually captured) of the packet. In effect this filters how much of each packet gets into Snort, where the default is 1514 bytes. Thus the -P switch must be followed by an integer that defines the snaplen.

8.1.4.18 The -q Switch The lowercase -q switch places Snort in its quiet mode, surpressing its banner and status report. To illustrate the use of a few switches consider the following example, which uses the -d switch to dump the application layer, the -v switch to enable the program's verbose mode, the -q switch to surpress its banner and status report, and exit after receiving 1 packet by using the -n switch.

```
C:\Snort\bin>snort -d -q -v -n1
04/01-12:42:43.735414 192.168.2.3:6646 ->
192.168.2.255:6646
UDP TTL:128 TOS:0x0 ID:3436 IpLen:20 DgmLen:198
Len: 170
00 00 00 A6 00 00 00 04 00 00 00 00 00 00 00 08
...............
00 00 00 18 4D 00 63 00 4E 00 41 00 55 00 6E 00
....M.c.N.A.U.n.
69 00 71 00 75 00 65 00 49 00 64 00 0B 00 00 00
i.q.u.e.I.d.....
24 00 00 00 31 63 31 30 37 38 66 61 2D 35 62 36
$...1c1078fa-5b6
65 2D 34 34 32 30 2D 62 34 35 63 2D 61 36 33 63
e-4420-b45c-a63c
65 64 30 37 30 33 31 61 01 00 00 00 18 4D 00 63
ed07031a.....M.c
00 4E 00 41 00 55 00 6E 00 69 00 71 00 75 00 65
.N.A.U.n.i.q.u.e
00 49 00 64 00 0B 00 00 00 24 00 00 00 38 63 33
.I.d.....$...8c3
31 34 31 63 64 2D 66 63 65 39 2D 34 64 39 32 2D
141cd-fce9-4d92-
```

```
62 61 33 36 2D 37 65 33 32 30 37 39 33 63 33 33  ba36-
7e320793c33
33 01 7B DE F7 BD 00 00 00 2C              3.{......,
= + = + = + = + = + = + = + = + = + = + = + = + =
+ = + = + = + = + = + = + = + = + = + = + = + = +
= + = + = + = + = + = + = + = + = +
```

Note that although you could enter the preceding command as snort –dqvn1, this author prefers to separate entries for clarity.

8.1.4.19 The –r and –R Switches   The lowercase -r switch is used to read and process a previously created tcpdump file. Thus the -r switch is followed by the location and file name of the tcpdump file. In comparison, the uppercase -R switch is used to include "id" in the snort_intf<id>.pid file name; thus it is followed by the ID.

8.1.4.20 The –s and –S Switches   The lowercase -s switch is used to log alerts to the system log (syslog), while the uppercase -S switch is used to set the Rules file variable n equal to value v; thus the -S switch is followed by the expression n = v.

8.1.4.21 The –T Switch   The uppercase -T switch is used to test and report on the current Snort program configuration. The test mode must be run with a Snort configuration file. Thus you need to use the -c option on the command line to specify a configuration file.

8.1.4.22 The –U Switch   The uppercase -U switch is employed to use UTC for timestamps. UTC stands for Coordinated Universal Time, which is a 24 h time standard and is the same as Greenwich Mean Time.

8.1.4.23 The –v and –V Switches   The lowercase -v switch places the program into its verbose mode, while the uppercase -V switch results in the version number of the program being displayed.

8.1.4.24 The –W Switch   The uppercase -W switch is only applicable to the 32-bit version of Windows, showing the list of available interfaces.

8.1.4.25 The -X and -x Switches The uppercase -X switch is employed to dump raw packet data commencing at the link layer. In comparison, the lowercase -x switch results in a program exit if configuration problems occur.

8.1.4.26 The -y Switch The lowercase -y switch results in the year being added to the timestamp in the alert and log files.

8.1.4.27 The -Z Switch At the end of the alphabet is the uppercase -Z switch. This switch is used to set the performonitor preprocessor file path and name; hence it is followed by the location of the file and its name.

8.1.5 Network Intrusion Detection System Mode

While all of the prior switches affect the operation of the program, its key utilization is when it is used in its NIDS mode. Thus in the remainder of this section we focus our attention on its NIDS mode of operation.

To run Snort in its NIDS mode you need to alter the snort.conf file that by default is located in the snort\etc directory. First, returning to Figure 8.5, which showed the first page of the snort.conf file, you need to go through the file to make applicable changes. Perhaps the first thing you need to do is rename the sample snort.conf file, perhaps as snort.confbak, so you will have a backup of the original file. Next, you need to go through the setup section, where you will enter the network you are protecting, the external network addresses, and various server addresses, if applicable. If you're in doubt about your computer's IP address or the IP address of the DNS server, use of the ipconfig command should help. For other servers, the technical control center should have a list of servers and their IP addresses. In this example the IP address of this author's computer was 192.168.2.2. Thus in the setup section he would adjust the setting of the address as follows:

```
# Setup the network addresses you are protecting
ipvar HOME_NET 192.168.2.2/24
```

Since the external network addresses reference all the other networks, this author did not make any changes to the next setup sequence. However, through the use of ipconfig it was determined that the DNS server's IP address was 192.168.2.1. Thus the next change made to the snort.conf file was:

```
# List of DNS servers on your network
ipvar DNS_SERVERS 192.168.2.1
```

Assuming that no changes are made to other servers or to the default ports we now come to the Rules section of the file. The Rules section uses a Unix directory structure, so it must be changed to conform to the DOS structure. In fact, in the snort.conf file the following note is most important:

Note for Windows users: You are advised to make this an absolute path,

```
# such as: c:\snort\rules
```

In the Rules section you would make the following changes so that Unix settings are now converted into DOS settings that will work under Windows.

```
var RULE_PATH c:\snort\rules
var SO_RULE_PATH c:\snort\so_rules
var PREPROC_RULE_PATH c:\snort\preproc_rules
```

After you make the change to the Rules directory you will more than likely not have any changes until you reach the area after step 4, which is the path to dynamic preprocessor libraries. Here the first entry is as follows in Unix form:

```
dynamicpreprocessor directory/usr/local/lib/snort_
dynamicpreprocessor/
```

Since the Windows version of Snort locates the library in c:\snort\ libl\ snort_dynamicpreprocessor you would replace the snort.conf file entry as follows:

```
dynamicpreprocessor c:\snort\lib\snort_dynamicprepro-
cessor
```

Next we need to change the path to the base preprocessor engine from its Unix form to its DOS form. In the snort.conf file we would encounter the following:

```
# path to base preprocessor engine
```

dynamicengine/usr/local/lib/snort_dynamicengine/libsf_engine.so

which we would change to:

```
# path to base preprocessor engine
dynamicengine c:\snort\lib\snort_dynamicengine\sf_
engine.dll
```

Now you want to capture packets. You would then change the applicable entries in step 6 in the snort.conf file. For example, we might add the following statement:

```
output alert_fast: alerts.ids
```

You also need to create a file in the log directory that will have the same name so it will be associated with the alerts.ids file we just created. To do so you can use Notepad and simply go to the snort\log directory and save a 0-byte file as alerts.ids.

Next there are two statements prior to Section 7 in the version of snort.conf downloaded by this author that require changes to conform to the structure of Snort on Windows devices. Although you will note that Snort says "Do not modify these lines," you need to change those lines to reflect the fact that Snort has the classification and reference config files in the directory labeled Etc under the Snort directory. Thus after the "Do not modify" line you would make the following changes to the two following lines:

```
# metadata reference data. do not modify these lines
include c:\snort\etc\classification.config
include c:\snort\etc\reference.config
```

Now with the previously made changes to the snort.conf file it's time to save those changes and work with the Rules file. To do so direct your browser to https://www.snort.org/snort-rules/.

Depending upon whether you're a subscriber or registered user, it's possible you may have different versions of a zipped tar file; however, a subscriber appears to be at most a month ahead of a registered user according to Snort documentation. You can download and extract Rules files to the snort\rules folder. Once this is completed you are ready to run Snort in its NIDS mode of operation. Then you would enter into the Command Prompt the following partial command:

```
c:\snort\bin\snort -A console -c c:\snort\etc\snort.
conf
```

which uses the uppercase -A switch to direct alerts to the console, while the lowercase -c switch causes the snort.conf file we previously altered to be loaded. Now because we probably want to log data, we would add the following to the previous command line entry:

```
-l c:\snort\log\ -K ascii
```

where the lowercase -l switch causes logging while the uppercase -K switch causes the logging mode to occur in ASCII as specified. Thus our command line entry would become:

```
c:\snort\bin\snort -A console -c c:\snort\etc\snort.
conf -l c:\snort\log\ -K ascii
```

The preceding will result in Snort running as a basic NIDS system. By altering its configuration file you can then adjust its NIDS capability to your specific requirements.

8.2 Using SpywareBlaster

A product of Javacool Software, SpywareBlaster represents a program designed to protect your computer from downloading spyware and other types of malicious software. This program has a number of features that make its use most interesting and effective.

8.2.1 Obtaining the Program

If you point your browser to the URL of http://www.javacoolsoft-ware.com/spywareblaster.html you will access the home page of Javacool Software, which has a prominent green button labeled Free Download with the version number of the program. When this author downloaded his copy of SpywareBlaster the currect version of the program was version 4.6. If you click on the Free Download button you will see a screen similar to the one illustrated in Figure 8.6, which provides you with several options. You can either continue with the download by clicking on the gray button with that label or select to obtain an automatic update so that your program will always represent the latest version of the program.

Since this author did not want to have automatic updates he selected the button labeled Continue Download, which resulted in a new page being displayed that provided links to two sites from which the program could be downloaded, Download.com, which would result in having a new tab being opened at http://download.cnet.com/SpywareBlaster/3000-8022-10196637.html?part = dl-SpywareBl&subj = dl&tag = button, or Major Geeks, whose selection would result in a tab opening at http://www.majorgeeks.com/SpywareBlaster_d2859.html. For either selection you would be able

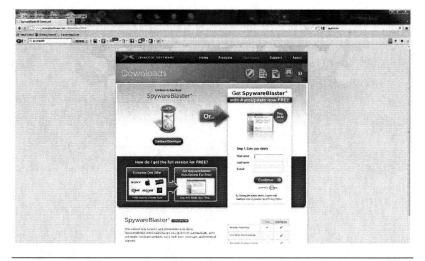

Figure 8.6 The Javacool Software download page.

to download the laterst version of the program. Figure 8.6 illustrates the Javacool Software download page.

The SpywareBlaster program is an executable binary file that operates under Windows and does not require the use of the Command Prompt. When you download the program you will be prompted for the location where it should reside, for which this author uses the directory labeled Download for obvious reasons. Once downloaded a simple double-click on the file will generate a warning about whether or not to allow it to run. Assuming you let it execute and make changes to your computer the program will use a setup wizard that will prompt you to accept the licensing agreement prior to proceeding. Assuming you accept the licensing agreement the wizard will propose a location for the program's installation that you could change but rarely need to do. Next you will be given the option to add a shortcut to the desktop, after which you will be allowed to install the program, and you will have a dialog box display informing you the program was installed and asking if you wish to run it at this time. Assuming you do, two windows will quickly pop up on your screen. In the background will be a list of your browsers and their SpywareBlaster protection status, while in the foreground a SpywareBlaster tutorial screen will be displayed. Figure 8.7 illustrates the initial SpywareBlaster tutorial screen. Note that you can also display the tutorial screen from the main SpywareBlaster

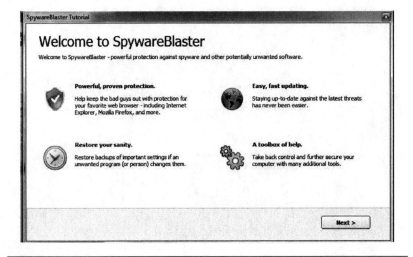

Figure 8.7 The SpywareBlaster tutorial screen.

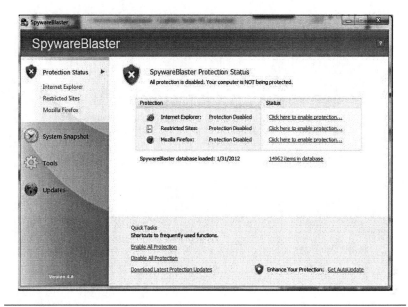

Figure 8.8   The initial SpywareBlaster protection status display with protection disabled.

screen, which we review shortly. However, when you first install SpywareBlaster you probably should use the tutorial since if you did not select an updating option you will be given another chance by clicking on the button labeled Next in the tutorial screen shown in Figure 8.7.

Once you click on the button labeled Next you will be able to select an updating option, either automatic updating or manual updating. This will be followed by a "Thank you!" which displays a button labeled Finish. Now that we briefly discussed the SpywareBlaster tutorial we can move on a bit backwards to the screen that was quickly overwritten by the tutorial screen. That screen is the initial program screen, which when operating on this author's computer is shown in Figure 8.8.

8.2.2 Adding Protection

Initially as shown, all protection is disabled. To add protection you can simply click on an entry to the right of the browser entry or the restricted sites' entry. In addition to providing information about your computer's protection status this screen also allows you to select from several entries located on the left portion of the screen, such as

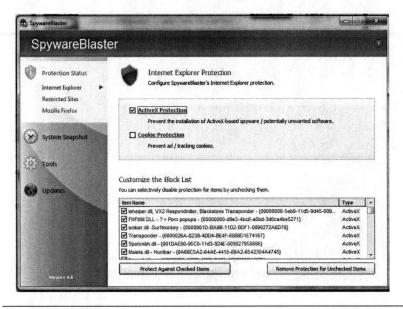

Figure 8.9 Adding ActiveX protection to Internet Explorer.

System Snapshot, Tools, and Update. This screen also informs you when the program's database was loaded and the number of items in the database. At the lower portion of Figure 8.8 you find a shortcut to frequently used functions as well as entries to enable or disable all protection as well as to download the latest protection updates.

To illustrate the use of this program as well as its ease of use let's protect Internet Explorer. To do so you simply need to click on the entry to the right of the Internet Explorer Protection Disabled status. Doing so results in the program requiring you to select either ActiveX or Cookie protection or both. In the example shown in the top portion of Figure 8.9 ActiveX protection is shown being added as protection to Microsoft's Internet Explorer. As a personal aside, this author belives that if organizations wish to add cookies to track his website visits they can have at it and will probably wonder about his visits. Note that after this author selected ActiveX protection the program listed items in a block list that you could selectively disable by placing a checkmark into each applicable square associated with an item name. At the bottom of Figure 8.9 you can either protect every item or remove any previously protected item in the customized block list. What this author did to show how some programs are redundant is to add a porn pop-up by going to a website known for its infection.

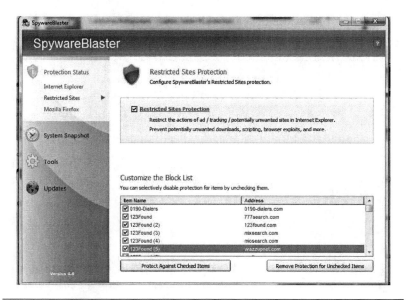

Figure 8.10   SpywareBlaster's restricted site protection screen.

Because my web browser blocks pop-ups, adding protections against specific pop-ups is a bit redundant.

8.2.2.1 Restricted Site Protection   After configuring SpywareBlaster to protect Internet Explorer this author was curious about its restricted sites capability, so the next item on the agenda was to select it from the entry on the left column of Figure 8.9. This action results in a new window being displayed concerning restricted sites protection, as shown in Figure 8.10. By selecting the box to enable restricted sites protection, this action not only restricts the action of ad and tracking sites, but also blocks dialers from doing some nasty things, such as dialing Tierra del Fuego and other locations at exorbitant telephone rates.

If we focus on the left portion of any illustration between Figures 8.8 and 8.10 we can note the left gray appearing area shown here (which is a colored area in real life) column with a series of icons that are light at the top, to indicate the area we are working with. One icon in the shape of a clock is associated with what is referred to as system snapshot. When we select that icon the prior selected Protection Status icon and bar will lose its highlight, which will now be focused on system snapshot, with the System Snapshot screen now appearing in the main portion of the display, as shown in Figure 8.11. Note that this capability

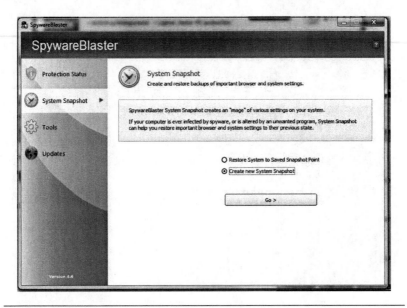

Figure 8.11   The system snapshot.

is similar to the system restore capability built in to modern versions of Windows. However, while system restore was developed to help you restore your computer's system files to an earlier point in time, in effect undoing system changes while maintaining the status quo for data files, SpywareBlaster's System Snapshop creates and restores backups of critical browser and system settings that could be adversely affected by an out-of-control virus or another type of software. Thus SpywareBlaster's snapshot capability is oriented toward a browser while Microsoft's restore point is oriented toward system changes.

8.2.2.2 System Snapshot   Returning our attention to Figure 8.11, note that you only have two options. You can either select the Restore option or create a new system snapshot. Of course, a third option is to simply ignore this capability and continue your exploration of the program by selecting the Tools entry on the left of the screen. However, if you progressed this far in the use of this program it is recommended that you use its System Snapshot capability. When you select the Creation option a new window will appear that will prompt you to enter a name for the saved snapshot, and by default a box will be checked that will add the date and time to the name. Although you can change this option this author would recommend keeping the date and time appended, as they serve as a guide to when the snapshot occurred. Concerning the snapshot, it occurs much faster than creating a system restore point, which one would expect due to its focus on a specific piece of software. If at a later date you decide you need to restore a previously saved system snapshop, after selecting the Restore option and clicking on the button labeled Go, previously saved snapshops will be listed. You can select a snapshop for deletion or proceed to have the snapshot used. Concerning the latter, the program will compare the selected snapshot to your current state, and if there are no changes it will allow you to go back and select a different snapshot.

8.2.3 *The Tools Menu*

The next item on our agenda for reviewing is the Tools menu. The default Tools page is shown in Figure 8.12, from which you can select five items. The first item is Browser Pages, which when selected allows you to view and change the browser's home page, search page, default page URL, and local page. In addition, you can display any unused or unassigned pages as well as add entries to any page. What is nice about this capability is that you can perform this for different users of a computer by simply selecting the users from a pull-down bar.

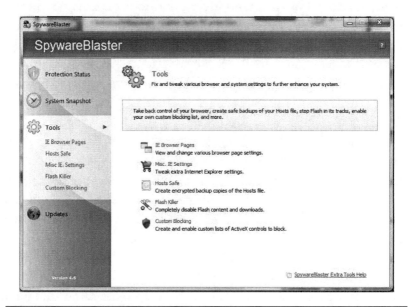

Figure 8.12 The SpywareBlaster Tools menu.

One item that was noted as a slight error was the placement of entries between the Tools selection menu and its main display. In the main display the next item was its miscellenous IE settings (Misc IE Settings), while in the left column Hosts Safe was the next item shown. Assuming you select the Misc IE Settings entry, shown as the second item in the main portion of Figure 8.12, you will be able to disable the IE home page settings if you so desire, as well as change the text to be displayed after the web page name in the Internet Explorer title bar.

The next option in the Tools main page is labeled Hosts Safe. Selecting this option allows you to store encrypted backup copies of the Hosts file. As a refresher for some readers, the Hosts file contains the association between host names (www.something.com) and their IP addresses, similar to a DNS server. Since the browser first checks the Hosts file for a name resolution to acquire an IP address, the potential corruption of this file can result in your browser going to addresses it shouldn't. Thus while the Hosts file can slightly enhance the speed of accessing web pages by eliminating the need for some name resolutions, it can also result in some potential problems, both inadvertent and by design. Concerning inadvertent problems, if a website has moved to a new IP address, an old entry in your Hosts file can render it inaccessible. Concerning the latter, some malicious programs will use the Hosts file to redirect browsers from a legitimate site to a phishing site where you might log on to a dummy website and provide information that could be used to wipe out your account. SpywareBlaster provides the ability to keep encrypted backup copies of your Hosts file as well as an easy method to restore a good backup copy of your Hosts file. In the event you think this is far fetched, according to a newspaper article this author read in April 2012 in the *Maui Times*, the FBI noted that a DNS software changer had infected a large number of host computers and as a result established a website where users could test their computers to determine if they were infected. The web URL is http://dns-ok.us/. For additional information regarding the DNS changer malware you should visit the FBI's website at http://www.fbi.gov/news/stories/2011/november/malware_110911.

8.2.3.1 *Flash Killer*   Another option provided by SpywareBlaster is the ability to disable the popular Macromedia Flash program. Under certain situations advertisers use Flash to place distracting advertisements on your computer, so this is a method to block those advertisements. Unfortunately, killing Flash also blocks some popular websites from their full potential, which is why the program easily allows you to revert back to allowing Flash.

8.2.3.2 Custom Blocking   The last entry in the Tools window is labeled Custom Blocking. Selecting this entry allows you to build your own list of ActiveX controls that should be blocked. As a warning to users, the program tells you to use caution when using a custom blocking list someone else has created.

8.2.4 *Checking for Updates*

In concluding our examination of SpywareBlaster we turn our attention to its Updates option, the main window of which is shown in Figure 8.13. The screen shown in Figure 8.13 resulted from clicking on the Updates icon in the highlighted left portion of the screen. This action allows you to check for updates to the program. Note that the last update attempt, version currently loaded, and a link for information about automatic updates are also on this page display. If you click on the Options entry under the Updates entry you can control how

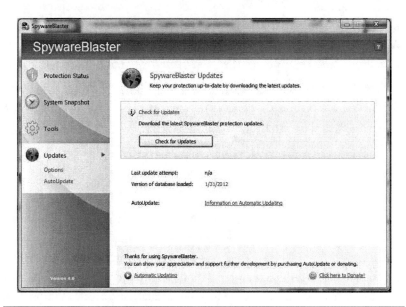

Figure 8.13   The main SpywareBlaster Updates window.

updates occur, via a direct connection to the Internet, which is the default setting, via system proxy settings, using a defined proxy setting, or via an alternative method, which should only be used when downloading results in a file corruption and the selection of an alternative method forces the program to use an alternative method for updates. The third and last entry in the Update section is Autoupdates. Selecting this entry allows you to receive automatic program updates as well as, if you desire, to support future development of the program.

8.3 Using Online Armor

If you are like this author you always wonder about someone placing a keylogger program on your computer and the effect it could have on your personal and work experience. This is because most office employees use the Internet to periodically make online purchases using their credit cards or log on to their stock account or perform other types of financial actions. While such actions are encrypted so data flowing between the computer and the destination are protected your keystrokes are not. Recognizing the need for a keyboard logger as well as adding firewall and web shield functions is a program from Emsisoft marketed as Online Armor, which can be downloaded from http://www.emsisoft.com/en/. As you will note when you visit that URL, there are three versions of the program: freeware, a full version, and an Internet security pack, which contains a firewall and antivirus software. This author will review the installation and operation of the Internet security pack, which was available on a 30-day trial basis at the time this book was written. You can obtain the free trial version of the program by either entering "online armor" into a search engine or going to http://www.online-armor.com/products-online-armor-free.php.

8.3.1 Installation

Similar to many programs Online Armor is obtained as a binary file. You should save the file in a relevantly named directory and once downloaded, double-click on the file. During the setup process you will be asked to select a language, after which the wizard will install the program on your computer. Figure 8.14 illustrates the Online Armor setup wizard, which was used to install version 5.5 of the program on this

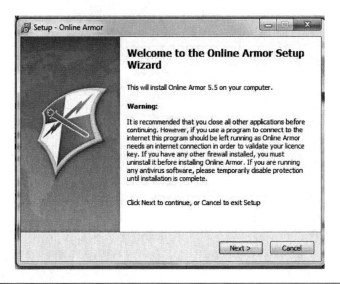

Figure 8.14 The Online Armor setup wizard.

author's computer. The setup wizard has the familiar license and main-tance agreement form that defaults to not accepting the agreement, so to install the program you need to accept it. Once this is accomplished the wizard program will display the location where it will install Online Armor and allow you to select a different location and program name if you so desire. Although the program will inform you of its space requirements, it appears not to check to determine if appplicable hard drive storage is available. Since the program required 67.3 MB of stor-age this was well within the author's available storage and should be of sufficient size to add to most modern computers that have drives beginning at 1 tetrabyte. Next, the setup wizard will create shortcuts in the Start Menu folder if you so desire, after which it will finish the installation process. However, as a delayed reaction Windows Security issued a prompt to install TLEM Network Service from the publisher Emsi Software GmbH, which was a driver associated with the pro-gram. Once this software is installed a safety check wizard will walk you through the configuration of the program.

The initial screen of the safety check wizard is shown in Figure 8.15. You basically have two options from this screen: to trust everything on your computer or use a step-by-step wizard that guides you through the steps necessary to detect installed programs on your computer. Although "Trust everything on this computer" was originally selected

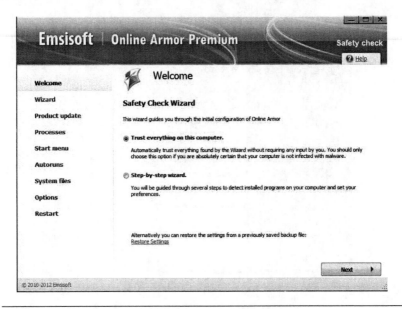

Figure 8.15   The initial screen of the Online Armor safety check wizard.

by this author for illustrative purposes, since most readers may have a variety of devices with potential problematic software or need a better understanding of the programs on their machines, you should consider selecting the second entry.

In Figure 8.16 readers will view the use of the Online Armor step-by-step wizard that was checking this author's computer. Note that in checking autoruns the message "Not Passed" was displayed. This author was using an HP TouchSmart computer with a wireless mouse and keyboard. Apparently software for the HP keyboard, which transmitted keystrokes to the computer, was considered a potential threat.

At the bottom of Figure 8.16 note that the step-by-step wizard was in the process of preparing a list of unknown files. If you have a comprehensive suite of programs chances are rather high that Online Armor will not recognize at least a few and possibly many of the programs you have. If either situation arises this program will prompt you when it protects your computer by displaying pop-up information about a program attempting to allow an Internet connection, invoke another program, or perform another function that could be detrimental to the health of your computer. Once the step-by-step wizard completes its action it will either walk you through a series of checkpoints that require attention or ask you to reboot your machine if the

Figure 8.16 Online Armor step-by-step wizard.

program recognizes every one of your programs, which to this author is an unlikely event. About the only negative the author feels this program has is its lack of recognition of many popular programs, such as the Apple Software Update program, Apple's Safari web browser, the NY Times reader, and similar programs. In a perfect world the developers might include recognition of those programs, but we do not live in a perfect world. Fortunately, the program allows you to select the programs you trust, which will then avoid the display of pop-ups when the program runs.

8.3.2 Operation

Figure 8.17 illustrates how Online Armor allows you to select the programs you have knowledge about and are comfortable with allowing to run when the computer is turned on. Note that if you have second thoughts about allowing a program you will still have an opportunity at a later time to decide whether or not to allow it to run. In the example illustrated in Figure 8.17 this author allowed HPAdvisor, a well-known program associated with most HP computers and which is highlighted in the referenced figure. As you examine Figure 8.17 note that in addition to the HPAdvisor.exe there are other recognizable

Figure 8.17   Allowing an unrecognized program to start when you turn on your PC.

programs that operate upon starting this author's computer. For example, HitachiBackupService.exe is used to back up the contents of several key directories, while several HP products, to include the HPAdvisor that was allowed and an HP Quick Synchronization Service, are also shown. Concerning the latter, this author believes in dual backups of important data and has both a built-in but removable HP backup drive as well as a stand-alone Hitachi backup drive. After all, having once experienced a computer failure and the inability of the backup drive to restore data, this author decided that it was worth a bit of performance to obtain a dual backup capability.

Once you select files for autorum and enable system files not recognized, Online Armor will display an Options screen. This screen will have six tabs labeled General, Firewall, Exclusions, Backup/Restore, Hotkeys, and License. The General tab allows you to launch the program at the next start-up as well as check for updates, change the interface language, and even enter a debug mode if you so desire. The Firewall has settings that allow trusted programs to access the Internet, notify you of access attempts, enable or disable logging based upon different events, look up external IP addresses, and other activities not found in most conventional firewalls that simply allow or deny based upon IP addresses or port values. The

Exclusions tab allows you to exclude folders from the program's protection, while the Backup/Restore tab allows you to back up and restore the program's settings. The Hotkeys tab shows the hotkeys used to control various aspects of the program. Online Armor uses Ctrl+Alt+ and a third character for many functions that are displayed in this tab, and if necessary you can change the hotkey. For example, Ctrl+Alt+F displays the firewall settings as well as shows three graphs labeled "inbound data," "outbound data," and "connections" at the top of the display. The last tab, License, shows you license information, such as how many days remain on your trial and how to activate a new program key. Once you work your way through these tabs and click on the button labeled Next you will be asked to restart your computer. The first time this happens will require you to more than likely authorize or deny one or more unrecognized programs. One example of a common program that was not recognized by Online Armor is bttray.exe, which represents a product from Bluetooth Software. Although you will need to allow or deny numerous programs, unlike many security programs that simply ask you to allow or deny a product or connection, this program describes the program and what it appears to be doing. An example of an Online Armor pop-up is shown in Figure 8.18. Once you click on the checkbox next to the label "Remember my decision," the program will not bother you again for that program. Thus after allowing HP to perform keylogging as well as allowing Bluetooth software and about 20 other programs, this author was able to use the protection afforded by the program without any intervention.

Once you install Online Armor you can easily change previous settings or check the status of the program by simply selecting the program from the Start Menu. Doing so will result in a screen similar to the one shown in Figure 8.19. In addition to providing you with the status of computer protection, you will see the date of the last update as well as obtain the ability to submit a suspect file to the company. In the example shown in Figure 8.19 a quick glance at the screen indicates that all four major features of the program are operating, to include its anti-keylogger capability. The last feature is perhaps the most important of the program. As a reminder, when you perform a financial transaction, view your holdings at a brokerage company, or purchase a book at an online store your transaction is encrypted from

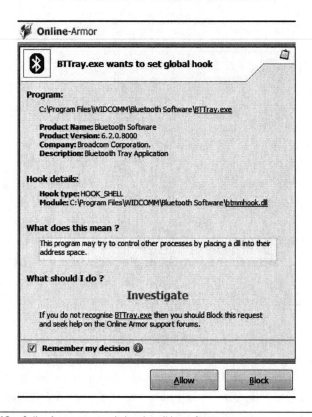

Figure 8.18   Online Armor pop-up window describing software programs.

your computer to a web server, with the URL appearing as https to indicate you are in a secure mode of operation—or are you? From your computer to the web server https does indeed indicate that transmission is secure; however, what can be said about entering data into your computer, such as entering a username and password or credit card information? While the result of the transmission is indeed secure, entering keystrokes is not. Thus a keylogger program could record your keystrokes and transmit such information to a third party, and hence the need for an anti-keylogger program.

8.4 AXCrypt File Encryption

While there are many security-related programs that can perform a variety of functions, most lack the ability to provide a mechanism to hide the content of key files and directories that you would not want to become observable by someone who may access your computer or

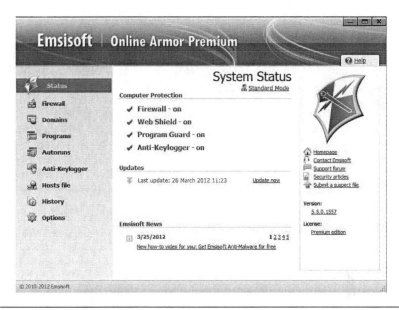

Figure 8.19   Viewing Online Armor's system status.

perhaps the technician that has a scope and is monitoring the contents of transmissions in a legitimate manner but should not observe clear text communications routed to the corporate treasurer or another official concerning key corporate information. For example, you would not want employees to know that as an exercise you were doing a cost-effective analysis concerning the closing of a plant in one location and opening another in a different location. If the economics do not make sense and your effort results in no action you wouldn't want employees to know that a potential plant closing was on the agenda, as it would be "water over the dam." Thus the ability to easily encrypt data is called for and is the focus of this section.

To understand the need for encryption we can simply relate this author's experience. In March 2012 a well-known silver and gold coin dealer's website was broken into. Although the follow-up email to this author indicated that credit card data were not stored on the computer, for some unknown reason the client list was. Perhaps this explains why my telephone was quite busy with calls from various bullion dealers even though I was on a do not call list. Thus if the coin dealer had encrypted its client list the probability that the hacker was able to use it would have been greatly diminished.

8.4.1 Installation

In this section we turn our attention to AXcrypt file encryption, a program from Axantum Software AB that can be obtained at http://www.axantum.com/axcrypt/Downloads.html.

When you install this program it will display its software license, similar to other programs, which you must accept to proceed. The next window to be displayed gave this author a bit of hesitation, as it at first appeared to make you install a "spam-free search bar" by its pre-checking the box acknowledging acceptance of the terms associated with a licensing agreement for the search bar. With three buttons labeled Back, Install, and Cancel this author, after thinking about the situation, unchecked the acceptance of terms and then clicked on the button labeled Install, which then installed the encryption program without having another search bar on his browser. Since the program is free, the search bar probably enables the Swedish firm to generate some revenue.

When you install AxCrypt patience is a virtue, as it takes a minute or so to install on a dual core computer. However, the wait is worth it as this program is easy to use and has many features that enable it to safeguard your email as well as necessary files and directories. Once the setup wizard completes its operation, information concerning how to encrypt a file is prominently displayed, simply requiring you to right-click a file in Windows Explorer and select AxCrypt and Encrypt, actions we demonstrate below. Note that this is an abbreviated explanation for this program; it also allows you to encrypt entire directories with a single operation as well as to generate self-extracting (.exe) files that can be emailed to persons that do not have the program.

8.4.2 Operation

Instead of starting a separate program AxCrypt is fully integrated into Windows Explorer where you browse your files and folders. Figure 8.20 illustrates the use of AxCrypt on this author's computer to encrypt a directory named CapitalCityStatements viewed with the last five letters replaced by dots, which contains financial records from a bank. Obviously this represents the type of records you may wish to encrypt.

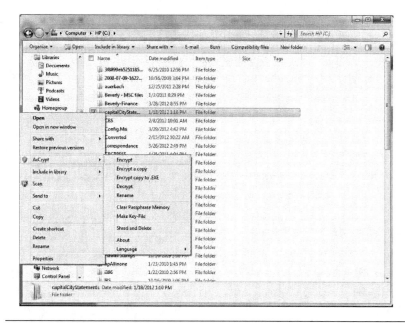

Figure 8.20 Working with AxCrypt.

As shown in Figure 8.20, right-clicking brings up the menu with AxCrypt added since it was just installed. Selecting that entry results in another menu with 10 entries, ranging from Encrypt at the top of the menu to Language at the bottom.

AxCrypt uses AES encryption with 128-bit keys. Once you select Encrypt you will be prompted to enter a passphrase as well as verify it. The resulting dialog box will, in addition to requesting you to enter and verify a passphrase, have two check blocks, with the one associated with "Remember this for decryption" checked, while the one labeled "Use as default for encryption" remains unchecked. If you unclick the top box when you go to access the file previously encrypted you will be prompted to enter the passphrase, after which the file will be opened, assuming you enter the correct passphrase. You can either click on a previously encrypted file or right-click and select AxCrypt and then select Decrypt to decrypt a previously encrypted file. Note that AxCrypt uses the file extension .axx and works with several versions of Windows from 2003 onward, to include 32- and 64-bit versions of Windows 7.

You can edit a previously encrypted file by simply double-clicking on it, resulting in a request to enter the passphrase if you unchecked the "Remember this for decryption" box. The second entry in the menu shown in Figure 8.20 allows you to make a copy of a file or directory that will be encrypted, while the third entry allows you to create a self-executing copy of a file or directory, with the latter very useful to send documents to persons that do not have AxCrypt. However, since a self-extracting file is obviously compromised if it falls into the wrong hands, it's far better to notify the receiving party of the passphrase and how to install the program from the Internet. While the next three menu options are obvious to most readers, the Make Key-File requires a bit of elaboration.

The use of a key file is optional; however, it provides a level of security typically much higher than that obtained from the use of a passphrase. This will generate random data in text format and save it as a key file. You should only store a key file on removable media and consider printing a backup copy, which should be stored in safe place. This is because if this file is lost it will be difficult to impossible to decrypt documents encrypted with it! To illustrate why it is important to print a copy of a key file in the event you remove a removable device to a location where your memory fogs up, the following illustrates the key file created by this author, a one-line text consisting of alphanumeric and special characters selected at random, to include upper- and lowercase and a special character thrown in for good measure. Just try remembering this:

```
711B EX3Q IfbR xkaZ qzWH mp2p PirO/Q38 FeR8 1qU8 dPM =
```

The third entry from the bottom of the menu shown in Figure 8.20 is labeled Shred and Delete. Selecting this entry does exactly what it says, after first prompting you to verify that you indeed want to overwrite the selected document. Thus instead of simply changing a bit setting to make space available and not actually deleting a file, the Shred and Delete option overwrites the file before making its space available for use by Windows.

The next entry in the menu, About, when selected provides you with information about the persons responsible for different aspects of the program as well as copyright information, while the last entry, Language, provides you with the ability to select from a list of languages.

As illustrated by this examination of AxCrypt, this program has several uses. In addition to securing data on a computer, you can use this program as a mechanism to transmit secure email as well as to completely delete files on your computer. Concerning the latter, unlike the operating system that simply toggles a bit to delete a file, AxCrypt's shred and delete capability ensures that a deleted file cannot be recovered.

Enhancing Network Performance

No book with the goal of providing readers with knowledge to diagnose networking problems would be complete without discussing the potential acquisition and utilization of a number of third-party and Windows built-in tools that can enhance the performance of a computer. In this chapter we turn our attention to the acquisition and utilization of several software products, some of which are included in Windows, that enable you to enhance the operational capability of your computer. For example, periodically running a built-in disk defragmentation program not only defragments your disks, but speeds up disk reading and writing, which will enhance file uploads and downloads as well as other disk-related operations. Thus while not directly related to networking operations, the tools covered in this chapter enhance many network operations.

In the first portion of this chapter we discuss several third-party products you can consider to both get a handle on communications and enhance your network performance. Because the Internet hardly remains static, this author also briefly discusses the use of search tools that can provide readers with the ability to locate different products. In the second portion of this chapter we turn our attention to a few facilities built in to Windows that can enhance our networking capability.

9.1 Third-Party Networking Tools

One of this author's favorite sites is Softpedia, which you can visit by going directly to the URL: http://www.softpedia.com/get/Network-Tools. As an alternative, entering "networking tools" into a search engine such as yahoo.com, bing.com, or google.com will more than likely have a link that takes you to the networking tools section of this website or to other sites where you can select from a variety of networking programs.

Figure 9.1   The Softpedia Networking Tools screen provides access to downloads in this category that are further subdivided into 11 subcategories.

Figure 9.1 illustrates the Networking Tools page of the Softpedia website in mid-2012. Note that this page is subdivided into 11 areas that you can select, ranging from Bandwidth Tools, located in the upper left portion of the screen, to Tracert/Whois tools, located in the lower right portion of the screen. By clicking on a particular entry a screen showing the latest downloads in the selected category will be displayed, from which you can either display additional information about a software product or download the product. While it might be presumptuous to select certain types of products over others, this author mentions a few that he uses and leaves further investigation of products to readers.

9.1.1 Bandwidth Tools

One series of products this author has found to be rather interesting are a variety of bandwidth monitors you can download from this site. In addition to providing a description of each program, Softpedia shows a sample screen, provides licensing information, indicates the latest update, and even provides a rating of the program. To access bandwidth tools you could simply click on the category shown in Figure 9.1. Doing so will result in a new web page labeled Bandwidth Tools, which will list the latest downloads in this selected category. Because this page will vary based upon the actions of program developers, you should probably visit each category periodically to determine what additions or revisions have occurred to programs you either are considering or are using. In addition to listing programs by their latest downloads, you can toggle the display to list programs in a defined category by their last update and also by their rating. One of the programs this author uses is Broadband Usage Meter, which when downloaded and installed places a small green display of your Internet data transfer rate. By right-clicking on the display you can change the color of the display to any Windows-supported color, change the size of the display, change the network that is actually the adapter being monitored, and perform other operations. Although Broadband Usage Meter represents a simple software solution designed to compute data transfers and display statistics, it also provides a mechanism to verify the connectivity promised by a communications carrier. While this author has used Broadband Usage Meter, which you can obtain from http://www.rackeys.com/, you might prefer to experiment with other broadband meters. Thus the Softpedia website as well as a search using "broadband meter" can provide you with the ability to locate numerous programs that may satisfy your requirements.

9.1.2 IP Tools

If you use the Softpedia website and click on the IP Tools section you will initially see a list first presented by the latest downloads of software programs that can be grouped under this category of IP tools. Included in this category are several programs designed to provide you with the IP address of a computer, and an application (NetSetMan) that allows you to enter network settings, including IP address, subnet mask, gateway, and DNS and Windows Internet Name Service (WINS) servers, and then save your settings. Additionally, this program also supports WiFi, printers, workgroups, PC names, and DNS domain settings. Other programs in this category include a virtual private network (VPN) client (FlyVPN); a program that includes support for managing ping and tracert utilities (Ping Manager); a program that monitors external IP addresses for changes every hour (IPSpy); a program that provides information about an IP address (IPInfoOffline), to include its IP block range, organization (RIPE, ARIN, APNIC, LACNIC, or AFRINIC), assigned date, country name, and country code; and a variety of other IP-related programs that allow you to hide your real IP address (IP Swapper), determine the host name for an IP address (DNS Lookup), and perform other operations under the IP tool category. In fact, at the time this book was written the Softpedia website had 13 pages of IP tools available for selection. While going through the IP Tools category this author located a tool that would block IP addresses and web addresses; however, from a security standpoint, for many users the opposite would be a good tool, that is, a program that only allows IP addresses and address blocks as well as web addresses. To add some utility, this type of program could automatically allow IP and web addresses that were first queried by the computer, in effect allowing responses. This might be equivalent to certain types of firewall and router access lists that could be beneficial for small organizations that cannot afford separate hardware and the personnel cost associated with training employees to become responsible for maintaining such hardware.

9.1.3 Miscellaneous Networking Tools

In this category Softpedia appears to lump a variety of programs that perform tasks ranging from a program developed to help system administrators manage their network (Foxy Admin) to an application designed to assist you in keeping track of your different network configurations (TCP/IP Manager). Concerning the latter, this program allows you to not only keep track of different network configurations, but also quickly change those configurations. Other programs in this category provide a wake-up for devices on a LAN (EMCO WakeOnLan Professional) that can be used to significantly save on electricity by allowing computers to be place in a sleep mode over the weekend and awakened on Monday mornings, or Tuesday if Monday was a holiday, turn a laptop into a virtual WiFi hotspot (Virtual

Hotspot), manage switch and router ports, and even create networking maps (StrikeNetworkDiagram). Thus miscellaneous really means a miscellaneous IP set of tools.

9.1.4 Network Information

In Softpedia the Network Information category is rather interesting, as it contains programs that were previously included under the IP Tools category as well as programs that use the TCP/IP Finger program. At the time this author accessed this category of software programs in mid-2012 there were a total of 10 pages with approximately 30 programs per page available for user selection. Thus this website favorably compares to a little boy or girl opening a door to a candy shop. While you know there are some good treats to find, each person has a different taste, so what will be good for one person may mot elicit a favorable response from another person that does not have a requirement for a particular program. Similarly, the reason we will not explore programs in any detail results from the fact that tools to access programs are more important than describing the operation of a particular program. Thus in the remainder of this section we discuss some additional download sites that have a variety of networking tools as well as examine the use of some search tools to locate networking tools that may be applicable to different readers.

9.1.5 Other Sites to Consider

In addition to softpedia.com there are other popular download sites that can be easily accessed to provide you with a variety of networking programs for Windows-based computers. One popular site is cnet.com, with the URL that takes you directly to Windows networking tools being http://download.cnet.com/windows/network-tools/. Another site you may wish to consider is http://www.paessler.com/tools, which is provided by Paessler, which goes by the motto "the network monitoring company." At this site you can obtain a variety of network-related programs, ranging from a billing tool to a Simple Network Management Protocol (SNMP) tester. Another major download site you may wish to consider is soft32.com, where by entering http://www.soft32.com/windows/network-tools you can go directly to a comprehensive list of networking programs available for downloading.

9.1.6 Using Search Tools

The previous section listed only a handful of sites where you can obtain networking-related programs. In actuality, by using one or more web search tools and applicable queries you can locate a large number of sites where you may be able to obtain the program or programs you require. To assist you in your search this section will focus on the use of applicable queries for such search engines as bing.com and google. com. This author excluded yahoo.com because Microsoft provides the search capability for yahoo.com under a long-term contract and should produce results similar to bing.com.

To begin our exploration of queries we can start with the term *networking tools*, which will provide the reader with approximately three-quarters of a million results. Obviously you wouldn't want to go through every link, so many persons either select a promising entry that may have read a description on the returned query that indicates that the URL will provide access to a number of programs. As an alternative you may decide to refine your query. Concerning the latter, since you want to download programs, one refinement of the search query could be "download networking tools," which produces approximately a half million hits. While still quite enough hits to keep you occupied for a while, let's suppose you are looking for a more specific type of program, such as a network billing program. If you entered "network billing program" as your query into bing.com the result would be over 100,000 hits. Thus you probably need a bit more clarity for your query, or do you?

Moving forward, let's assume you are looking for a program that traces routes to an IP address, operates under Windows 7, and has a graphic user interface in place of the command line tracert built in to most versions of Microsoft Windows. Entering the query "trace route Windows 7 GUI program" will, as shown in Figure 9.2, produce over 18 million matches; however, because we were pretty specific in our query the best matches actually occur on the first few pages. As illustrated in Figure 9.2 the first and third hits produced by Bing

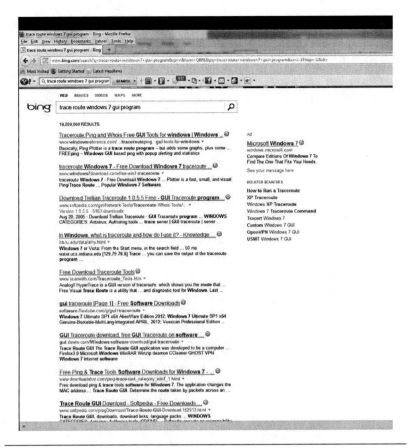

Figure 9.2   Using bing.com to search for a traceroute Windows 7 GUI program.

incorporate all six of the keywords in the query, while the second hit will require you to click on the link to determine if the program has a graphical user interface (GUI) capability. Remember, even though the result shows Windows 7, it's possible that the program runs in command mode. Thus you would need to click on the link to determine that the program is indeed a GUI program.

As you continue your examination of the results displayed in Figure 9.2 note that by being rather specific in your query you can locate many programs that will more than likely meet your criteria. For example, while the fourth entry describes how to access the built-in tracert facility included in Windows, which is not what we are searching for, entries 5 to 8 and many others provide links to the software that we are searching for. In general, the more specific the query, the better the chance that a search tool will locate what you are looking for. Remembering this, you need to structure your queries as specifically as possible. To assist you when you need to adjust your search, most search engines provide a list of related searches you can select from. In the example shown in Figure 9.2 using bing.com, the related searches are listed in the upper right portion of the screen.

9.2 Windows Built-In Networking Tools

In addition to networking tools that are used via the Command Prompt you can significantly enhance certain computers through the use of many Windows built-in GUI tools. These tools can be accessed by going to Start > Accessories > System Tools, with the resulting display shown in Figure 9.3. As illustrated in the figure, there are 13 system tools on the author's computer, and depending upon the version of Windows you use, you may have a slightly different number of built-in Windows system tools. The tools shown in Figure 9.3 range from Character Map, which enables you to copy and paste accented letters and other foreign language characters into any Windows application, to Windows Easy Transfer, which facilitates migrating from one version of Windows to another by transferring selected files. In between are several programs this author uses on a periodic basis to determine if there are computer-related problems that when alleviated may significantly enhance network operations. In the next few paragraphs we discuss the operation and utilization of several system tools that may enable you to enhance certain network operations, from file uploads and downloads to Internet browsing.

9.2.1 Disk Cleanup

Under System Tools in Figure 9.3 you will note icons labeled Disk Cleanup and Disk Defragmentation. You would select Disk Cleanup if you want to reduce the number of unnecessary files on your hard disk to free up disk space and help your computer run faster. Through the use of disk cleanup you may be able to remove temporary files, empty the recycle bin of its contents, as well as remove a variety of system files and other items that you no longer need. Thus through the use of disk cleanup you can free up storage space on any hard drive on

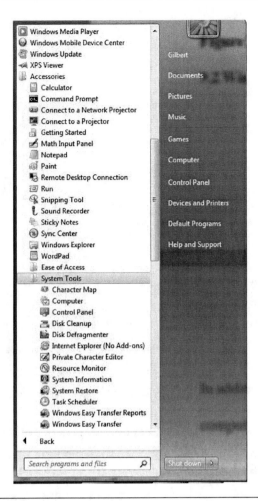

Figure 9.3 Accessing Windows System Tools.

your computer, which may allow you to avoid both the time involved and cost associated with migrating to a larger-capacity hard drive.

After you select the drive to be cleaned the program will display the amount of data storage on the selected device that could be removed, as well as allow you to select files to remove to reach the maximum amount of data storage. In Figure 9.4 the operation of disk cleanup on this author's computer is shown. Note that according to the program a maximum of 5.97 Gbytes of data storage could be recovered, with 306 Mbytes shown as preselected by the program, assuming you wish to delete temporary Internet files (214 MB), and if you scroll down on the right, you can then note that Thumbnails (92 MB) was also preselected,

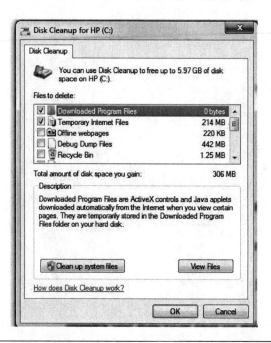

Figure 9.4   Running disk cleanup informs you of the amount of storage you may be able to free up on a drive.

for a total of 306 MB. By selecting such files as the recycle bin, temporary Internet files, system error memory dump files, and other files that you will more than likely never use you can easily recover between 5 and 10% of your drive's storage capacity. In addition, once you use disk cleanup to remove some files there is a good chance other files will now become unnecessary to have, further boosting recoverable data storage.

9.2.2 Why Disk Defragmentation Matters

To understand the benefits associated with disk defragmentation we need to appreciate what fragmentation is, how it occurs, and its effect upon computer operations, to include file uploading and downloading, which represent two common Internet activities. Fragmentation occurs to a hard disk over time as you save, modify, or delete files. Starting from the reverse, when you delete a file your computer actually sets a bit in each sector occupied by the file to inform the operating system that it is available for reuse. Suppose the size of the file was 14 sectors and you now need to save a file that requires 4 sectors of storage. If your computer overwrites the previously erased file, it leaves 10 sectors that are not used. Similarly, if you need to store 20 sectors of data, chances are high that the operating system will either look for 20 contiguous sectors, in effect leaving a hole of 14 sectors unused, or use the 14 sectors from the deleted file and then move the read/write heads of the hard drive to another location where the remaining 6 sectors will be written, causing the file to become fragmented. Over time, both the files and the hard disk itself will become fragmented, and your computer slows down, as it has to look in many different places to save or retrieve files. Thus disk defragmentation describes the process of consolidating fragmented files on your computer's hard disk.

One of the tools included within most versions of Windows is a disk defragmenter. This system tool rearranges the data on your hard disk and reunites fragmented files so your computer can run more efficiently. In the version of Windows used by this author the disk defragmenter can be run on a scheduled basis so you don't have to remember to run it, although you can still run it manually or change the schedule it uses.

Figure 9.5 illustrates the disk defragmenter program. Note that this author set the program so that it periodically operates, which explains why after several years of use fragmentation is shown to be at a level of 1% on his C drive. By clicking on the button labeled Configure Schedule you can easily set the frequency, disk to defragment, and when defragmentation should occur. The other two buttons in Figure 9.5, as their labels indicate, allow you to analyze a selected disk and to defragment a disk, doing so manually instead of at a predefined time. Note that if you previously set up a schedule and the program previously operated, your display will note the percent of defragmentation for each drive as well as when the program was last run against a particular drive.

9.2.3 Resource Monitor

Another built-in Windows system tool that is available on most versions of this operating system is the resource monitor. You can activate this program by clicking on the icon to the left of the label Resource Monitor. Figure 9.6 illustrates an example of its default display on this author's computer. Note that by default monitoring occurs when

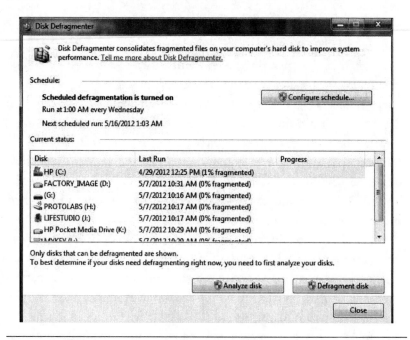

Figure 9.5 The Windows built-in disk defragmenter provides a set-and-forget capability, or you can run it manually.

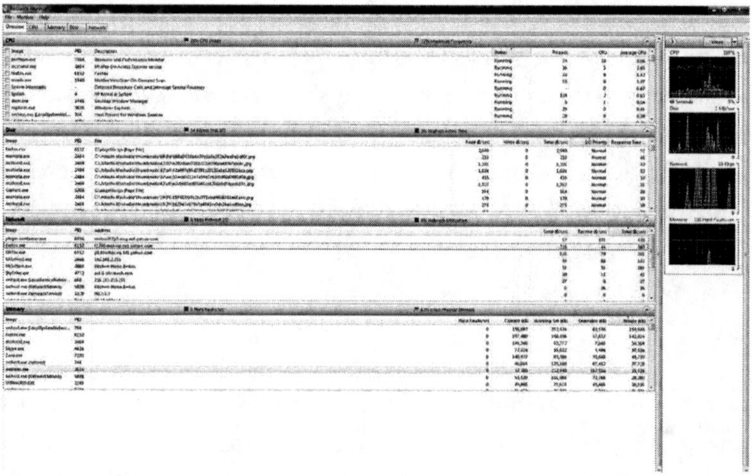

Figure 9.6 The Resource Monitor provides tabular and graphical information about the CPU, memory, disk, and network utilization.

you activate the program. If you want to display a snapshot of what is occurring on your computer, you could select the Stop Monitoring entry from the drop-down Monitor menu, which is to the left of the File menu.

The resource monitor, as its name implies, provides you with the ability to note CPU, memory, disk, and network activity. By selecting Stop Monitoring you can obtain a snapshot of what is occurring on your computer at a particular point in time. In Figure 9.6 under the CPU heading you can note the programs and processes, services, and associated handles running, while under the Disk heading you can obtain a feel for disk activity, as it displays such information as processes with disk activity, disk usage (kb/s), and disk queue length. Selecting Network results in the display of processes with network activity, general network activity, IP addresses and TCP port connections, listening ports, and data transmitted and received. Note that while some of the display occurs when you simply run the program, other aspects of the display require you to select the applicable tab under the menu bar. For example, if you select the tab labeled Memory, you will see a display showing both processes and physical memory; however, if you selected the Overview entry, which is the default when the program runs, you would note the number of faults and percent of physical memory in use as well as obtain a list of processes and data associated with each, such as hard faults per second and the size of the process in kilobytes, as well as the amount that is shareable and private.

The old adage a picture is worth a thousand words becomes important when you focus on the right area of Figure 9.6. By default when you use the program four graphs are shown, with the CPU utilization in the upper right corner, followed by the disk transfer rate, network throughput, and memory in terms of 100 hard faults per second. By clicking on a different tab than the default one of Overview the display will adjust according to the type of computer you are using and then tab selected. Thus clicking on a specific tab enables you to change both the tabular data and graphs shown. For example, this author was using a dual core processor-based computer. Thus when this author clicked on the tab labeled CPU the display showed four CPU-related graphs, with the top showing total CPU utilization and the second graph service CPU usage. Then the next two graphs provided utilization for each core. Moving forward, if you click on the tab labeled Network the resulting display would show in Tabular form processes with network activity, followed by network activity that indicates IP addresses and bytes transmitted and received, followed by TCP connections and listening ports, with the latter indicating the port number, protocol, and firewall status. To the right of the tabular data will be a series of graphs based upon the communications employed by your computer. While the top graph will show network utilization for a 60 s period, the remaining graphs will vary based upon the type of communications employed. Thus in this author's display the network graph was followed by graphs illustrating TCP connections, wireless LAN connections, Bluetooth network connections, and local area network connections that occurred over the past 60 s. Thus the Network tab can, with a simple click, provide you with an overview of network activity.

9.2.4 System Information

The last system tool we will examine in this concluding chapter is labeled System Information. System Information represents a utility built in to most versions of Windows, which when run provides you with a detailed view of the hardware installed on the computer, what is currently loaded into memory, as well as details about other Microsoft programs installed on the computer. From the data presented you can easily determine if the computer is operating correctly or if one or more hardware or software problems requires resolution.

The basic display of System Information is subdivided into four areas: System Summary, Hardware Resources, Components, and Software Environment. In addition, a search field in the display provides you with the ability to easily locate information about your computer. Figure 9.7 illustrates the initial display of the System Information utility for which the System Summary was selected and the Hardware Resources, Components, and Software Environment areas were exploded by clicking on a plus (+) sign associated with each category, resulting in each category now showing a minus sign (−), which when clicked upon will collapse each entry. As shown in Figure 9.7, the System Summary provides the display of general information about the computer, such as its operating system, OS version,

Figure 9.7   The System Information utility program provides hardware and software information that can be used to correct or alleviate many problems from occurring.

system name, manufacturer, model number, memory, page file data, and other information about the device, in one concise location.

Under the Hardware Resources category data concerning conflicts, direct memory access (DMA), and similar hardware-related information are displayed. This information can be important for determining if a hardware upgrade will or will not conflict with other hardware, as well as provide information about current or potential interrupt conflicts. As you select each item within a category the right window display will change to reflect the applicable entry selected. Some selected items, such as IO, Interrupt Requests (IRQs), and memory, will also display the status of the selected items. For example, selecting IRQs will display a list of computer interrupts and their status. Hopefully the status of each IRQ will be ok, but if not, then you will know a problem exists. Moving along, the Components category, as shown in the left window section of Figure 9.7, includes drives, the sound device, displays, modems, and other devices installed on your computer. Note that certain categories of devices, such as Multimedia, are shown with a plus (+) sign and need to be clicked upon to expand so you can select a device. For example, expanding Multimedia results in the ability to select either Audio Codecs or Video Codecs.

The last major grouping or category is the Software Environment. The Software Environment displays information about system drivers, environmental variables, print jobs, network connections, running tasks, loaded modules, and other program-related data. In fact, selecting Windows Error Reporting may shed light upon some repeating software problems that might otherwise be hard to diagnose. For example, an application program that repeatedly fails can easily be noted by selecting Windows Error Reporting from the Software Environment category. This can be especially helpful when the application runs on a monthly or quarterly basis and we tend to forget that a prior failure occurred. However, using this utility, it becomes possible to observe such failures over a period of time. Another helpful feature of System Information is the search bar at the bottom of the display. You can use this facility to search within a selected category or to search for a category name. Through the use of the System Information utility you can examine the computer system and try to either avoid a potential problem from occurring or locate the source of a problem. Note that by itself the System Information utility is most useful for learning what is installed on a computer as well as what is loaded into memory after Windows is initialized.

Index